The Films of

THE CISCO KID

by Francis M. Nevins

The World of Yesterday
Waynesville, North Carolina
1998

All photos used in this book are from private collections.

Copyright ©1998 by Francis M. Nevins

ISBN: 0-936505-14-1

Library of Congress Catalog Card Number: 98-61613

Published by
The World of Yesterday
104 Chestnut Wood Drive
Waynesville, NC 28786-6514
Phone (828) 648-5647

First Printing 1998 9 8 7 6 5 4 3 2 1

Manufactured in the United States of America

Contents

Duncan Renaldo was probably the best known Cisco playing Cisco both in movies and on TV. Here he is in the movie costume with his horse Diablo.

For: Bill Catching
Paul Landres
Troy Melton (1921-1995)

Duncan Renaldo loved children, not like some cowboy stars. He ran a ranch for troubled kids in Cisco, Texas.

Introduction

On the east coast in the early 1950s when I was growing up, we had seven channels' worth of television programming to choose from and precious little on any of them except Westerns. If I had a dollar today for every hour of my childhood and early teens that I spent hunched in front of the 12"-inch screen, soaking up old 60-minute B Western features and new 30-minute TV series in the same vein—well, I'd have a nice pile of dollars. Books have been written about lots of those pictures but none until now about the screen adventures of The Cisco Kid. I decided it was time.

The Films Of The Cisco Kid follows more or less the same format as my earlier book *The Films Of Hopalong Cassidy* (1988), but there are some differences too. Both the Cassidy character and the Cisco character first came to life in short stories written only a few years after the beginning of the twentieth century. But Clarence E. Mulford continued writing stories and novels about Cassidy until 1941: so many stories and novels, with such complex interconnections, that it took me a whole separate book to do justice to them. (That book, *Bar-20: The Life Of Clarence E. Mulford, Creator Of Hopalong Cassidy*, was published by McFarland & Co. in 1993.) The Cisco Kid on the other hand appeared in just one story, O. Henry's "The Caballero's Way" (1907), which is so short that I've included it in Chapter One of this book. The transformation of Cisco from his original incarnation into the hero of movies and TV was even more radical than the transformation of Mulford's Cassidy character. Mulford lived long enough to make a sort of retirement hobby out of ridiculing what the Hollywood types had done to his knight of the frontier. O. Henry died young and never saw his creation on the screen. I doubt he would have been pleased if he had.

Hopalong Cassidy was the hero of movies and TV episodes for exactly twenty years, from 1935 through 1954, during which he was portrayed by

one man, William Boyd. The Cisco character has shown up on large and small screens for just over eighty years, from 1914 through 1994, and has been played by either seven or eight actors (depending on how you classify the 1917 feature **Betrayed** that we'll discuss in Chapter Two). Not only was each portrayal different from the others but the best-known of the screen Ciscos played the role in three different ways. If *The Films Of The Cisco Kid* seems to be a looser, less unified book than *The Films Of Hopalong Cassidy*, this is the reason why. But I hope it's just as enjoyable and informative as the Cassidy book and, knowing the publishers as I do, I'm sure it will be just as stunning visually.

I owe deep thanks to many people who helped but especially to Maris Allen, Pamela Boyer, Robert E. Briney, Bill Catching, Mary Dougherty, the late William K. Everson, Will Hutchins, Paul Landres, John Langellier, Boyd Magers, the late Troy Melton, William Nadel, Milton and Sharon Obrock, Mark Rudman, Sondra Schol, Anthony Tollin, Jon Tuska and Nick Williams. *Muchas gracias, amigas y amigos*!

Francis M. Nevins
St. Louis, Missouri
September 1996

Publishers Acknowledgements:

The publisher wishes to thank all those collectors who were nice enough to dig in to their collections and loan us photos for this book: Boyd Magers, Don Cantrell, Bobby Copeland, Buck Rainey, Dan Stumpf, Phil Loy, Charles K. Stumpf, Troy Melton, Bill Catching, Ron and Linda Downey.

We wish to thank James Neuenschwander for designing the front cover.

This is a photo of O. Henry as used on the dust jacket of one of the collections of his works.

One • O. Henry, Father of All Ciscos

"Here's adventure! Here's romance! Here's O. Henry's famous Robin Hood of the Old West—THE CISCO KID!"

When Duncan Renaldo and Leo Carrillo (or their doubles) came thundering across the desertscape to the tune of vaguely Latin-flavored agitato music, we grammar school kids of the 1950s sitting glued in front of our parents' 12–inch TV screens knew next to nothing about what we were watching. Those of us who were too young to have seen any of the Cisco movies in theaters had never heard of the character before. We didn't know that the 30-minute telefilms we were seeing in black-and-white had been shot in color, or that the music score beneath the front and end titles had been composed by a never-credited Albert Glasser. Few of us had ever heard of O. Henry except as a candy bar.

Later, when we took American Lit in high school and had to read "The Ransom of Red Chief" and "The Gift of the Magi," most of us learned a little about who O. Henry was. In those days nobody would dare ask their teachers about the connection between O. Henry and The Cisco Kid, and frankly, not many teachers would have known the answer.

So who was O. Henry?

He was probably the most popular American short story writer in the first half of this century. In ten years' time he wrote close to three hundred tales which, according to the entry on him in Volume 19 of *Twentieth-Century Literary Criticism* (1986), featured "familiar, conversational openings, circumlocutory dialogue, plots hinging on improbable coincidence, and variations on the surprise or twist ending...." For twenty-odd years after his death his stories were studied in colleges as marvelous examples of short fiction. Then opinion shifted and his tales were dismissed as clever commercial concoctions. Some recent critics are finding links between his stories and the work of various avant-garde writers who wouldn't know a well-constructed plot if it bit them. The pendulum is sure to swing some more as we move into the twenty-first century.

O. Henry of course is not the name he was born with. William Sidney Porter was born in Greensboro, North Carolina on September 11, 1862 to Dr. Algernon Porter and his wife, who died of pneumonia when her second son was three. The doctor and his children moved in with his mother. Raised by his grandmother and an aunt, William Sidney left school at age 15 and went to work in his uncle Clarke Porter's drugstore, earning a pharmacist's license in 1881. Throughout his adolescence he was terrified of catching the pneumonia that had killed his mother. When he developed a persistent cough he moved to southwest Texas and worked for two years on a cattle ranch managed by the sons of the doctor who had taken over Algernon's practice. One of these sons was Lee "Red" Hall, a Texas Ranger who helped run down Sam Bass and other legendary outlaws. Around 1884, resettling in the state capital at Austin, Porter worked as a clerk and bookkeeper, as a draftsman in a state land office, and finally as a teller at the First National Bank. He married his first wife, the former Athol Estes, in July 1887.

In 1894 Porter bought a defunct weekly humor magazine for $250, retitled it The Rolling Stone and tried to put it on its feet by the simple ploy of writing almost every word he published in it. The magazine failed and he began submitting humorous stories and sketches to other periodicals. Meanwhile he'd been fired from his bank job when shortages were discovered in his accounts, and in 1895, believing he was about to be arrested and charged with embezzlement, he left his wife and spent a year on the run, holing up in Houston and New Orleans, then crossing the border and taking cover in Honduras and Mexico, traveling part of the time with the fugitive American outlaw Al Jennings. In 1897, when word reached Porter that his wife was seriously ill, he went back to Austin and surrendered. She died later that year.

Porter was convicted of embezzlement—whether rightly or wrongly is still disputed by his biographers—and sentenced to five years in the federal ward of the Ohio state pen. He worked the midnight shift in the prison pharmacy and spent his days writing stories which he submitted to magazines using his in-laws' Pittsburgh address and the pseudonym of O. Henry, which apparently came from Orrin Henry, one of the prison guards. In July 1901, after serving three years and three months, he was released. After a brief stay with his late wife's parents he relocated to New York City in the spring of 1902 at the urging of the Ainslee's Magazine editors who'd bought some material from him.

From then on he wrote like a demon, turning out well over 200 stories before the end of the century's first decade. The New York World, a paper with a readership of half a million, paid him a staggering $100 a week to write a story for each of its Sunday issues. He turned out copy at white heat, spent money lavishly, gave huge tips to waiters and generous handouts to derelicts, whiled away hours in bars and restaurants ad-libbing stories about the people around him, drank two quarts of whisky a day. Somehow he found time to get married again—in November 1907, to the former Sara Coleman---but the marriage was quickly wrecked by his philandering and alcoholism. His greatest fear during his time as a literary superstar was that someone would go public with the hidden years of his life, so he falsified his biography to hide the fact that he'd been in prison. He died on June 5, 1910, of a combination of diabetes and cirrhosis of the liver, literally in the middle of his latest story, which was published incomplete in Cosmopolitan a few months later.

What was the secret of his success? At his best he was an astonishingly vivid writer. According to critic Hyder E. Rollins' essay "O. Henry" (Sewanee Review, Spring 1914): "No other writer has excelled him in the use of suggestive description." Perhaps more important was the care and skill with which he constructed his stories. Rollins described everything in an O. Henry tale as "a careful preparation for the denouement, even if the most searching reader can seldom detect it...." Or, as Vachel Lindsay put it in his 1912 poem "The Knight in Disguise":

He always worked a triple-hinged surprise
To end the scene and make one rub his eyes.

"Twist ending" is the catchphrase that has remained associated with O. Henry's name from the beginning of this century to the end.

Tastes have changed over ninety years, and much of what made O. Henry what he was isn't fashionable anymore. The outlandish coincidences that fuel his plots tend to make us either laugh or groan. The grandiose circumlocutions he loved not wisely but too well—like having A tell B to get off his mule by saying "Segregate yourself from your pseudo-equine quadruped"—strike today's readers as the prose equivalents of lead balloons. On the other hand his realistic yet sympathetic portraits of con men, Western outlaws, rogues of every description, sent blasts of critical heat his way while he was alive but today would be counted among his abiding strengths.

Most of his tales are set in the places he knew best: South America, the area around the Texas-Mexico border, the Appalachians, turn-of-the-century New York, and prison cells. He probably wrote "The Caballero's Way" in the Caledonia Hotel, which still exists in New York City today as an apartment house. The story was first published in Everybody's Magazine for July 1907 and included later that year in the O. Henry story collection *Hearts Of The West*. With its vivid description of Cisco's ride through the pear flat, its identification with a vicious protagonist, its occasional heavy-handed circumlocutions, its central technical problem—how can a cold-blooded killer whose code forbids violence to any woman get even with the woman who betrayed him?—the tale demonstrates just about every element that critics have discovered in O. Henry's work.

It also, of course, gave birth to the film saga that we'll explore in this book, but the Cisco of movies and TV has nothing in common with O. Henry's Cisco except a name. The character as Porter conceived him was not at all a Robin Hood of the Old West, indeed not even a Mexican, but a murderous little Anglo probably modeled on Billy the Kid, while Cisco's nemesis Sandridge—at least in the opinion of William Nadel, a fan and distant relative of Porter—was based on Texas Ranger "Red" Hall. But O. Henry's tale was the original if remote starting point for twenty-three theatrical films, 156 half-hour TV films, a feature-length TV movie, a radio series, comic books, tons of tie-in items and even a rock-n-roll song.

So let's read the story.

The Caballero's Way
by O. Henry

The Cisco Kid had killed six men in more or less fair scrimmages, had murdered twice as many (mostly Mexicans), and had winged a larger number whom he modestly forbore to count. Therefore a woman loved him.

The Kid was twenty-five, looked twenty; and a careful insurance company would have estimated the probable time of his demise at, say, twenty-six. His habitat was anywhere between the Frio and the Rio Grande. He killed for the love of it—because he was quick-tempered—to avoid arrest—for his own amusement—any reason that came to his mind would suffice. He had escaped capture because he could shoot five-sixths of a second sooner than any sheriff or ranger in the service, and because he rode a speckled roan horse that knew every cow-path in the mesquite and pear thickets from San Antonio to Matamoros.

Tonia Perez, the girl who loved the Cisco Kid, was half Carmen, half Madonna, and the rest—oh, yes, a woman who is half Carmen and half Madonna can always be something more—the rest, let us say, was humming-bird. She lived in a grass-roofed *jacal* near a little Mexican settlement at the Lone Wolf Crossing of the Frio. With her lived a father or grandfather, a lineal Aztec, somewhat less than a thousand years old, who herded a hundred goats and lived in a continuous drunken dream from drinking *mescal*. Back of the *jacal* a tremendous forest of bristling pear, twenty feet high at its worst, crowded almost to its door. It was along the bewildering maze of this spinous thicket that the speckled roan would bring the Kid to see his girl. And once, clinging like a lizard to the ridge-pole, high up under the peaked grass roof, he had heard Tonia, with her Madonna face and Carmen beauty and humming-bird soul, parley with the sheriff's posse, denying knowledge of her man in her soft mélange of Spanish and English.

One day the adjutant-general of the state, who is, *ex officio*, commander of the ranger forces, wrote some sarcastic lines to Captain Duval of Company X, stationed at Laredo, relative to the serene and undisturbed existence led by murderers and desperadoes in the said captain's territory.

The captain turned the color of brick dust under his tan, and forwarded the letter, after adding a few comments, per ranger Private Bill Adamson, to ranger Lieutenant Sandridge, camped at a water hole on the Nueces with a squad of five men in preservation of law and order.

Lieutenant Sandridge turned a beautiful *couleur de rose* through his ordinary strawberry complexion, tucked the letter in his hip pocket, and chewed off the ends of his gamboge moustache.

The next morning he saddled his horse and rode alone to the Mexican settlement at the Lone Wolf Crossing of the Frio, twenty miles away.

Six feet two, blond as a Viking, quiet as a deacon, dangerous as a machine gun, Sandridge moved among the *jacales*, patiently seeking news of the Cisco Kid.

Far more than the law, the Mexicans dreaded the cold and certain vengeance of the lone rider that the ranger sought. It had been one of the Kid's pastimes to shoot Mexicans "to see them kick": if he demanded from them moribund Terpsichorean feats, simply that he might be entertained, what terrible and extreme penalties would be certain to follow should they anger him! One and all they lounged with upturned palms and shrugging shoulders, filling the air with *"quién sabe"s* and denials of the Kid's acquaintance.

But there was a man named Fink who kept a store at the Crossing–a man of many nationalities, tongues, interests, and ways of thinking.

"No use to ask them Mexicans," he said to Sandridge. "They're afraid to tell. This *hombre* they call the Kid—Goodall is his name, ain't it?—he's been in my store once or twice. I have an idea you might run across him at–but I guess I don't keer to say, myself. I'm two seconds later in pulling a gun than I used to be and the difference is worth thinking about. But this Kid's got a half-Mexican girl at the Crossing that he comes to see. She lives in that *jacal* a hundred yards down the arroyo at the edge of the pear. Maybe she–no, I don't suppose she would, but that *jacal* would be a good place to watch, anyway."

Sandridge rode down to the *jacal* of Perez. The sun was low, and the broad shade of the great pear thicket already covered the grass-thatched hut. The goats were enclosed for the night in a brush corral near by. A few kids walked the top of it, nibbling the chaparral leaves. The old Mexican lay upon a blanket on the grass, already in a stupor from his *mescal*, and dreaming, perhaps, of the nights when he and Pizarro touched glasses to their New World fortunes—so old his wrinkled face seemed to proclaim him to be. And in the door of the *jacal* stood Tonia. And Lieutenant Sandridge sat in his saddle staring at her like a gannet agape at a sailorman.

The Cisco Kid was a vain person, as all eminent and successful assassins are, and his bosom would have been ruffled had he known that at a simple exchange of glances two persons, in whose minds he had been looming large, suddenly abandoned (at least for the time) all thought of him.

Never before had Tonia seen such a man as this. He seemed to be made of sunshine and blood-red tissue and clear weather. He seemed to illuminate the shadow of the pear when he smiled, as though the sun were rising again. The men she had known had been small and dark. Even the

Kid, in spite of his achievements, was a stripling no larger than herself, with black, straight hair and a cold, marble face that chilled the noonday.

As for Tonia, though she sends description to the poorhouse, let her make a millionaire of your fancy. Her blue-black hair, smoothly divided in the middle and bound close to her head, and her large eyes full of the Latin melancholy, gave her the Madonna touch. Her motions and air spoke of the concealed fire and the desire to charm that she had inherited from the *gitanas* of the Basque province. As for the humming-bird part of her, that dwelt in her heart; you could not perceive it unless her bright red skirt and dark blue blouse gave you a symbolic hint of the vagarious bird.

The newly lighted sun-god asked for a drink of water. Tonia brought it from the red jar hanging under the brush shelter. Sandridge considered it necessary to dismount so as to lessen the trouble of her ministrations.

I play no spy; nor do I assume to master the thoughts of any human heart; but I assert, by the chronicler's right, that before a quarter of an hour had sped, Sandridge was teaching her how to plait a six-strand rawhide stake-rope, and Tonia had explained to him that were it not for her little English book that the peripatetic *padre* had given her and the little crippled *chivo*, that she fed from a bottle, she would be very, very lonely indeed.

Which leads to a suspicion that the Kid's fences needed repairing, and that the adjutant-general's sarcasm had fallen upon unproductive soil.

In his camp by the water hole Lieutenant Sandridge announced and reiterated his intention of either causing the Cisco Kid to nibble the black loam of the Frio country prairies or of haling him before a judge and jury. That sounded business-like. Twice a week he rode over to the Lone Wolf Crossing of the Frio, and directed Tonia's slim, slightly lemon-tinted fingers among the intricacies of the slowly growing lariat. A six-strand plait is hard to learn and easy to teach.

The ranger knew that he might find the Kid there at any visit. He kept his armament ready, and had a frequent eye for the pear thicket at the rear of the *jacal*. Thus he might bring down the kite and the humming-bird with one stone.

While the sunny-haired ornithologist was pursuing his studies, the Cisco Kid was also attending to his professional duties. He moodily shot up a saloon in a small cow village on Quintana Creek, killed the town marshal (plugging him neatly in the centre of his tin badge), and then rode away, morose and unsatisfied. No true artist is uplifted by shooting an aged man carrying an old-style .38 bulldog.

On his way the Kid suddenly experienced the yearning that all men feel when wrong-doing loses its keen edge of delight. He yearned for the woman he loved to reassure him that she was his in spite of it. He wanted her to call his bloodthirstiness bravery and his cruelty devotion. He wanted Tonia to bring him water from the red jar under the brush shelter, and tell him how the *chivo* was thriving on the bottle.

The Kid turned the speckled roan's head up the ten-mile pear flat that stretches along the Arroyo Hondo until it ends at the Lone Wolf Crossing of the Frio. The roan whickered; for he had a sense of locality and direction equal to that of a belt-line street-car horse; and he knew he would soon be nibbling the rich mesquite grass at the end of a forty-foot stake-rope while Ulysses rested his head in Circe's straw-roofed hut.

More weird and lonesome than the journey of an Amazonian explorer is the ride of one through a Texas pear flat. With dismal monotony and startling variety the uncanny and multiform shapes of the cacti lift their twisted trunks and fat, bristly hands to encumber the way. The demon plant, appearing to live without soil or rain, seems to taunt the parched traveler with its lush gray greenness. It warps itself a thousand times about what look to be open and inviting paths, only to lure the rider into blind and impassable spine-defended "bottoms of the bag," leaving him to retreat, if he can, with the points of the compass whirling in his head.

To be lost in the pear is to die almost the death of the thief on the cross, pierced by nails and with grotesque shapes of all the fiends hovering about.

But it was not so with the Kid and his mount. Winding, twisting, circling, tracing the most fantastic and bewildering trail ever picked out, the good roan lessened the distance to the Lone Wolf Crossing with every coil and turn that he made.

While they fared the Kid sang. He knew but one tune and sang it, as he knew but one code and lived it, and but one girl and loved her. He was a single-minded man of conventional ideas. He had a voice like a coyote with bronchitis, but whenever he chose to sing his song he sang it. It was a conventional song of the camps and trails, running at its beginning as near as may be to these words:

Don't you monkey with my Lulu girl
Or I'll tell you what I'll do--

and so on. The roan was inured to it, and did not mind.

But even the poorest singer will, after a certain time, gain his own consent to refrain from contributing to the world's noises. So the Kid, by the time he was within a mile or two of Tonia's *jacal*, had reluctantly allowed his song to die away—not because his vocal performance had become less charming to his own ears, but because his laryngeal muscles were aweary.

As though he were in a circus ring, the speckled roan wheeled and danced through the labyrinth of pear until at length his rider knew by certain landmarks that the Lone Wolf Crossing was close at hand. Then, where the pear was thinner, he caught sight of the grass roof of the *jacal* and the hackberry tree on the edge of the arroyo. A few yards farther the Kid stopped the roan and gazed intently through the prickly openings. Then he dismounted, dropped the roan's reins, and proceeded on foot, stooping and silent, like an Indian. The roan, knowing his part, stood still, making no sound.

The Kid crept noiselessly to the very edge of the pear thicket and reconnoitered between the leaves of a clump of cactus.

Ten yards from his hiding-place, in the shade of the *jacal*, sat his Tonia calmly plaiting a raw-hide lariat. So far she might surely escape condemnation; women have been known, from time to time, to engage in more mischievous occupations. But if all must be told, there is to be added that her head reposed against the broad and comfortable chest of a tall red-and-yellow man, and that his arm was about her, guiding her nimble small fingers that required so many lessons at the intricate six-strand plait.

Sandridge glanced quickly at the dark mass of pear when he heard a slight squeaking sound that was not altogether unfamiliar. A gun-scabbard will make that sound when one grasps the handle of a six-shooter suddenly. But the sound was not repeated; and Tonia's fingers needed close attention.

And then, in the shadow of death, they began to talk of their love; and in the still July afternoon every word they uttered reached the ears of the Kid.

"Remember, then," said Tonia, "you must not come again until I send for you. Soon he will be here. A *vaquero* at the *tienda* said to-day he saw him on the Guadalupe three days ago. When he is that near he always comes. If he comes and finds you here he will kill you. So, for my sake, you must come no more until I send you the word."

"All right," said the ranger. "And then what?"

"And then," said the girl, "you must bring your men here and kill him. If not, he will kill you."

"He ain't a man to surrender, that's sure," said Sandridge. "It's kill or be killed for the officer that goes up against Mr. Cisco Kid."

"He must die," said the girl. "Otherwise there will not be any peace in the world for thee and me. He has killed many. Let him so die. Bring your men, and give him no chance to escape."

"You used to think right much of him," said Sandridge.

Tonia dropped the lariat, twisted herself around, and curved a lemon-tinted arm over the ranger's shoulder.

"But then," she murmured in liquid Spanish, "I had not beheld thee, thou great, red mountain of a man! And thou art kind and good, as well as strong. Could one choose him, knowing thee? Let him die; for then I will not be filled with fear by day and night lest he hurt thee or me."

"How can I know when he comes?" asked Sandridge.

"When he comes," said Tonia, "he remains two days, sometimes three. Gregorio, the small son of old Luisa, the *lavandera*, has a swift pony. I will write a letter to thee and send it by him, saying how it will be best to come upon him. By Gregorio will the letter come. And bring many men with thee, and have much care, oh, dear red one, for the rattlesnake is not quicker to strike than is '*El chivato*,' as they call him, to send a ball from his *pistola*."

"The Kid's handy with his gun, sure enough," admitted Sandridge, "but when I come for him I shall come alone. I'll get him by myself or not at all. The Cap wrote one or two things to me that make me want to do the trick without any help. You let me know when Mr. Kid arrives, and I'll do the rest."

"I will send you the message by the boy Gregorio," said the girl. "I knew you were braver than that small slayer of men who never smiles. How could I ever have thought I cared for him?"

It was time for the ranger to ride back to his camp on the water hole. Before he mounted his horse he raised the slight form of Tonia with one arm high from the earth for a parting salute. The drowsy stillness of the torpid summer air still lay thick upon the dreaming afternoon. The smoke from the fire in the *jacal*, where the *frijoles* bubbled in the iron pot, rose straight as a plumb line above the clay-daubed chimney. No sound or movement disturbed the serenity of the dense pear thicket ten yards away.

When the form of Sandridge had disappeared, loping his big dun down the steep banks of the Frio crossing, the Kid crept back to his own horse, mounted him, and rode back along the tortuous trail he had come.

But not far. He stopped and waited in the silent depths of the pear until half an hour passed. And then Tonia heard the high, untrue notes of his unmusical singing coming nearer and nearer, and she ran to the edge of the pear to meet him.

The Kid seldom smiled; but he smiled and

waved his hat when he saw her. He dismounted, and his girl sprang into his arms. The Kid looked at her fondly. His thick, black hair clung to his head like a wrinkled mat. The meeting brought a slight ripple of some undercurrent of feeling to his smooth, dark face that was usually as motionless as a clay mask.

"How's my girl?" he asked, holding her close.

"Sick of waiting so long for you, dear one," she answered. "My eyes are dim with always gazing into that devil's pincushion through which you come. And I can see into it such a little way, too. But you are here, beloved one, and I will not scold. *Qué mal muchacho!* not to come to see your *alma* more often. Go in and rest, and let me water your horse and stake him with the long rope. There is cool water in the jar for you."

The Kid kissed her affectionately.

"Not if the court knows itself do I let a lady stake my horse for me," said he. "But if you'll run in, *chica*, and throw a pot of coffee together while I attend to the *caballo*, I'll be a good deal obliged."

Besides his marksmanship the Kid had another attribute for which he admired himself greatly. He was *muy caballero*, as the Mexicans express it, where the ladies were concerned. For them he had always gentle words and consideration. He could not have spoken a harsh word to a woman. He might ruthlessly slay their husbands and brothers, but he could not have laid the weight of a finger in anger upon a woman. Wherefore many of that interesting division of humanity who had come under the spell of his politeness declared their disbelief in the stories circulated about Mr. Kid. One shouldn't believe everything one heard, they said. When confronted by their indignant men folk with proof of the *caballero's* deeds of infamy, they said maybe he had been driven to it, and that he knew how to treat a lady, anyhow.

Considering this extremely courteous idiosyncrasy of the Kid and the pride that he took in it, one can perceive that the solution of the problem that was presented to him by what he saw and heard from his hiding-place in the pear that afternoon (at least as to one of the actors) must have been obscured by difficulties. And yet one could not think of the Kid overlooking little matters of that kind.

At the end of the short twilight they gathered around a supper of *frijoles*, goat steaks, canned peaches, and coffee, by the light of a lantern in the *jacal*. Afterward, the ancestor, his flock corralled, smoked a cigarette and became a mummy in a gray blanket. Tonia washed the few dishes while the Kid dried them with the flour-sacking towel. Her eyes shone; she chatted volubly of the inconsequent happenings of her small world since the Kid's last visit; it was as all his other homecomings had been.

Then outside Tonia swung in a grass hammock with her guitar and sang sad *canciones de amor*.

"Do you love me just the same, old girl?" asked the Kid, hunting for his cigarette papers.

"Always the same, little one," said Tonia, her dark eyes lingering upon him.

"I must go over to Fink's," said the Kid, rising, "for some tobacco. I thought I had another sack in my coat. I'll be back in a quarter of an hour."

"Hasten," said Tonia, "and tell me—how long shall I call you my own, this time? Will you be gone again tomorrow, leaving me to grieve, or will you be longer with your Tonia?"

"Oh, I might stay two or three days this trip," said the Kid, yawning. "I've been on the dodge for a month, and I'd like to rest up."

He was gone half an hour for his tobacco. When he returned Tonia was still lying in the hammock.

"It's funny," said the Kid, "how I feel. I feel like there was somebody lying behind every bush and tree waiting to shoot me. I never had mullygrubs like them before. Maybe it's one of them presumptions. I've got half a notion to light out in the morning before day. The Guadalupe country is burning up about that old Dutchman I plugged down there."

"You are not afraid—no one could make my brave little one fear."

"Well, I haven't been usually regarded as a jack-rabbit when it comes to scrapping; but I don't want a posse smoking me out when I'm in your *jacal*. Somebody might get hurt that oughtn't to."

"Remain with your Tonia—no one will find you here."

The Kid looked keenly into the shadows up and down the arroyo and toward the dim lights of the Mexican village.

"I'll see how it looks later on," was his decision.

At midnight a horseman rode into the rangers' camp, blazing his way by noisy "hallo"s to indicate a pacific mission. Sandridge and one or two others turned out to investigate the row. The rider announced himself to be Domingo Sales, from the Lone Wolf Crossing. He bore a letter for Señor Sandridge. Old Luisa, the *lavandera*, had persuaded him to bring it, he said, her son Gregorio being too ill of a fever to ride.

Sandridge lighted the camp lantern and read the letter. These were its words:

Dear One: He has come. Hardly had you ridden away when he came out of the pear. When he first talked he said he would stay three days or more.

Then as it grew later he was like a wolf or a fox, and walked about without rest, looking and listening. Soon he said he must leave before daylight when it is dark and stillest. And then he seemed to suspect that I be not true to him. He looked at me so strange that I am frightened. I swear to him that I love him, his own Tonia. Last of all he said I must prove to him I am true. He thinks that even now men are waiting to kill him as he rides from my house. To escape he says he will dress in my clothes, my red skirt and the blue waist I wear and the brown mantilla over the head, and thus ride away. But before that he says that I must put on his clothes, his *pantalones* and *camisa* and hat, and ride away on his horse from the *jacal* as far as the big road beyond the crossing and back again. This before he goes, so he can tell if I am true and if men are hidden to shoot him. It is a terrible thing. An hour before daybreak this is to be. Come, my dear one, and kill this man and take me for your Tonia. Do not try to take hold of him alive, but kill him quickly. Knowing all, you should do that. You must come long before the time and hide yourself in the little shed near the *jacal* where the wagon and saddles are kept. It is dark in there. He will wear my red skirt and blue waist and brown mantilla. I send you a hundred kisses. Come surely and shoot quickly and straight.

Thine Own Tonia

Sandridge quickly explained to his men the official part of the missive. The rangers protested against his going alone.

"I'll get him easy enough," said the lieutenant. "The girl's got him trapped. And don't even think he'll get the drop on me."

Sandridge saddled his horse and rode to the Lone Wolf Crossing. He tied his big dun in a clump of brush on the arroyo, took his Winchester from its scabbard, and carefully approached the Perez *jacal*. There was only the half of a high moon drifted over by ragged, milk-white gulf clouds.

The wagon-shed was an excellent place for ambush; and the ranger got inside it safely. In the black shadow of the brush shelter in front of the *jacal* he could see a horse tied and hear him impatiently pawing the hard-trodden earth.

He waited almost an hour before two figures came out of the *jacal*. One, in man's clothes, quickly mounted the horse and galloped past the wagon-shed toward the crossing and village. And then the other figure, in skirt, waist, and mantilla over its head, stepped out into the faint moonlight, gazing after the rider. Sandridge thought he would take his chance then before Tonia rode back. He fancied she might not care to see it.

"Throw up your hands," he ordered, loudly, stepping out of the wagon-shed with his Winchester at his shoulder.

There was a quick turn of the figure, but no movement to obey, so the ranger pumped in the bullets—one—two—three—and then twice more; for you never could be too sure of bringing down the Cisco Kid. There was no danger of missing at ten paces, even in the half moonlight.

The old ancestor, asleep on his blanket, was awakened by the shots. Listening further, he heard a great cry from some man in mortal distress or anguish, and rose up grumbling at the disturbing ways of moderns.

The tall, red ghost of a man burst into the *jacal*, reaching one hand, shaking like a *tule* reed, for the lantern hanging on its nail. The other spread a letter on the table.

"Look at this letter, Perez," cried the man. "Who wrote it?"

"*Ah, Dios!* it is Señor Sandridge," mumbled the old man, approaching. "*Pues señor*, that letter was written by 'El chivato,' as he is called—by the man of Tonia. They say he is a bad man; I do not know. While Tonia slept he wrote the letter and sent it by this old hand of mine to Domingo Sales to be brought to you. Is there anything wrong in the letter? I am very old; and I did not know. *Valgame Dios!* it is a very foolish world; and there is nothing in the house to drink—nothing to drink."

Just then all that Sandridge could think of to do was to go outside and throw himself face downward in the dust by the side of his humming-bird, of whom not a feather fluttered. He was not a *caballero* by instinct, and he could not understand the niceties of revenge.

A mile away the rider who had ridden past the wagon-shed struck up a harsh, untuneful song, the words of which began:

Don't you monkey with my Lulu girl
      Or I'll tell you what I'll do—

Photo of Herbert Stanley Dunn, sporting the original Cisco Kid hat, and Mr. Marion Stoneking, an administrator with the North Orange County Community College District. The picture was taken by Don Cantrell in 1975 in the backyard of Dunn's Costa Mesa home to publicize his selection as an Americana Award winner by Cypress College. The ceremonies were held January 6, 1976. (Photo courtesy of Mr. Cantrell.)

Two • Cisco in the Silents

How and when did the vicious Cisco of O. Henry's story, who wasn't even Mexican, evolve into the Latino Robin Hood of movies and TV? Everyone before now who has discussed the question says that the transformation took place in 1929 and credits Raoul Walsh, the original director and intended star of **In Old Arizona**. The truth is that a good deal of the process happened long before 1929, but Walsh still deserves much of the credit; more in fact than anyone has realized.

As of this writing Cisco's career on the screen has lasted for eighty years, beginning not long after O. Henry's death and extending through the time I've worked on this book. The saga began in March 1914 when the French-owned Eclair studio released **The Caballero's Way**, a three-reeler featuring J. W. Johnston as Sandridge, Herbert Stanley Dunn (whom reference books sometimes call Arthur Dunn or Herbert Stanley) as Cisco, and Edna Payne as Tonia. Dunn was born in Brooklyn, New York on November 24, 1891 and died in Costa Mesa, California on April 14, 1979. We would know nothing about his portrayal of Cisco beyond these bare facts except for a stroke of luck. Decades after his time in the movies and about a year before his death, Dunn was interviewed in his Costa Mesa home by reporter Don Cantrell. Apparently the interview was never published but Cantrell turned over his notes to John Langellier of the Gene Autry Western Heritage Museum, and thanks to him we can hear Stan Dunn reminisce about his time as Cisco as if we were in his home with him.

Dunn's father was a ship captain of Irish descent and his mother an Algonquin Indian who, along with all four of her children, found work in early silent movies. (One of Stan's brothers, Eddie Dunn, wound up as a gag writer and bit player in Laurel & Hardy comedy shorts.) After appearing on the stage in various stock companies, 13-year-old Stan was hired by Vitagraph Films as a property boy in 1905. He moved to Biograph five years later and acted in countless one- and two-reelers. Then in 1913 or early 1914 he was hired by Societé Francaise de Films et Cinematographes Eclair, a New York firm backed by French investors, and was sent to Tucson to be a prop man and actor in the company's Westerns. Some time after Stan arrived, Eclair director Webster Cullison was preparing to make **The Caballero's Way**. Cullison was testing other actors for the part of Cisco, Dunn said, but "finally decided they were too old. He wanted a young kid. So he picked me."

The film proved such a hit that Eclair's front office wired Cullison to drop whatever else he was doing and make a series of Cisco shorts with Dunn in the lead. Whether O. Henry's estate was notified isn't known but I suspect no one at Eclair thought it was necessary. Over the next year or so, until the pressures of World War I in Europe caused the studio's collapse, Dunn starred in a cycle of Cisco shorts that presumably were structured along the same general lines as the long-running Broncho Billy Anderson series. (How many were made is impossible to tell but Dunn's estimate of 200 seems way too high.) Except for two days of filming in Tombstone and one junket to California, all the Eclair Ciscos were shot in the Tucson area. They have long since crumbled to dust and survive only in Stan Dunn's recollections of almost sixty-five years later.

"After **The Caballero's Way** my wife Bertha and I wrote the rest of the scripts. I had the ideas and she wrote them out in longhand. She called herself Bert. A lot of people thought she was a man. She was a very pretty girl. She passed away in 1966 but we had a terrific life.

"We were the first ones [to make movies] in Tucson....I was the first film cowboy to use two guns. [The fancy gloves he wore as Cisco] and the two-gun bit was Cullison's idea. I couldn't roll a cigarette or do much of anything while wearing that hot leather but I finally slit a few glove fingers and that worked out a little better. I

This was one of the last formal photographs of Herbert Stanley Dunn in the den of his Costa Mesa, California home a year before his death in mid-april of 1979. He died at age 87. Photo was taken by the Orange County Register Newspaper. (Courtesy of Don Cantrell, last editor of the Tombstone Epitaph.)

couldn't ride a horse in the beginning or shoot a gun either but we were firing blanks so it really didn't matter.

"....They had ordered this leather costume from El Paso, Texas, and I had to get into it with a shoehorn, it was so tight. I never had to put my foot into a stirrup to mount a horse. I only grabbed hold of the pommel, started him off and threw myself into the saddle. I didn't have a mustache either but they made one up.

"My pay soon jumped from thirty-five to forty-five dollars a week, and that was big money in those days. You could buy a steak dinner in Tucson for twenty-five or thirty cents. We were paid in pieces of gold or silver since there was no paper money down there at that time."

Early in Dunn's stint as Cisco a horse fell on him and broke his leg, leaving him with a limp for the rest of his life.

"I was lucky. There were no stunt men in those days. We did our own fistfighting and took our own falls. A lot of the actors suffered more serious injuries. Some were killed. The leg hurt me for quite a while....and I went through a lot of pain using it. I had to walk but I worked it out by using it. Trouble is, that same leg had been broken three times before. It wasn't so bad when I was younger but it's bothering me more and more as I get older.

"Another funny thing. I was riding into the San Xavier mission area from out in the hills. My horse was trotting along at a fast pace and he stepped in a hole. I went over his head and when I came to it was so funny. All these people, Papago Indians, were looking down at me. I must have hit my head, I went out of that saddle so fast. Then I got up and went back to my horse. The Indians thought that was great. The mothers and fathers were going: 'That guy is great, he's going to do it again.' They were hollering and cheering, even the kids.

"The people in Tucson accepted us very well. They took [moviemaking] as something new and fascinating. It excited them....Downtown was about four blocks square then. There was about a hundred and fifty townspeople and there was a lot of consumptives, you know, tubercular cases. They had a sanitarium out there too but it was out to the east about twenty miles.

"Oh, it was beautiful country. It was still a little wild in 1913 but there was no hardship in finding local people to work in a picture....We didn't use many but the ones we wanted we got: Mexicans, white men, white women. They all wanted to get in. These people worked for nothing, the extras I mean. They didn't get any money at all that I ever saw.

"As for fun, well, there was only one place there and that was the old Tucson Hotel. The restaurant closed around seven or eight o'clock. If you wanted a drink....Tucson was dry. There were no liquor stores or anything. I didn't see any bar. [But if] you ordered it, you got it. At the restaurant, I mean....You sort of got it under the table.

"There wasn't any free time to get away or ride off into the hills. We got enough of that during the week. We actually worked seven days a week....We could get off if we had something to do but there was no place to go. We had horses to curry down and wash, and take care of the feeding. Each one of us had our own horses and we took care of them. There were no guys to take care of horses. Oh, there was so much to do.

"The location shooting was right around Tucson, all around the mountain areas there in different places. You see, in those days you could take a camera and move it all over and get a different location. We had no automobiles. All we had was horses and you couldn't run a horse too far, then work them all day and bring them back again. You wouldn't have a horse.

"Once we went up Sabino Canyon, that was fifteen miles from town. The trail goes up a mountainside, it goes up to a gold mine there. We passed a small stream and it was very funny, because it had garnet stones. They're red stones, little bitty things. They're all over. When you first look at them they look like blood. It was fascinating to me because here I was a Brooklyn boy out on the prairie, and I knew nothing about those things. Sometimes we'd get so far out and the horses would get worked so hard that I'd just lie down there at night with my horse and go to sleep. I was used to sleeping on the ground.

"The old studios were at Congress and Main Streets. Seems they were on the northwest corner. There was a house there, a two-story house, and in back of it was an adobe house but it was vacated....We utilized that by putting a stage in

Herbert Stanley Dunn, here in costume, was the first Cisco Kid. (Courtesy of Bobby Copeland.)

there. [The property Eclair rented] was a couple of acres, and you had a corral in there for your horses, and you had a stable. We did quite a lot of the building. It took all the actors together because we had no carpenters but ourselves....

"Generally this is how we would work. In the mornings we would get out on the land, then in the afternoon we'd have the overhead lights in the studio. We had canvas over the rigging of the stage. That was to cut the sunlight down or diffuse it. We'd film along that whole range of mountains. There was the Santa Ritas, Catalina, and what they call the Big A today....Then there was the saguaro forest. It was east of Congress Street and way out. There was a big bed of them there....Some of those things must be a thousand years old.

"We went down to Tombstone once....And I said: 'Gee, that's a long ride for a horse. What about the horses?' [Cullison or someone else replied]: 'No, we got horses down there.' So we went down there in a car. Very seldom I traveled in a car, very seldom. I don't remember much about Tombstone but Boot Hill wasn't filling up nearly as fast as it had back in the 1870s and

1880s. It was still pretty wild-looking to us New Yorkers, and it did give us a feeling of reality for the kind of shoot-em-ups we were filming. I remember the old Cochise County Court House and we filmed around there.

"We went down to Nogales on our horses once because Pancho Villa had taken the town. They were fighting the Carranza forces. They were also fighting with American soldiers....The American soldiers told the Mexicans they better shoot the other way or they were going to dry them up. No bullets came our way because we were off at a distance. But I had the great pleasure of seeing Pancho Villa on a big white horse with a silver saddle and bridle. He had a white shirt on, a big brown sombrero and it looked to me like he had lots of pistol belts....He was quite a showman anyway, you know.

"Territorial days ended about a year before we came. I think Arizona became a state in 1912. The natives were talking about it. Yeah, they felt it was a great idea. It gave them a feeling of being something, of being more secure. Now they had the government behind them. They figured the government people would be coming in to take over the things they wanted, like running the water through. We had to rely on wells in those days. We had no electricity either, we used oil lamps.

"The studio people stayed at the Tucson Hotel until they could find themselves a home to live in. They all went into private homes like I did. I lived in an old judge's home on Congress Street....He was my friend too. He was related to the rich people, the management. They all had nice homes. The people who had the space were glad to have us there. They loved the prestige....

"There was a movie house in Tucson....I was in it once, the time they showed the first Cisco Kid picture. The company had sent it out for us to see it. We saw it first, then they let the local people see it....Now they were seeing what they had worked in, so that made them feel big.

"There was no dialogue in those days. We made it up as we went along. They inserted the words in New York when they put the picture together. Every day we had to send some cans in because it took three days to get there...."

After Eclair's collapse Dunn acted off and on in both Hollywood and New York. Eventually Columbia Pictures hired him as a property master for $500 a week, much more than he'd ever earned as an actor. Twice during his subsequent career he was sent back to the area where in his early twenties he'd played Cisco: in 1940, to help construct Old Tucson for the filming of **Arizona**

(Columbia, 1940, directed by Wesley Ruggles and starring William Holden and Jean Arthur), and in 1943, on loanout to Howard Hughes for **The Outlaw**. "Do I miss Arizona?" he was asked near the end of his life by Don Cantrell. "Yeah, I'd love to move back there. But I couldn't move from here if I wanted to. I can't walk!"

In 1935, Dunn remembered, he happened to meet Warner Baxter, who six years earlier had won an Oscar for his performance as Cisco in the first feature about the character, **In Old Arizona**. When Dunn claimed that he himself had been the first to play the part, Baxter wouldn't believe him until Stan showed some stills from the 3-reel version of **The Caballero's Way** the next day. "They told me I was first!" an unhappy Baxter exclaimed. What is strongly suggested by this anecdote, and supported by Don Cantrell's 1975 photograph of Dunn wearing the original Cisco hat, is that the 1914 version of the character, like Baxter's of fifteen years later, was a Latino. So let's tip our own hats to that long-forgotten director Webster Cullison for transforming O. Henry's murderous Anglo into the ethnic rogue-hero who still survives in our century's final years.

Everyone well versed in Western-film history knows that the first person to make a feature-length movie with O. Henry's character turned into a Latino was Raoul Walsh (1887-1980), whose Hollywood career endured for more than half a century. What no one has realized until now is that the movie in which he did it was not **In Old Arizona**.

Walsh was born in New York City on March 11, 1887. His mother's people were of Irish and Spanish descent and his father was an immigrant from Dublin who became a clothing cutter and later the co-owner of a prosperous wholesale garment business. Among the many celebrities of the late 19th century who frequently visited the Walsh home on East 48th Street was actor Edwin Booth, the brother of Lincoln's assassin.

Like every later movie hero with Irish-Spanish roots, Raoul had a zest for adventure. At sixteen he dropped out of school to sail to Cuba on a cargo schooner with his uncle. He went on from there to Mexico, learned riding and roping, joined the drovers pushing a trail herd north to Texas, then found work breaking remounts for the cavalry. Recuperating in San Antonio after a horse fall injured his leg, he was hired by a theatrical troupe to ride a cayuse across a treadmill in its production of *The Clansman*, the play based on Thomas Dixon's pro-Ku Klux Klan novel.

In 1909, after he'd returned to New York,

Walsh was signed by Pathé Freres as an actor in the one-and two-reel shorts that the studio was filming in the wilds of New Jersey. A chance meeting with Christy Cabanne, who was directing the same sort of pictures for the rival Biograph company, brought Walsh to the attention of the legendary D.W. Griffith. The result was that the young actor found himself among the group Griffith took with him to California when he launched his own production company. Before long Walsh was not only acting in but also scripting and directing two-reel action flicks.

Late in 1913 or early in 1914, Griffith sent Walsh back to the Rio Grande country to shoot footage of Pancho Villa and his rebel army as they fought battles across Mexico. On Walsh's return the studio expanded his material into a 7-reel feature, **The Life Of General Villa** (Mutual, 1914), by splicing it together with fiction footage directed by Christy Cabanne—another Griffith protégé who went on to figure in the Cisco saga—and with Walsh himself decked out in Mexican garb (not for the last time in his career) as Pancho Villa. Walsh's best known screen performance came soon afterwards, in Griffith's 1915 classic **The Birth Of A Nation**, based on the same Thomas Dixon novel in whose San Antonio stage version Walsh had appeared as a rider in the Ku Klux Klan. The role he played in Griffith's film was John Wilkes Booth, whose brother Edwin he had met years before in the Walsh home on East 48th Street.

Late in 1915 Walsh parted company with Griffith and joined the newly formed Fox studio as a writer-director. He spent the next five years making an incredible twenty full-length features, everything from exotic romances starring Theda Bara to actioners with his younger brother George as the hero. It is the eighth of his early Fox pictures that concerns us here.

Betrayed (Fox, 1917), a five-reeler which Walsh both wrote and directed, is set along the Texas-Mexico border. Carmelita Carrito (Miriam Cooper), a lovely señorita engaged to Pepo Esperanza (Monte Blue), finds herself falling in love with Leopoldo Juarez (Hobart Bosworth), a bandit who takes refuge in her father's hacienda. When Leopoldo rides away, Carmelita stares out the window after him and eventually falls asleep. William Jerome (Wheeler Oakman), a U.S. Army officer also hunting for Leopoldo, comes to the hacienda and Carmelita, infatuated once again, tells him that the bandito has made a date to meet her by a certain brook. At the climax Leopoldo discovers that he's been betrayed and makes Carmelita put on his coat and sombrero so that Jerome mistakes her for his quarry and shoots her

down. This is when the señorita wakes from her siesta—that's right, the whole sequence lifted from "The Caballero's Way" has been a dream—and finds that Leopoldo is still hiding in the hacienda, and that a squad of U.S. troopers led by none other than her fiancé Pepo are surrounding the house. The film ends with Pepo capturing the bandit, earning a nice reward and re-establishing himself in Carmelita's affections.

O. Henry was still one of America's most widely read story-tellers seven years after his death, and the reviewer for at least one trade paper pointed out that part of **Betrayed**'s plot was a rip-off. If O. Henry's estate took any legal action it was quickly settled and never led to a reported judicial opinion. Perhaps Walsh's decision twelve years later to direct and star in **In Old Arizona** was his way of making amends.

Between his two screen versions of the O. Henry tale came a long-forgotten two-reeler, **The Border Terror** (Universal, 1919), one of hundreds of shorts released in the late Nineteen Teens. Harry Harvey directed from a scenario by H. Tipton Steck which both the film's credits and Universal's copyright registration acknowledged as adapted from "The Caballero's Way." I presume this means that it was made with permission from O. Henry's estate. Cisco was played by Vester Pegg (1889-1951), a puncher who around the same time had small parts in some of the earliest films of John Ford. Tonia was portrayed by Yvette Mitchell. Whether the Cisco character had reverted to his Anglo origins in this 20-minute version or was still presented as Latino is anyone's guess.

Vester Pegg played the Cisco Kid in **Border Terror** (Universal, 1919). (Courtesy of Bobby Copeland.)

A publicity photo of Warner Baxter in costume as the Cisco Kid, dated 1933.

Three • Cisco Talks: Warner Baxter

For the lover of Westerns, moviegoing in the 1920s was cowboy heaven. Between 1917 and 1923 traditionalists could enjoy Paramount's cycle of features starring William S. Hart, which as often as not were written and directed by a man destined to play a meaty part in the Cisco saga later on: Lambert Hillyer. From 1918 through 1928 the Fox studio presented a series of slicker, more action-packed shoot-em-ups with Tom Mix (three directed by Hillyer and two by the young John Ford) and, between 1920 and 1927, another popular series with Buck Jones (including two non-Westerns helmed by Ford, half a dozen by William Wellman and a few late oaters by Hillyer). Universal's longest-running series (1921-30) showcased the stunting and comedic skills of Hoot Gibson, who was directed twice by Ford but most often by actionmaster B. Reeves Eason. Other Universal Western series featured stars like Jack Hoxie (1923-27) and Art Acord (1925-27). After Paramount's **The Covered Wagon** (1923, directed by James Cruze) and Fox's **The Iron Horse** (1924, directed by John Ford) created the frontier epic, MGM launched an elaborate cycle of Westerns with Tim McCoy and First National an equally well-made series with Ken Maynard, both running from 1926 through 1929. Paramount followed up **The Covered Wagon** with a set of generously budgeted pictures based (at least nominally) on novels by Zane Grey and usually starring Richard Dix or Jack Holt. Harry Carey, the first actor groomed to stardom by John Ford, played the lead in dozens of Westerns at various studios through the Twenties. FBO presented Tom Tyler (1925-29), Bob Steele (1927-29) and teenage Buzz Barton (1927-29) in three separate rangeland series. Lesser stars like Al Hoxie, Fred Humes, Buffalo Bill Jr. and Buddy Roosevelt hung their Stetsons at low-rent outfits like Action Pictures, Anchor and Rayart. It seemed as if the cornucopia of Western fare would never go dry.

And then almost overnight it did. Between the middle of 1926 and the end of 1929, the period chronicled in Alexander Walker's *The Shattered Silents* (Morrow, 1979), the printing of sound on film evolved from a technical novelty to a revolutionary development that brought one era of movie history to an end and gave birth to another. What seemed most drastically threatened by the coming of talking pictures was outdoor moviemaking in general and the Western in particular because Hollywood's new gurus, the sound technicians, insisted again and again that it was impossible to record sound except indoors under tightly controlled conditions. Most of the studios resigned themselves to the death of the Western and ended their output of oaters.

John Ford, under contract to Fox at the time, was not convinced. As he told Peter Bogdanovich almost forty years later: "They said it couldn't be done, and I said, 'Why the h... can't it be done?' They said, 'Well, you can't because---' and they gave me a lot of Master's Degree talk. So I said, 'Well, let's try it.'" (50) The result was **Napoleon's Barber** (1928), a 22-minute short that Ford claimed to be "the first time anyone ever went outside with a sound system."

Raoul Walsh was directing at Fox then too. It was apparently in mid-1928 (although he doesn't give the date) when studio head Winfield Sheehan frantically summoned Walsh back from a Mexican vacation and sent him to the Beverly Theater to take in his first talking picture. "The triteness of the sets and the obvious nervousness of the female lead made me want to jump up and start shouting. Then a thought struck me. If the tedious dialogue could be supplemented and broken up by more action, the result might be thrilling instead of soporific." (219) As he was leaving the theater he heard "a burst of sound" from a Fox Movietone newsreel dealing with a dockworkers' strike, felt a rush of inspiration, and went back to Sheehan's office with the announcement: "I'm going to make the first outdoor sound feature." The film he made, or rather started to make as both director and leading man until a terrified jackrabbit entered his life, was **In Old Arizona** (1929), first and best known of the twenty-three full-length cinematic exploits of The Cisco Kid.

The source of the Beverly Theater anecdote is Walsh's autobiography, *Each Man In His Time* (Farrar, Straus & Giroux, 1974), prepared with the help of veteran screenwriter John Twist and published when the director was in his late eighties. It's a vividly written book but Walsh is hopelessly unreliable on facts and seems to have forgotten more than he remembered. In his recollection, neither he nor Sheehan know anything about John Ford (who rates just three passing mentions in the entire Walsh memoir) having made or being about to make a short with full sound for Fox that same year. Walsh claims it was his idea to make the first full-length talkie and to call it **In Old Arizona** but tells us three pages later that originally the "agreed length" of the film had been "two reels"—the same length as **Napoleon's Barber**—but that Sheehan liked the rushes of the first two days' shooting so much "that he demanded a five-reeler instead of the shorter footage." (222) You'd never know from Walsh's account that the finished picture ran almost ninety minutes. According to Walsh, the Cisco character as created by O. Henry "was a Mexican." (222) **Betrayed**, the 1917 feature where the character had been turned into a Mexican by Walsh himself, gets dropped down the memory hole. Walsh in his autobiography claims to have written the script for **In Old Arizona** himself. "Poor O. Henry. I hoped he would not turn over in his grave. After I finished with this version of his story, it would be a tossup who wrote what." (223) Whatever contributions were made by Tom Barry, who is credited on screen for adaptation and dialogue, are studiously ignored. Walsh describes shooting a scene for **In Old Arizona** with a stagecoach being chased by Indians. There's no such scene in the picture. He has Sheehan telling him: "Remember that scene where you fried the bacon? That g...... sizzling was so real it made me hungry." (222) No bacon is fried in the movie, although Alexander Walker and countless other film commentators have described it vividly.

What is known for sure is that Walsh himself was playing Cisco in the picture, as witness the photograph of him in costume on horseback that he prints in his book, and that he was making the outdoor sequences in and around Bryce Canyon, Utah, with a Fox Movietone newsreel truck to capture naturalistic sound. When the truck was damaged beyond repair, Walsh shut down production, phoned Sheehan in Los Angeles and made plans to finish the film on the Fox back lot. "I'll have to rewrite some of the end sequences to fit because there aren't any mountains. Build me some adobe house fronts, and I'll need one interior. Better get started right away because we're pulling out of here tonight." (224)

Walsh was in the front passenger seat of the lead car racing much too fast across the starlit Utah desert to the nearest Union Pacific rail link. "We missed outcrops and cattle and once scattered a herd of deer. The only thing we did not miss was a big jack rabbit. The headlights must have dazzled him, because he jumped at the windshield on my side and came crashing through it. There was no safety glass—Ford began to install it the next year—and the jack, dead from the impact, hit me squarely in the face, accompanied by a shower of glass splinters." (224-225) Walsh was hospitalized in Salt Lake City, where Tom Mix visited him with a bottle of five-star Hennessy cognac hidden under a basket of fruit. Eventually he was sent to a New York specialist to have his right eye removed. Fox contract director Irving Cummings took over **In Old Arizona**, with Warner Baxter and Dorothy Burgess cast as Cisco and his *inamorada*. "They were able to save all the long shots I had made, in which my face was not too distinguishable, and they used the same chase scenes through Bryce Canyon." (229) Walsh never comes out and says it but what follows from his account is that every bit of **In Old Arizona** with Warner Baxter in front of the camera—in other words the vast majority of the film we have today—was directed not by Walsh but by Irving Cummings, who must certainly be credited for Baxter's Oscar-winning performance.

Cummings was one of the countless directors who put in long years at his trade but never broke out from the pack to become either a household name like John Ford or a cult figure. Born in New York City on October 9, 1888, he started acting on the stage in his teens. One of his earliest parts was that of a man 70 years old. In September 1908, a month before his twentieth birthday, he was leading man opposite the legendary Lillian Russell in *Wildfire*. His first movie role was in **The Window**, a primitive one-reeler shot in New York. In one of his earliest feature-length pictures, **Uncle Tom's Cabin** (World, 1914), he donned blackface for the part of runaway slave George Harris. He had a minor role in one of the earliest cliffhanger serials, **The Million Dollar Mystery** (Thanhouser, 1914, 23 chapters), and played the male lead opposite Lottie Pickford in that 30-chapter cinematic marathon **The Diamond From The Sky** (North American Film, 1915). By the end of the decade he'd been seen in more than forty silent features, usually under directors and alongside fellow actors who have been forgotten for generations but occasionally opposite an immortal like Ethel Barrymore, with whom he co-starred in **An American Widow** (Metro, 1917).

Early in the Twenties he co-founded the Cummings & Smith production company and made his debut as director in its first offering, **The Man From Hell's River** (1922), which he also starred in. The enterprise collapsed a year later but Cummings had no trouble getting work as a director at the established studios: first Universal, then First National, finally Fox, which was to be his home for most of the next twenty years. His earliest Fox features were **The Johnstown Flood** (1926), starring George O'Brien and introducing Janet Gaynor, and **Rustling For Cupid** (1926), an O'Brien Western. Cummings was a solid unpretentious craftsman who could be relied on to direct from two to five films a year with minimal fuss. Most of his silents and early talkies were melodramas. Between 1935 and 1945 he specialized in musicals, directing four with Shirley Temple, three with Alice Faye and Don Ameche, and four starring Betty Grable, who headed the cast of **The Dolly Sisters** (1945), the last film of his long stay at what had become 20th Century-Fox. Near the end of his tenure, in 1943, he received a gold medal for outstanding achievement in the arts and sciences from the Thomas A. Edison Foundation. The last film he directed was the feeble **Double Dynamite** (RKO, 1951), starring Jane Russell, Frank Sinatra and Groucho Marx and produced by his son, Irving Cummings Jr. He officially retired in 1954 and died in Cedars of Lebanon Hospital on April 18, 1959.

Except that he never became a director, Warner Baxter's career vaguely resembles that of the man under whom he earned an Oscar. He was born in Columbus, Ohio on March 29, 1893 and, after graduating from high school, got a job selling farm implements. His first acting experience was in Louisville, Kentucky when a stock company performer took sick and Baxter was more or less drafted to fill in. Four months later his mother found out young Warner was on the stage and made him come home. He went into the insurance business, became head of the Philadelphia office of Travelers, then decided to chuck it all and go west. In Oklahoma he invested his meager savings in a garage and lost every penny. In Dallas he joined a stock company at a salary of $30 a week. He spent the next several years acting all over the country and, in the fall of 1917, starred on Broadway in Frederic and Fanny Hatton's *Lombardi, Ltd*. Appearing in the Morosco Theatre production

with the man who would be the talkies' first Cisco was the last and greatest of the Cisco sidekicks, Leo Carrillo.

Baxter's Hollywood career began in 1921 at the small Realart studio. He advanced quickly from featured player to male lead opposite stars like Constance Binney, Ethel Clayton, Madge Bellamy, Alice Calhoun and Colleen Moore, hopping from studio to studio and from one director to another. (Lambert Hillyer, who directed him in the 1924 **Those Who Dance**, was to become a central figure in the Cisco saga long after Baxter left the role.) Late in 1924 he settled in at Famous Players-Lasky, which would eventually merge into Paramount, and stayed there, with occasional loanouts to other studios, until 1928. Perhaps his best role at Paramount was as the lead in **The Great Gatsby** (1926, directed by Herbert Brenon). Sandwiched among the pictures he played in at Paramount were two Westerns: **A Son Of His Father** (1925, directed by Victor Fleming) and **Drums Of The Desert** (1927, directed by John Waters). Near the end of his time at Paramount he was loaned out to play the romantic Mexican Indian Alessandro opposite Dolores Del Rio in **Ramona** (Inspiration/United Artists, 1928). Before the end of that year he was at Fox, replacing Raoul Walsh in the role of The Cisco Kid, and would remain under contract to the studio till the end of 1939. His peak year during the talkie era was 1936, when he starred back-to-back in probably the finest films of his career—as Dr. Mudd in John Ford's **The Prisoner Of Shark Island** and, at MGM, as Joaquin Murietta in William Wellman's **The Robin Hood Of El Dorado**—and was reportedly the highest paid actor in Hollywood.

But his time at the top soon ended. He suffered a nervous breakdown in the late Thirties, went into psychoanalysis and, looking considerably older and more ravaged, spent most of the Forties at Columbia starring in a "B" detective series as Robert Ordway, The Crime Doctor. His medical problems kept getting worse and he gradually withdrew from Hollywood, moving to Malibu where he went into the real estate business and served a term as mayor. His arthritis became so severe he had to retire from acting. The last film he appeared in was **State Penitentiary** (Columbia, 1950), a low-budget prison flick directed by Lew Landers, who a few years later would figure in the Cisco TV series. In April of 1951 Baxter entered St. John's Hospital in Santa Monica for a partial lobotomy which it was hoped would relieve his arthritis. He developed bronchial pneumonia and died three weeks later, on May 7, survived by actress Winifred

Bryson, his wife for 33 years.

Playing Baxter's **In Old Arizona** nemesis was Edmund Lowe, a native Californian born in San Jose on March 3, 1892. His father was a lawyer and judge while his Irish Catholic mother had no time for anything but motherhood, giving birth to a grand total of two daughters and twelve sons. The most famous of them was reportedly named for the hero of Dumas' **The Count Of Monte Cristo** but if so his mother must have forgotten to check the book before filling out the paperwork because the Dumas protagonist spelled his name not with a u but the French way, Edmond, with an o. Lowe graduated from Santa Clara University, earned a master's degree in pedagogy, then began acting in Los Angeles stock companies and on Broadway, beginning around 1912. His first movie appearances were in 1915. Three years later he began getting roles as featured player or male lead in a variety of silent melodramas and adventure films. As chance would have it, one of these (**Barbara Frietchie**, 1924) was directed by later Cisco stalwart Lambert Hillyer and another (**East Of Suez**, 1925) by Raoul Walsh.

Lowe signed a long-term contract with Fox, where he enjoyed his best known silent role as Sergeant Flagg opposite Victor McLaglen's Captain Quirt in Walsh's ribald comedy about World War I, **What Price Glory** (1926). Before **In Old Arizona** his only work under Irving Cummings had been as star of the gangster flick **Dressed To Kill** (1928). He stayed at Fox till 1932, reprising his Sergeant Flagg role three more times—for Walsh in **The Cock-eyed World** (1929) and **Women Of All Nations** (1931) and for the undistinguished John Blystone in **Hot Pepper** (1933)—and playing Sergeant Mickey Dunn one more time for Cummings in **The Cisco Kid** (1931). During the Thirties he bounced from studio to studio and, when not teamed with Victor McLaglen in other pictures about feuding friends in macho professions, was usually cast as either a suave detective in the Nick Charles manner or a tough sleuth in the tradition of Sam Spade. (Dashiell Hammett, creator of both characters, wrote the screen story that was adapted into one of Lowe's finest crime pictures, Universal's 1935 **Mister Dynamite**.) As the Thirties yielded to the Forties and Lowe himself approached and then passed the half-century mark, the demand for his services fell off. By 1945, the last year in which he had any leading roles at all, he was relegated to Poverty Row outfits like Monogram, which by then had taken over the Cisco series, and PRC. Lowe tried to carve a niche for himself in early television as star of *Front Page Detective* (1951-52), whose production values made PRC look like

MGM. In his sixties he did a few notable TV guest shots, for example as the villain in "War of the Silver Kings" (ABC, Sept. 22, 1957, directed by Budd Boetticher), the premiere episode of *Maverick*. His final appearance on the big screen was in **Heller In Pink Tights** (Paramount, 1960), directed by George Cukor and starring Sophia Loren and Anthony Quinn. His first and third wives had divorced him, his second (actress Lilyan Tashman) had died in 1934, and he had never had any children. Financially secure but alone and in poor health, he died in the Motion Picture Country Home on April 29, 1971.

The career of Dorothy Burgess proved less lucky than those of her male co-stars. She was born in 1907 and had never appeared in a feature before she was signed for **In Old Arizona** where she played the treacherous Tonia. After a few more roles in long-forgotten Fox pictures she was let go and began free-lancing, usually in small parts at the major studios, once in a while as female lead in a Poverty Row quickie. Her big moment after **In Old Arizona** was as co-star with Leo Carrillo and Johnny Mack Brown in **Lasca Of The Rio Grande** (Universal, 1932), one of the many Latin-themed Westerns that poured out of Hollywood in the wake of the first Cisco feature's success. (Those films will be covered in the next chapter.) Burgess left the business in 1935 but came back five years later for tiny parts in half a dozen more pictures, the last of which was **Girls In Chains** (PRC, 1943), directed by the low-budget legend Edgar G. Ulmer. Then she dropped out of sight for keeps and died in 1961.

So much for the three stars and two directors who were responsible for **In Old Arizona**. Now let's take a look at the film.

The year, we learn from an offhand remark about the coming invasion of Cuba, is 1898. A stagecoach pulls into a nameless Arizona town and picks up a load of talkative passengers—including two Irish immigrants, an attractive young woman and a ZaSu Pitts-like hag—while a Mexican street band makes music. The notorious Cisco Kid (Warner Baxter), on whose head there's a $5,000 reward, intercepts the coach on the desert (for no apparent reason dismounting from his black stallion Yaqui to do it), takes the Wells Fargo box but refuses to steal anything from the passengers. "I never rob the individual," he declares, although he does make the pretty woman sell him the brooch she's wearing. The coach rolls on with the horses' harness gear jingling like sleighbells and the holdup is reported at the nearest Army post to the background noise of a military barbershop quartet. The colonel (Roy Stewart) assigns Sergeant Mickey Dunn (Edmund

Lowe), a homesick refugee from the sidewalks of Noo Yawk, to take a squad, hunt Cisco down and kill him.

In another distant Arizona town, the Italian barber (Henry Armetta) bewails having lost $87 savings in the theft of the Wells Fargo box and the citizens are forming a vigilante committee to go after the bandit. "I hate to see workingman lose so much money," says the customer being shaved in the barber chair, who we discover is Cisco. (This sequence seems so much like the **Napoleon's Barber** two-reeler that I can't help wondering whether it was meant to tweak John Ford's nose.) Cisco, who is sprucing up for a visit to his *inamorada*, promises a generous tip if he can take a bath in the Italian's tub. While the barber is drawing hot water, a dust-caked Dunn arrives in town and stops off at the shop for a shave. Cisco and the sergeant trade macho banter in the manner of Walsh's Quirt & Flagg war-buddy movies, with an astonishing display of sexual innuendo as each man admires the size of the other's gun. After Cisco takes his bath he introduces himself to Dunn by the full name he will bear throughout the Fox series, Gonzalo Sebastiano Rodrigo Don Juan Chicuelo, and confides that women call him Conejito, which means little rabbit. "Are you that fast?" Dunn asks in awe, and boasts that his own nickname among "goils" is Big Casino. As he promised, Cisco gives the barber a $100 tip. He and Dunn agree to meet in the local saloon for drinks at 3:00 P.M. Until then, Cisco says, he'll be with his girl. "I like lots of señoritas but I love only one." After he's ridden out of town, the blacksmith (James Marcus) who's been shoeing Dunn's horse tells the sergeant that the Latino he's befriended is the bandit he's been hunting. "Well, I'll be d......!" Dunn exclaims, while a jackass brays.

Whichever director is in charge brings us to the home of Tonia Maria (Dorothy Burgess) a little ahead of Cisco. "El Conejito is coming!" screeches the old lady (Soledad Jiminez) who keeps house for her, and Tonia hastily chases another man out of the way before Cisco arrives. "Someday he will catch you," the old lady warns, and then, she predicts, prefiguring the film's climax, "you will have a flower in your hand but you will not smell it."

There follows a long drawn out sequence of romantic byplay between Cisco and Tonia, spiced with vino and a plate of ham and eggs. (Walsh and countless commentators have misremembered the sizzling eggs on the soundtrack as the sound of bacon frying.) "You got something for me?" Tonia wheedles, and Cisco gives her the brooch he took from the stagecoach. After they

unmistakably have sex, he sends her to town to break his date with Dunn and lies down for a no doubt well-earned nap.

Tonia finds the sergeant in the saloon and makes a play for him but he snubs her and they exchange insults. "Don't get sore," he advises her. "Anybody can make a mistake. That's why they have rubbers on lead pencils." After she flounces out, Dunn discovers from another bar patron that he's been talking with Cisco's woman. Meanwhile a refreshed Cisco is strumming a guitar for the old housekeeper and philosophizing. "Music, wine and love. I don't know which one I could give up if I have to. Maybe I would do without music and wine, but love I got to have always." Telling the origin story that will be repeated through the subsequent Cisco films with first Baxter and then Cesar Romero as the lead, he says that his father came from Portugal and his mother from San Luis Obispo. "I run away from Portugal when I was sixteen. I never see them no more. Now, well, I am sorry." "You are very mysterious," the old woman remarks. "Mysterious?" he says. "Life is full of mysterious. Yesterday and tomorrow. The rainbow's end and the moonbeam's kisses. Who knows?" Later he becomes even more reflective. "What is life after all? The warm breath of a few summers, and the cold chill of a few winters, and then—by golly, I think I need a drink, huh?" And: "The most precious things in the world cannot be bought with gold. The tender touch of a little baby's fingers, the light in a woman's eyes and the love in a woman's heart." When Tonia returns from town, he gives her a handful of gold and says he's going off to steal a cattle herd in Guadalupe. (One that presumably does not belong to an individual.) "Then," he promises, "we go far across the sea to Portugal." Or to any place else that appeals to her. "You got to be happy always. That is what I say to myself." In another line that anticipates the picture's climax, "I always like to see you wave to me when I ride away," he says.

Hardly is Cisco out of sight when Tonia starts bragging to the old lady about how Dunn at the saloon threw himself at her feet. At this precise moment the sergeant shows up, hunting either Cisco or sex or both, and in fact does apologize to her until she invites him into her house. "I'm practically in," he chortles, then sings "There'll be a hot time in the old town tonight." The same overlong scene of romantic byplay she enjoyed with Cisco is now repeated with Dunn, culminating in her reading his fortune with cards and predicting that he'll fall madly in love with her. "You got much money, eh?" she asks. The sergeant offers to take her with him next month when he's reassigned to a New York post at

Governor's Island and rhapsodizes about the Bowery, "finest street in the woild." Hoping to drum up more business with his squad, Tonia asks to be taken to his encampment. "Are there nice soldiers in the camp, eh?" "Yeah," he assures her. "Poifectly nice."

Now comes a sequence that, except for intercut close-ups of Baxter, was clearly shot by Walsh in Utah before his accident. Cisco pockets $4,000 for the Guadalupe cattle he's stolen and is followed across the desert by three toughs (Frank Campeau, Tom Santschi and Pat Hartigan) who plan to shoot him in the back, take the cattle money and collect the bounty on him too. In the film's single and all too brief action scene, Cisco plays dead, turns the tables on the hijackers and kills two of them. "Hey! You coyote you!" he calls after the survivor. "Tell them you meet The Cisco Kid. These other two fellows don't talk no more."

Meanwhile at the squad's camp, while Dunn and two privates (James Bradbury Jr. and Jack Dillon) are belting out a hearty rendition of "The Bowery," Tonia searches the sergeant's tent and finds the reward poster offering $5,000 for Cisco. Knowing that Dunn wants Cisco and not her, she is still overcome by greed and offers a deal: if he'll give her all the reward money, she'll let him know when Cisco returns from Guadalupe so Dunn can kill him. "I'll get a promotion out of this," he tells her. "And a gal! That's enough for me, baby. You get the money." Elsewhere in camp the two privates are discussing how Dunn feels towards Tonia. "He's serious this time," insists the older. "This morning he asked me if I knew anything about buying furniture on the installment plan. Wanted to know how much it would cost to furnish a flat in Flatbush." The younger is unconvinced. "Say, listen, he buys wedding rings like you and me buy bananas. That is, if we bought bananas."

On his way back to Tonia Cisco stops at a gypsy wagon to buy her a beautiful white mantilla but still returns earlier than expected. He finds Dunn's horse in front of her house, sees him leave after unmistakably having had sex with her and overhears her betray herself: "I love no one but you....The Cisco Kid? I never, never loved him, I swear to you...He is a pig. I wish he was dead...Will I get this reward money soon?" She promises to send Dunn a note by the housekeeper as soon as Cisco arrives. "I am not as good as I think I am," Cisco confides to his horse, "and maybe I never was."

He enters the house and engages Tonia in dialogue full of operatic irony. "I was afraid you might not come back," she says. "I would not disappoint you," he replies. "I know how anxious you have been for me to come back." He offers her a last chance to leave for Portugal with him that night but she puts him off till the next day. "You get ready for long, long journey." he tells her solemnly. While he's tending to Yaqui, Tonia writes her note to Dunn. Cisco intercepts the old woman in the stableyard and reads the message, which ends very much like the note in O. Henry's story: "Do not fail, my love. Shoot quick and straight." He tears up the message and substitutes another to the effect that Cisco is terrified of being captured and will try to elude pursuit by leaving Tonia's place at 10:00 P.M. dressed in her clothes and wearing a white mantilla. When the note is delivered to Dunn, he rides off to kill Cisco as one of the privates reminds another that the sergeant is the best shot in the Army.

Cisco is still with Tonia, waiting for the clock to strike ten. "You got something for me?" she demands. "The surprise of your life," he says, wrapping the mantilla around her. Then he pours wine and offers a toast. "To you, my faithful, loyal, constant sweetheart. To your eyes with their warm devotion, and to your lips with their warm kisses, and to the hearts of you and all the other girls in the world who—who are true, I drink." Hearing the hoofbeats of Dunn's horse outside, he prepares to leave. "Adios, my beautiful angel. That is what you are and what you will be—an angel. When I ride away, you stand outside where I can see you, and wave goodbye to me. Then I know you love me. If it is to be the end, I want to know that you are thinking only of me." He mounts and rides away while Tonia stands outside and waves. We hear a shot and a scream and see the woman fall over but are left to imagine Dunn's reaction when he discovers whom he's killed. Bent over in the saddle, a grim heartbroken look in his eyes, Cisco rides slowly into the night as the film's theme song, "My Tonia" by DeSylva, Brown & Henderson, fills the sound track.

Seen from the perspective of generations later, **In Old Arizona** is something less than unanimously acclaimed. Jon Tuska in *The Filming Of The West* (Doubleday, 1976) says that "Baxter invested his portrayal of Cisco with such complexity and lighthearted romance" that he richly earned the Oscar he won for the performance. (440) William K. Everson in *The Hollywood Western* (Citadel Press, 1992) takes a negative view. "There are few exteriors in the film, and many of those take place at night, so they could as easily have been shot in the studio, and probably were. There's very little action, and so much talk that the film seems far longer than it is....What probably caused the excitement....was the fact that Warner Baxter, a very staid and unexciting player

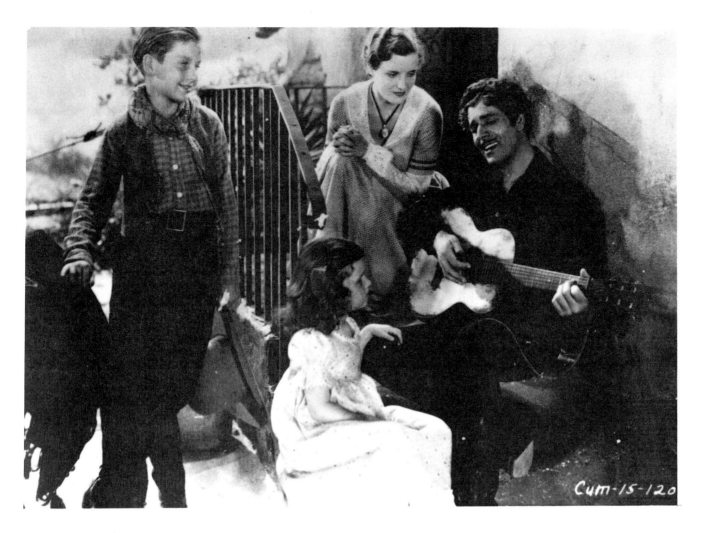

Looks like Cisco (Warner Baxter) is enjoying serenading Sally Benton (Nora Lane) and her two children Billy and Ann (Douglas Haig and Marilyn Knowlden) in this scene from **The Cisco Kid** (Fox, 1931).

in silents, here had a colorful role with a Mexican accent. That in itself probably provided the novelty that won Baxter the Academy Award....., though it was a routine piece of acting at best." (130-132) My own opinion is somewhere between these poles. Baxter's Cisco projects a convincing philosophic sadness and his Latino accent is far superior to that of the other Anglo actors who played romantic bandito roles in the early Thirties. The scenes that were clearly directed by Walsh in Utah are physically beautiful and, in an unselfconscious way lacking all trace of today's political correctness mania, reflect the multicultural ambience of the late 19th century West, for example in the bits with the Russian immigrant waiting for the stagecoach and the Chinese in the crowd at the vigilantes' harangue. But the film is sadly deficient in action and betrays the story it's nominally based on by telegraphing O. Henry's surprise ending long before the climax. Some of the dialogue is rather

poetic but there's far too much of it and at times it's drowned out by the orgy of background noises—everything from a saloon piano to a bawling baby to an ancient gramophone to the horses' jingling harness gear to the famous sizzling eggs—which constantly scream at us: "Listen! These are real sounds you're hearing!" In that sense **In Old Arizona** is the aural counterpart of those 3-D movies from the early Fifties that bombarded audiences with chairs, flaming arrows and anything else that could be hurled at a camera.

Whatever we think of the film today, the Fox executives in 1929 and their competitors at other studios knew very quickly that **In Old Arizona** was a winner. Over the next few years Hollywood launched a tidal wave of Latin-themed Westerns—including two more Fox features starring Warner Baxter, **Romance Of The Rio Grande** (1929) and **The Arizona Kid** (1930)—which we will consider in Chapter Four. But before any more Cisco Kid films could be made, a new arrangement had to be negotiated with O. Henry's estate. Once that process was completed, Fox began work on **The Cisco Kid** (1931), with Irving Cummings as both producer and director, and a screenplay by Alfred A. Cohn that picks up on and creatively varies the themes from **In Old Arizona**. Warner Baxter and Edmund Lowe of course were back as Cisco and Sergeant Dunn, and Cummings even rehired James Bradbury Jr. and Jack Dillon to reprise their roles as the two privates who try to help Dunn catch his man. This time Cisco had two love interests, the Latina played by Conchita Montenegro and the Anglo by Nora Lane, and also two sidekicks. Lopez was played by Charles Stevens, a grandson of Geronimo who enjoyed a long career in Hollywood playing Indians, Mexicans, South Sea witch doctors and other ethnic types, while the part of Gordito went to a grossly overweight actor who was to be involved with Cisco films for many years to come.

Ysabel Ponciana Chris-Pin Martin Piaz was born in Tucson in 1894 of a Yaqui father and a Mexican mother. In his teens he held menial jobs as a water boy and a barber's assistant until 1911, when he joined a troupe of Indians headed for Hollywood and movie work. He spent years as an extra or an unbilled bit player in countless silents and early talkies, most of them Westerns. At the time he appeared as Gordito in **The Cisco Kid** his screen name was Chris Martin but he changed it to Chris-Pin Martin later in the Thirties and, under his new byline, continued to play Gordito as long as 20th Century-Fox released Cisco pictures and briefly came back in the part during Gilbert Roland's tenure as Cisco. In the spring of 1953, soon after returning from a personal appearance tour of Europe and the Middle East, he was hospitalized with a mild heart attack. He seemed to recover and was resuming his normal life when he collapsed with another heart seizure after addressing a meeting of the Montebello Moose Lodge. He died on June 27, 1953 at age 59, survived by a widow and five children, and already thirty times a grandfather and twice a great-granddad.

The Cisco Kid opens on a bright morning during the administration of President McKinley when Sergeant Mickey Dunn (Edmund Lowe) and Privates Dixon and Bouse (James Bradbury, Jr. and Jack Dillon) are sent out to capture Cisco, who's back in Arizona territory committing robberies despite the $5,000 price still on his head. Meanwhile Cisco is running stolen cattle over the border with his compadres Gordito (Chris-Pin Martin) and Lopez (Charles Stevens).

Seeing the three troopers after him, Cisco has his pals shoot at him and pretend to be the owners of the cattle. The troopers chase Cisco to the accompaniment of agitato music, a genuine rarity in Westerns of the very early 1930s, but his black stallion Yaqui outdistances them and Cisco then heads for the town of Carrizo and the pleasures of women and wine.

In the local saloon, the sheriff (Frederick Burt) and banker Hankins (Willard Robertson) are at a balcony table, plotting to take over widowed Sally Benton's Star Bar ranch. Carmencita (Conchita Montenegro), with whom the sheriff is infatuated, performs a fiery Spanish dance for an appreciative audience including Cisco, who has a balcony seat across the saloon. Seeing romantic byplay between the dancer and the Mexican stranger, the jealous sheriff shoots across the room at Cisco. A gun battle breaks out and Carmencita keeps the sheriff from chasing after Cisco, then meets the stranger in a secluded spot for an interlude of amore. "When I look at jou," Cisco says, "then I drink from the fountain of joung. I love only the beauty and I trust no woman. No woman are faithful." This of course is a reference to his betrayal by Tonia Maria in **In Old Arizona**. "All women I hate," he declares just before taking Carmencita into his arms.

That same evening, Dunn and the two enlisted men ride into Carrizo. As soon as he steps inside the saloon, Dunn is mobbed by dance hall girls. Learning that his favorite Carmencita has gone off to dally with "the king of Mexico," Dunn suspects his rival is Cisco and sets out after them. One saloon girl slips away to warn Carmencita and Cisco. Racing out of town, Cisco is chased by the troopers and wounded. The next morning he falls off Yaqui in the front yard of the Star Bar ranch. Sally Benton (Nora Lane) and her children Billy and Ann (Douglas Haig and Marilyn Knowlden) nurse him back to health. Meanwhile in Carrizo, Dunn repeats his behavior with **In Old Arizona**'s Tonia by inviting Carmencita to return to his native New York City with him in three months when his hitch is up and he's collected the $5,000 on Cisco's head. More faithful than Tonia, the dancer sends him off on a wild goose chase by claiming Cisco told her he was headed for California.

During the next two weeks, while Dunn and the privates are hunting Cisco in all the wrong places, our romantic bandit is recovering at the Star Bar and befriending Sally and her children, who call him Tio (Spanish for uncle). Gordito and Lopez show up at the ranch with a note to Cisco from Carmencita, explaining how she threw the troopers off the scent. Billy confides in his Tio

Warner Baxter as the Cisco Kid and Nora Lane in a gripping scene from the conclusion of **The Cisco Kid** (Fox, 1931).

that banker Hankins will take over the ranch unless Sally can come up with the $5,000 her late husband had owed him. Sergeant Dunn happens to drop by the Star Bar, is invited by Sally to stay for supper, and soon learns that a wounded Mexican has been living there for the past two weeks. Luckily Cisco and his compadres have left the ranch that afternoon to visit Carrizo and take care of Sally's financial problem.

Before going into action, Cisco stops off at Carmencita's place for another romantic interlude. ("For one sweet kiss from jou, *mi adorada*, I would spend a dozen years in purgatory.") Carmencita begs to be taken along when he returns to Mexico but, distrusting women as much as ever, he promises nothing. While Gordito and Lopez stage a gun battle on the main street to distract the townspeople, Cisco steals $5,000 from the bank. Dunn rides in during the excitement, just in time to see Carmencita apparently get shot by Hankins as he's firing at the fleeing Cisco, but this turns out to be another diversion so that the romantic rogue can get away.

Cisco returns to the Star Bar and gives Sally the $5,000 he claims he "withdrew" from the bank for her. Seeing Dunn riding up, he races off the property. But as Yaqui leaps a fence barrier where little Ann is standing, the child falls over. Cisco comes back to make sure she isn't hurt and Dunn arrests him. When the sergeant learns of his prisoner's good deeds for the Bentons, he abandons all hope of collecting the reward, pretends to Sally that he's convinced he had the

wrong man, and allows Cisco to go back across the border.

Prints of **The Cisco Kid** are hard to come by, and no book on Westerns discusses it in any detail. In *Hollywood Corral* (Popular Library, 1976), by all odds the most knowledgeable volume ever written on the "B" Western, Don Miller dismisses the picture as "a throwaway production running a bare hour and [one that] made little impression." (182) The most extensive discussion I've seen comes from one of the program notes prepared by William K. Everson for his New School film series (May 1, 1981). Everson describes **The Cisco Kid** as "by far the best of the early ones [i.e. the three Ciscos in which Baxter starred], partly because it is the shortest. There is no padding, no excess of dialogue, no novelty prolongation of Baxter's Spanish accent. True, there is not very much real action, but the story itself keeps on the move, and when there is some traditional action, it is punctuated both by music and first-class photography. The night chase near the beginning is beautifully done, and the short street shootup near the end is given added excitement by intelligent camera mobility. In fact the camera is mobile throughout, unusual both for the period and for the normally rather dull director...." For whatever reason, Fox put no more Cisco exploits on its shooting schedules. But Westerns of the same general type as **In Old Arizona** and **The Cisco Kid** continued to pour out of other studios as the early Thirties rolled on.

A newspaper ad from 1930. (Courtesy of Charles K. Stumpf.)

Four • Los Otros Caballeros: Latin-Themed Westerns from the Teens to the Fifties

In the golden decade of silent movies between the end of World War I and the coming of sound, Latino actors and characters figured prominently. The first superstar of the Twenties was Rudolph Valentino, whom William K. Everson in *American Silent Film* (Oxford University Press, 1978) ranks with Clark Gable as "the most clear-cut romantic idol that the movies ever created." (166) Other studios hoping to match the success of the Valentino pictures concocted star vehicles for actors like Antonio Moreno, Ramon Novarro and, down on poverty row, Don Alvarado. None of these men were identified with Westerns, although Valentino just missed starring in one. According to Richard Schickel's *D.W. Griffith: An American Life* (Simon & Schuster, 1984), Griffith had seriously considered the not yet famous Valentino for the male lead, loosely based on bandit Joaquin Murietta, in his 1919 Western **Scarlet Days**, but had rejected him in favor of Richard Barthelmess, who played the dashing rogue Alvarez with "his hair plastered down and a goatee and a mustache plastered on...." (411) The period's best known Western with Hispanic motifs was **The Mark Of Zorro** (Fairbanks/United Artists, 1920, directed by Fred Niblo), whose star Douglas Fairbanks was no more Latino than Barthelmess. Clearly by the time Warner Baxter was first cast as The Cisco Kid, the tradition of making Latin-themed Westerns with Anglo leads had been solidly established. As silents gave way to talkies, that tradition continued.

About six months after **In Old Arizona**'s release, Fox followed it up with another romantic Western featuring a Latin ambience and Warner Baxter. **Romance Of The Rio Grande** (Fox, 1929) was directed by Alfred Santell from a screenplay by Marion Orth based on Katharine Fullerton Gerould's 1923 novel *Conquistador*. Pablo Wharton Cameron (Warner Baxter), whose grandfather Don Fernando (Robert Edeson) disowned Pablo's mother years before for marrying a gringo, is injured by bandits and brought to Don Fernando's hacienda to recover. There he falls in love with the Don's adopted daughter Manuelita (Mona Maris) and defeats the scheme of a fortune hunter (Antonio Moreno) to marry the young woman and take over the family estates. A dozen years later, as we'll see, an almost completely different adaptation of Gerould's novel became the basis for a Cisco picture with the same title as this film.

One of the earliest talkies to show a trace of **In Old Arizona**'s influence was a low-budget serial produced by Mascot Pictures, the poverty-row outfit specializing in quickie cliffhangers that entrepreneur Nat Levine had founded in 1927. The company's first all-talking release, **The Lone Defender** (Mascot, 1930), was directed by Richard Thorpe and starred the legendary Rin-Tin-Tin. Silent serial hero Walter Miller played the human lead, a reputed outlaw by the name of Ramon Roberto who joins Rinty and a plucky teenager (Buzz Barton) to track down the killers of a Mexican prospector and recover the treasure map the dead man had concealed in his pocket watch. At the end of Chapter 12 we discover that Ramon isn't a bandito at all but a special agent of the Justice Department!

The first of the larger studios to enter the Latino Robin Hood genre in Fox's footsteps was RKO, the new incarnation of what in the silent era had been known as FBO. **Beau Bandit** (RKO, 1930) was directed by Lambert Hillyer, who had turned out several of the William S. Hart features for Paramount during the Twenties, and the screenplay was by Wallace Smith, based on his own magazine story "Strictly Business" (Cosmopolitan, April 1929). It's in this film that the idea of giving the Cisco figure a sidekick seems to have originated. The outlaw Montero (Rod LaRocque) and his deaf-mute partner Coloso (Mitchell Lewis) are being pursued by Sheriff Bobcat Manners (Walter Long) and a posse. Montero decides to replenish his funds by holding up a bank but changes his plans when the corrupt

George Cooper, George E. Stone and Frank Fay in a publicity still for **Under A Texas Moon** (Warner Brothers, 1930).

banker Perkins (Charles Middleton) offers him money to kill the fiancé (George Duryea, later and better known as Tom Keene) of music teacher Helen Wardell (Doris Kenyon), whom he wants for himself. Montero pretends to commit the murder, collects his blood money, then lets Perkins know he's been scammed and forces the banker, who happens also to be a justice of the peace, to unite the music teacher and her lover in wedlock. This is precisely the kind of story that in the late Thirties and early Forties would serve the Cisco series well. As luck would have it, Lambert Hillyer ended up directing one Cisco feature (after the series moved from 20th-Fox to Monogram) and dozens of 30-minute Cisco TV films.

Meanwhile the people at Warners were treading on RKO's tail with **Under A Texas Moon** (Warner Bros., 1930), the first talkie in the Cisco mold to be shot in color. The screenplay was by Gordon Rigby, based on Stewart Edward White's short story "Two-Gun Man" (<u>Famous Story</u> <u>Magazine</u>, October 1925), and the director was Hungarian-born Michael Curtiz, who would stay longer at Warners and helm more of the studio's Golden Age classics (including **Captain Blood, The Charge Of The Light Brigade, The Adventures Of Robin Hood, Angels With Dirty Faces, Dodge City, The Sea Hawk, Casablanca** and **Mildred Pierce**) than any other film-maker. **Under A Texas Moon** however keeps far from the roster of Curtiz' greatest hits. While hunting some stolen Texas cattle whose recovery will net him a huge reward, that dashing caballero Don Carlos (Frank Fay) dallies with four separate and distinct señoritas (Armida, Raquel Torres, Mona Maris and Myrna Loy) before stowing the bad guys in a food cooler and galloping back to Mexico with the luckiest of the quartet (Loy) by his side. Frank Fay's freckled Irish mug makes him hard to buy as a Hispanic.

Early in 1930 Fox began planning a sequel to **In Old Arizona** with Warner Baxter again cast as

GRAND Playing Now

A newspaper clipping from **The Arizona Kid** (Fox, 1930). (Courtesy of Charles K. Stumpf.)

Cisco and Edmund Lowe as his adversary the cavalry sergeant, but just before shooting was to commence, the studio discovered that all it had ever purchased from O. Henry's estate was the right to make a single movie about the Cisco character. This is why **The Arizona Kid** (Fox, 1930), directed by Alfred Santell from a screenplay by Ralph Block, looks and feels like a second full-length Cisco exploit but in fact isn't: Baxter's character was renamed and Lowe's scrapped at the last minute. In the picture as released, the notorious Arizona Kid (Warner Baxter) poses as a wealthy Mexican mine owner and romances the beautiful Lorita (Mona Maris) while pursuing his career as a thief. Then he falls in love with Virginia Hoyt (Carole Lombard), an Eastern woman who's come West with her brother Nick (Theodor von Eltz). When bandits raid the mine that's supposed to be the source of his wealth and kill two of his compañeros, the Kid discovers that behind the murders are Virginia and Nick, who is not her brother but her husband. After the Kid takes appropriate revenge, he and Lorita make their getaway. "Considering the relative paucity of spectacular action," says William K. Everson, "**The Arizona Kid** does keep nicely on the move. The outdoor locations are excellent, the saloon and other interiors big and colorful, and full of busy extras. Scenes never run too long so that the stress on dialogue doesn't slow it down, and it does move steadily towards a good climax. It's a handsome film, and the only disappointing aspect is the miscasting of Carole Lombard, and her resulting rather pallid performance."

By this time other studios had come to believe they too might profit from romantic bandito movies and were rushing to put their own variations on the theme into release. Paramount weighed in with **The Texan** (Paramount, 1930), directed by John Cromwell from a screenplay by Daniel Nathan Rubin based on Oliver H.P. Garrett's adaptation of another O. Henry story, "A Double-Dyed Deceiver" (Everybody's Magazine, December 1905; collected in *Roads Of Destiny*, 1909.) On the run after killing a gambler he'd caught cheating at poker, the Llano Kid (Gary Cooper) boards a train and is persuaded by fellow passenger Thacker (Oscar Apfel) that he's the perfect man to impersonate Enrique, the long-lost son of wealthy Señora Ibarra (Emma Dunn), and become her heir. At the Ibarra hacienda, however, the Kid falls in love with the Señora's niece Consuelo (Fay Wray) and learns that the genuine Enrique is none other than the man he killed over the poker game. The Kid breaks with Thacker, is framed for a robbery at the hacienda and has to go on the run again, with his old friend the Bible-quoting sheriff John Brown (James Marcus) in hot pursuit. After the Kid kills Thacker, the sheriff lets him go and identifies Thacker's body as that of the young fugitive. This may sound like a rip-off of the climax from King Vidor's **Billy The Kid** (MGM, 1930) where (in defiance of historical fact) Pat Garrett pretends to have killed Billy and lets him escape across the border, but **The Texan** actually came out several months earlier.

On almost anyone's list of Western stars who should never have been allowed to play Latinos, Ken Maynard would surely rank near the top. But that's precisely what he played in **Song Of The Caballero** (Universal, 1930), directed by Harry Joe Brown. The adaptation of this picture was by Bennett Cohen, the dialogue by Lesley Mason and the story by Kenneth C. Beaton and Norman Sper. Juan (Ken Maynard), a bandit who preys only on the properties of the Madera family because of the way Don Pedro Madera (Francis Ford) mistreated Juan's mother, falls in love with Anita (Doris Hill), the fiancé of Don Pedro's worthless son José (Gino Corrado). After fighting a duel with José, Juan reveals that he's Don Pedro's nephew. William K. Everson in *The Hollywood Western* describes this 60-minute quickie as "about the most bizarre Western ever made. It looks for all the world like an imitation-Fairbanks swash-

35

buckling script....[which was converted] into a Western with no changes other than that of transposing a (presumably) European locale into California. The most curious aspect of it all, perhaps indicative of haste, is that all of the dialogue was taut and stilted, as though the players were limited to mouthing the original subtitles. There was an endearing quality to the bemused heroine ....listening to Maynard's declarations of love, couched in phrases better suited to Valentino or Fairbanks, and which Maynard delivered as though reading them for the first and only time, which he probably was. Even casual expressions retained the flavor of a different locale and period; Maynard constantly refers to his pals as 'Comrades,' and the dusty trail is always 'the King's Highway.' Fisticuffs are jettisoned in favor of rapiers, and in the climactic set-to, Maynard is leaping over balconies and dueling with a half dozen of the villain's cronies.... Maynard's distinctly clumsy swordplay is far from convincing." (129-130) It does not seem a great injustice that except for Everson's discussion **Song Of The Caballero** remains unsung.

Next out of the cinematic frijole pot came the low-budget, low-action **Rogue Of The Rio Grande** (SonoArt WorldWide, 1930), starring Argentine actor José Bohr as, to quote film historian Jon Tuska, "a glamorous road agent dressed in black and bedecked in tooled leather and silver, who steals from the rich and provides for the poor and who is finally reformed from his wayward life through the love of a beautiful señorita." The screenplay was by prolific B Western scripter Oliver Drake and the director was Spencer Gordon Bennet, at his best a maker of superb serials and Westerns but so often nowhere near his best. The notorious bandit El Malo (José Bohr) and his men rob the safe of Seth Landport (Gene Morgan), the mayor of Sierra Blanca. Sheriff Rankin (Walter Miller, who starred in several of Bennet's silent cliffhanger serials for Pathé) offers a reward for the thief. Later El Malo and his sidekick Pedro (Raymond Hatton) come back to town for romantic interludes with the cantina dancers Carmita (Myrna Loy) and Dolores (Carmelita Geraghty). Eventually El Malo witnesses the mayor committing a stagecoach robbery, denounces Landport to the sheriff, escapes arrest himself by the skin of his teeth and, in company with Pedro and Carmita, heads for the border. In his essay on Spencer Bennet, reprinted in revised form in *A Variable Harvest* (McFarland, 1990), Tuska has little good to say about the film. "Bohr spoke in a labored, exaggerated accent and this only made the long, static indoor sequences move even more

slowly. Myrna Loy sang a couple of songs... but they were ineptly staged and proved tedious." (128)

The title character in **Captain Thunder** (Warner Bros., 1930) was not a comicbook superhero as the name suggests but one more Latino rogue in the Cisco mold. Capitán Tronido (Victor Varconi), a romantic scoundrel being hunted by Commandante Ruiz (Charles Judels), becomes involved with beautiful Ynez Dominguez (Fay Wray) and her impoverished lover Juan Sebastian (Don Alvarado). When Ynez is pressured by her father (John Sainpolis) to marry wealthy and corrupt rancher Pete Morgan (Robert Elliott), Juan vows to earn money and win his amorada by collecting the price on Captain Thunder's head. The Captain has been smitten by Ynez himself and almost falls into the Commandante's trap when he visits the señorita but she hides him and helps him escape. Morgan, to whom Captain Thunder owes a favor, compels the bandito to make prisoners of Ynez and Juan as they're on their way to be married and then to force Ynez into marrying Morgan himself. Man of honor that he is, the Captain keeps his word. As the film ends, Ynez hears a shot and Captain Thunder informs her that she's just become a widow. Alan Crosland directed from a screenplay by Gordon Rigby and dialogue by William K. Wells, based on Pierre Couderc and Hal Davitt's original story "The Gay Caballero." It's not clear whether the picture was meant to be funny.

The last of the year's bandito films and one of the most ambitious was **The Lash** (First National, 1930), an attempt at a wide-screen epic along the lines of Fox's **The Big Trail** and MGM's **Billy The Kid**. Frank Lloyd directed from a screenplay by Bradley King based on Lanier and Virginia Stivers Bartlett's 1929 novel *Adios!* Don Francisco Delfino (Richard Barthelmess), whose father has been murdered by corrupt land commissioner Peter Harkness (Fred Kohler), creates the identity of the outlaw El Puma in his quest for revenge. Sheriff David Howard (James Rennie) falls in love with Fernando's sister Dolores (Marian Nixon) and, after Fernando has killed Harkness, allows him to escape and rejoin his sweetheart Rosita (Mary Astor). Everson in *The Hollywood Western* calls the picture "a pedestrian ... Western in which only a fairly large cattle stampede sequence could in any way be said to justify big-screen treatment." (140) But this strange mix of elements from **Billy The Kid, In Old Arizona** and **The Mark Of Zorro** was by no means the poorest of the Ciscoesque early talkies.

After the deluge of such pictures that came out in 1930, it seems amazing that only three more joined the ranks in 1931. (Fox's **The Cisco Kid**, the first official sequel to **In Old Arizona**, was also a 1931 title but isn't being considered here.) Columbia's Western star Buck Jones played the lead in **The Avenger** (Columbia, 1931), directed by that fine visual stylist Roy William Neill from a screenplay by George Morgan based on an original story by Jack Townley. The time is 1849, and on the stagecoach taking him to visit his brother, Joaquin Murietta (Buck Jones) strikes up a friendship with Helen Lake (Dorothy Revier), who is coming to California to teach school. Later in town, Joaquin gets into a fight with three vicious Anglo gold hunters led by Al Goss (Walter Percival). The trio follow Joaquin to the claim being worked by his younger brother Juan (Paul Fix), get the drop on the Muriettas, beat Joaquin brutally, tie him to a tree and make him watch them hang Juan. Later they file on the Murietta claim and take over the mine. Forging a Zorroesque identity for himself as The Black Shadow, Joaquin attacks every stagecoach containing profits from the claim and secretly leaves placards in town, threatening Goss and his partners with death. Assigned to track down The Black Shadow is none other than Helen Lake's father (Edward Hearn), an Army captain. Ultimately Joaquin manipulates events so that the three killers wind up dead but not by his hands, and on learning the facts Captain Lake agrees to let Joaquin go free and take Helen with him. Everson in *The Hollywood Western* describes **The Avenger** as "a grim little film played for tension rather than action, [with] superb lighting and camera work..., (161) while Tuska in **The Filming Of The West** rhapsodizes about "one stunning shot when Buck, a black silhouette against a clouded horizon behind which the setting sun blazes, rides off into a diffused haze." (226) It's a shame that Roy William Neill (who is best known for Universal's Sherlock Holmes series starring Basil Rathbone and Nigel Bruce) never again directed a Western, and even more of a shame that this stunningly made little film was spoiled by Buck Jones' ludicrous stabs at a Mexican accent.

In the fall of that year and about a month after the release of Fox's **The Cisco Kid**, Universal offered its second entry in the Latin Western sweepstakes but, like most of the later 1930s Westerns with Latin protagonists or backgrounds, this one wasn't a romantic bandito picture and owed little to the Cisco films except **In Old Arizona**'s female lead Dorothy Burgess. **Lasca Of The Rio Grande** (Universal, 1931) was directed by Edward Laemmle from a screenplay by Randall Faye and a story by Tom Reed with roots in, of all unlikely things, a poem: "Lasca" by the English-born cowboy writer Frank Desprez. Both Texas Ranger José Santa Cruz (Leo Carrillo) and handsome young Miles Kincaid (Johnny Mack Brown) are in love with Lasca (Dorothy Burgess), a dance hall girl wanted for murder. At the end of this strange picture, Lasca saves Santa Cruz from having to choose between love and duty by diving into a herd of stampeding cattle and killing herself.

The next few salsa-flavored Westerns had even less of a Cisco connection than that one. In **Two Gun Caballero** (Imperial, 1931, directed by Jack Nelson), Robert Frazer starred in a dual role as an Anglo cowboy framed for murder and a Mexican who happens to be his identical double. The plot of course has Frazer returning to the States in Latino disguise to root out the real killer.

Hardly had a new year begun when the studio that had started the bandito cycle released **The Gay Caballero** (Fox, 1932), directed by Alfred Werker from a screenplay by Philip Klein and Barry Connors based on Tom Gill's 1931 novel *The Gay Bandit Of The Border*. No matter how much this may sound like another unofficial sequel to **In Old Arizona**, it isn't, and Fox action star George O'Brien is cast as an Anglo. College football hero Ted Radcliffe (George O'Brien) comes West to inspect the inherited cattle ranch that's supporting him and falls in love with Adela Morales (Conchita Montenegro). The señorita's father Don Paco (C. Henry Gordon) and his henchman Jito (Weldon Heyburn) are behind the systematic looting of Ted's ranch. The mysterious outlaw El Coyote who's been fighting Don Paco's schemes to rule the territory turns out to be another Anglo, Don Bob Harkness (Victor McLaglen). Except for the title there's no similarity whatever between this film and 20th-Fox's 1940 Cisco feature of the same name.

The next entry in Columbia's Buck Jones series borrowed somewhat from **The Avenger**, with Buck not only playing another Mexican but again seeking vengeance for the death of a younger brother played by Paul Fix. This time, however, he stays on the side of the law all the way. **South Of The Rio Grande** (Columbia, 1932) was directed by Lambert Hillyer, who had helmed **Beau Bandit** two years before, from a screenplay by Milton Krims and a story by Harold Shumate. Carlos Valderez (Buck Jones), an officer in the Mexican rurales, pursues the cantina dancer Consuela (Mona Maris) who's responsible for the death of his brother Juan (Paul Fix). As coincidence would have it, Consuela's latest target is Carlos' best friend, Ramon Ruiz (George J. Lewis), whom she's trying to ruin so that her partner Clark (Philo McCullough) can take over the oil-rich Ruiz lands. "Buck Jones does a Warner Baxter in this one," Variety commented, "and gets away with it nicely."

Tom Mix half-heartedly worked the same territory in **The Texas Bad Man** (Universal, 1932), directed by Edward Laemmle, who had helmed **Lasca Of The Rio Grande** the previous year. Mix plays a ranger posing as an outlaw to infiltrate the gang he's been assigned to break up, but about halfway through the picture and for no particular reason he dresses up as a Mexican and spends the next scenes inadvertently amusing us with his Pennsylvania Spanish accent. Maybe Mix's experience taught Buck Jones a lesson. In his next Western with Latin motifs, **The California Trail** (Columbia, 1933), directed by Lambert Hillyer from a screenplay by Jack Natteford, the setting is California prior to 1849 and just about everyone else in the cast is supposed to be Latin but Buck plays an Anglo scout, Santa Fe Stewart, who becomes a sort of Zorro figure to help free a province from the tyrannical rule of two brothers (Luis Alberni and George Humbert).

If a prize were offered for the most obscure oater of the Thirties that owed a debt to the Cisco saga, one of the prime contenders would be **Call Of The Coyote** (Imperial, 1934, directed by Patrick Carlyle). This 50-minute hunk of junk, which Everson in *The Hollywood Western* describes as "memorably inept" (278), stars Kenneth Thomson as Don Adios, a sombreroed Robin Hood who tries to save a hidden gold mine for its murdered owner's baby daughter. Our hero's sidekick, portrayed by Charles Stevens (Warner Baxter's compadre from **The Cisco Kid**), is called Pancho.

Another candidate for the prize, **The Pecos Dandy** (Security, 1934), starred George J. Lewis in the title role of a fancily garbed caballero who's framed as a horse thief by his rival for a woman's love. The screenplay, assuming there was one, seems to have been by L.V. Jefferson, and the director was either Victor Adamson (a grade-Z hack also known as Denver Dixon and Art Mix) or Horace B. Carpenter. A reviewer for England's Kinematograph Weekly (November 5, 1936) described the film as "so badly mutilated in the cutting that it is only with difficulty that the plot can be followed, while added to this there are players of little standing or ability, and dialogue that is more often than not out of sync...[S]o clumsily edited is the picture that it is impossible to know which [actor] plays the part of the villain." That George J. Lewis' character was Latino is an educated guess: he'd been born in Mexico and appeared mainly in Spanish-language features until he became established as a character actor in B Westerns. He had substantial roles opposite both Duncan Renaldo and Gilbert Roland in Monogram's Cisco films of the middle 1940s, and in the late Fifties he was seen regularly on the Disney *Zorro* teleseries as Guy Williams' father.

Among the Westerns from 1935 that deserve a moment of our attention are a pair of long-forgotten quickies that sound less like films in the Cisco tradition and more like romantic musicals with a Latin flavor. **Under The Pampas Moon** (Fox, 1935) gave Warner Baxter yet another chance to show off his accent as Cesar Campo, who follows the trail of his stolen horse to Buenos Aires and a fling with singer Yvonne LaMarr (Ketti Gallian). James Tinling directed from a screenplay by Ernest Pascal and Bradley King, based on an original story by Gordon Morris, with additional dialogue by Henry Johnson. Featured in the cast of this tuneful trifle were Tito Guizar (who would play the Ciscoesque lead in **The Llano Kid** four years later) and the fattest of all Cisco sidekicks, Chris-Pin Martin. In more or less the same vein was **Hi, Gaucho!** (RKO, 1935), directed by Tommy Atkins from a screenplay by Adele Buffington based on Atkins' original story. In his first starring role, John Carroll as the heroic Lucio sets out to save lovely but naive Inez (Steffi Duna) from an impostor posing as the man to whom she's been promised in marriage. The villain was portrayed by Rod LaRocque, who had played a spiritual cousin of Cisco five years before in the same studio's **Beau Bandit**.

Another strong contender for the Most Obscure Latin Oater award is **The Irish Gringo** (Keith, 1935), directed by veteran B-movie cinematographer William C. Thompson from a screenplay by "Patrick Petersalia," apparently a joint alias for Thompson himself and Patrick Carlyle, who also starred as Irish-Mexican adventurer Don O'Brien. (Did the makers of this atrocity think Gringo was another word for Latino?) While roaming the West with his pals Pancho and Buffalo, the Don is framed for the murder of old prospector Pop Wiley (William Farnum), who before his death had drawn a map showing the location of the Lost Dutchman mine in his little granddaughter's blouse. As if that weren't trouble enough, O'Brien has to contend with the jealousy of a girlfriend who mistakenly believes he's romancing another woman. In February 1936 the trade press reported that unpaid creditors had foreclosed on the negative of this picture. Small loss.

So little is known about **The Tia Juana Kid** (Sunset, 1936) that even the three-volume

Harold Huber, Nino Martini and Leo Carrillo have the other players with their hands up in this scene from **The Gay Desperado** (United Artists, 1936).

American Film Institute Catalog covering features of the Thirties isn't much help. The picture was directed and written by Jack Nelson, who had also been responsible for the 1931 **Two Gun Caballero**. The hero, a gallant bandito calling himself El Capitán, seems to have been played by Patrick Carlyle, who directed **Call Of The Coyote** and starred in **The Irish Gringo**. The release date, or maybe I should say the date it escaped, was sometime in January 1936. I wouldn't want to bet money that anyone actually saw it.

Of all the decade's films with roots in the Cisco saga the best was **The Robin Hood Of El Dorado** (MGM, 1936), directed by William A. Wellman from a screenplay by himself, Joseph Calleia and Melvin Levy based on Walter Noble Burns' heavily fictionized biography of Joaquin Murietta, **The Robinhood Of El Dorado** (1932). In perhaps the finest performance of his career, Warner Baxter starred as the honest farmer who turns revolutionary outlaw after his wife (Margo)

is murdered by Anglos with designs on the Murietta property. Everson in *The Hollywood Western* describes the film as a "romanticized but still very rugged" account of the historic character whom Buck Jones had played in **The Avenger** with much less conviction.

The actors most of us identify with the saga made separate if minor contributions to the pseudo-Cisco cycle later that year. In **Rebellion** (Crescent, 1936), directed by Lynn Shores from a screenplay and original story by John Thomas Neville that seems somewhat indebted to **The Robin Hood Of El Dorado**, the setting is California in 1850. Sent to protect the new American territory's Mexicans from Anglo raiders, Captain John Carroll (Tom Keene) falls in love with Paula Castillo (Rita Cansino) and helps her brother Ricardo (Duncan Renaldo) and his guerrilla band defeat the oppressors. Cansino was to become better known as Rita Hayworth and Renaldo as The Cisco Kid. In release at around the same time

39

was **The Gay Desperado** (Pickford-Lasky/United Artists, 1936), a musical comedy directed by Rouben Mamoulian, in which a crooning Mexican theater usher (Nino Martini) is drafted into a post-Prohibition outlaw group whose leader Braganza (Leo Carrillo), taking his cue from American movie gangsters, has decided to specialize in kidnapping. The singing draftee falls in love with the ring's first victim (Ida Lupino) and the rest is romance and music. Thirteen years later Carrillo would join forces with Renaldo and inaugurate what for my generation anyway is the golden age of the Cisco legend.

One of the last Ciscoesque features to be released was actually one of the first to be shot. **The Phantom Of Santa Fe** (Burroughs-Tarzan, 1936), directed by Jacques Jaccard from a scenario by Charles Francis Royal, starred Twenties matinee idol Norman Kerry as a sort of cross between Cisco and Zorro. By day he poses as the spineless idler Miguel Morago, but when romantic banditry beckons, he leaves a servant behind disguised as himself to furnish an alibi and rides out at the head of his caballeros, calling himself The Hawk, or sometimes The Phantom of Santa Fe. Both he and Anglo entrepreneur Steve Gant (Frank Mayo) are romancing Teresa Valarde (Nena Quartaro), daughter of the district's wealthiest ranchero, although Gant is also involved with Lola (Carmelita Geraghty), a cantina girl. Framed by his rival for the theft of priceless religious treasures from the local mission, Miguel enlists the jealous Lola to expose Gant's treachery. At the climax as Gant pulls a gun and tries to escape from the Valarde hacienda, a padre cries out "In the name of the Lord, stop!" and a crucifix magically drops from the wall to knock the pistol from the villain's hand. According to Everson in *The Hollywood Western*, the film was made at Universal around 1929, as a silent in Cinecolor, but was then shelved for several years before being sold to the short-lived Burroughs-Tarzan, which released the picture in 1936 as a talkie "with most of the key roles curiously redubbed by other actors." (140)

From late 1936 through 1940 the figure who dominated Latin-themed Westerns was not Cisco but Zorro. Republic Pictures resurrected the black-garbed swashbuckler in **The Bold Caballero** (1936), directed in color by Wells Root with Robert Livingston in the lead, and followed up that weak effort with two excellent 12-chapter serials about the character: **Zorro Rides Again** (1937), starring John Carroll, and **Zorro's Fighting Legion** (1939), starring Reed Hadley. Both cliffhangers were directed by the action powerhouse team of William Witney and John

English. Once 20th Century-Fox came back in the Cisco business, its moguls decided to corner the Latin Western market by presenting Tyrone Power in a big-budget remake of **The Mark Of Zorro** (1940), directed by **The Gay Desperado**'s Rouben Mamoulian.

Over the next few years there appeared an occasional B Western with marginal ties to the Cisco films. In **Law And Lead** (Colony, 1937), directed by Robert F. Hill from a screenplay by Basil Dickey based on an original story by Hill under his writing pseudonym Rock Hawkey, Rex Bell starred as cattle detective Jimmy Sawyer, who helps reformed bandito Pancho Gonzales (Donald Reed) track down the people responsible for resurrecting Pancho's old outlaw identity as The Juarez Kid. Tim McCoy took a hand in the game playing ranger Tim Carson in **Two Gun Justice** (Monogram, 1938), directed by Alan James from a screenplay by Fred Myton. Posing as an infamous rogue who calls himself The Vulture, Carson joins the outlaw gang led by Bart Kane (John Merton) in order to destroy it. Later that year Tim again played a lawman posing as a Mexican in **Lightning Carson Rides Again** (Victory, 1938), directed by Sam Newfield from a screenplay by E.R. O'Dasi (a byline of veteran scripter Isadore Bernstein), this time passing himself off as gambler José Hernandez while working to prove his vanished nephew (Robert Terry) innocent of a bank theft charge.

During the years when Zorro supplanted Cisco, the most notable Hollywood feature with ties to the Cisco tradition was **Thunder Trail** (Paramount, 1937), a superb entry in Paramount's long cycle of films more or less based on the works of Zane Grey. This one was directed by Charles Barton from a screenplay by Robert Yost and Stuart Anthony adapted from Grey's 1932 novel *Arizona Ames*. The protagonist, Arizona Dick Ames (Gilbert Roland), was separated in childhood from his brother Bob (James Craig) when villainous Lee Tate (Charles Bickford) killed their father and stole Bob to raise as his own son. Fifteen years later, Dick finds Tate transformed from just plain robber into a robber baron, determined to drive Amy Morgan (Marsha Hunt) and her father from their gold mine. Then Dick discovers that the man Amy loves is his long-lost kid brother, who still believes himself to be Tate's son. Everson in *The Hollywood Western* calls this film one of the best of all Paramount's Zane Grey adaptations. "[I]t ran a mere fifty-six minutes, yet despite almost constant action, it found time for good writing, subtle characterizations, a modicum of romance and comedy, some superb locations, an excellently staged runaway ore wagon sequence, and a well-sustained action climax." (165) If the storyline seems familiar to B Western fans it's because the same Zane Grey novel was also the uncredited inspiration for three first-rate series shoot-em-ups of the same decade: **Westward Ho** (Republic, 1935, directed by Robert N. Bradbury and starring John Wayne), **Across The Plains** (Monogram, 1939, directed by Spencer Bennet and starring Jack Randall), and **Saga Of Death Valley** (Republic, 1939, directed by Joseph Kane and starring Roy Rogers). My only excuse for covering **Thunder Trail** here is that its star, Gilbert Roland, was a genuine Latino and a future Cisco. The Arizona Ames character of course is not meant to be Hispanic but the filmmakers account for his accent by having him raised after his father's murder by a kindly Mexican prospector (J. Carrol Naish).

Director Charles Barton shot **Thunder Trail** at the same time and on the same locations with another Zane Grey-based feature, **Born To The West** (Paramount, 1937), starring John Wayne and Johnny Mack Brown. When those pictures were finished, Paramount handed over the production reins on the last films in its Grey cycle to Harry Sherman, who was also producing the classic Hopalong Cassidy series for release by the studio. After 20th Century-Fox revived the Cisco character in **The Return Of The Cisco Kid**, Sherman managed to squeeze into his production schedule **The Llano Kid** (Paramount, 1939), a remake of Paramount's 1930 feature **The Texan**. The director of the new version was Edward D. Venturini, an Argentinian of Italian descent whose only other English-language feature was **In Old Mexico** (Paramount, 1938), a powerful entry in the Cassidy series. The screenplay by Wanda Tuchock was based, as **The Texan** had been, on O. Henry's 1905 story "A Double-Dyed Deceiver." Tito Guizar played the singing bandit who teams up with scheming Lora Travers (Gale Sondergaard) to bilk wealthy old Doña Teresa (Emma Dunn, reprising her role in **The Texan**) by posing as her long-lost son. After falling in love with the old woman's adopted daughter Lupita (Jane Clayton), he breaks with Lora and turns over a new leaf.

Once the flood of Cisco imitations from the early Thirties had subsided, Latino characters other than Cisco himself and Zorro were rarely the heroes of Westerns, but several of the decade's oaters included a strong supporting role for a Latino who was either framed for crimes he didn't commit or bent on avenging a loved one's murder. Character actor Julian Rivero played such a part opposite Bob Steele in **Western Justice** (Supreme, 1934, directed by Robert N. Bradbury),

Ted Adams opposite Jack Randall in **Gunsmoke Trail** (Monogram, 1938, directed by Sam Newfield), and Noah Beery opposite Gene Autry in **Mexicali Rose** (Republic, 1939, directed by George Sherman). Any B Western fan worth his salt can add others to this list. No less surprising is the number of Thirties oaters in which the hero had a Hispanic sidekick. When the part was serious, as it tended to be in the decade's early and middle years, the man directors usually signed was again Julian Rivero. When the role was to be played for laughs, as was typical a few years later, more often than not it went to Frank Yaconelli, who in the mid-1940s was to play the sidekick in four of the Monogram Ciscos with Gilbert Roland in the lead. During the late Thirties the "straight" Mexican sidekick was confined to one studio, Republic, and one actor, future Cisco star Duncan Renaldo. For the 15-chapter serial **The Lone Ranger Rides Again** (1939), which owed much of its format to Republic's Three Mesquiteers series of trio Westerns, directors William Witney and John English signed Renaldo as Juan Vasquez to join Bob Livingston as the masked man and Chief Thundercloud as Tonto. Later the same year Renaldo joined the Mesquiteers series, playing Rico opposite Livingston as Stony Brooke and Raymond Hatton as Lullaby Joslin, and kept the role throughout the 1939-40 season.

At the end of the decade, soon after 20th Century-Fox had brought back Warner Baxter in **The Return Of The Cisco Kid**, Leo Carrillo played a vaguely Ciscoesque character in **The Girl And The Gambler** (RKO, 1939), directed by Lew Landers from a screenplay by Clarence Upson Young based on Willard Mack's 1925 stage play *The Dove*. Carrillo as the bandit El Rayo is smitten by cantina dancer Dolores Romero (Steffi Duna) and, in the guise of wealthy José Maria Lopez y Tostado, attempts to win her heart, unaware that it has already been won by Johnny Powell (Tim Holt), a dealer at the cantina's card tables. At the climax our noble outlaw stifles his emotions and lets the lovers elope. In the silent movie **The Dove** (Schenck, 1928), based on the same stage play, the members of the triangle had been played by Norma Talmadge, Noah Beery and future Cisco Gilbert Roland, while in the earlier talking remake, **Girl Of The Rio** (RKO, 1932), the parts had gone respectively to Dolores Del Rio, Carrillo himself, and Norman Foster, who would later turn director and helm one of 20th-Fox's Cisco features with Cesar Romero in the title role. Lew Landers, who helmed the 1939 movie version of Mack's play, was to direct Duncan Renaldo as Cisco and Carrillo as Pancho in some of their TV adventures of the Fifties.

Once 20th Century-Fox resumed making Cisco films, many of the Latino actors who eventually would figure in the saga found work in trio Westerns. Perhaps the most generously budgeted picture of this sort was **Rangers Of Fortune** (Paramount, 1940), directed by Sam Wood and starring Fred MacMurray, Albert Dekker and, in the part of Sierra, Gilbert Roland. In **Road Agent** (Universal, 1941), directed on a more modest scale by Charles Lamont, the trio was played by Dick Foran, Leo Carrillo and Andy Devine. It's a sober historical fact that Carrillo's character in this film was called Pancho. But when 20th-Fox dropped its Cisco series other studios lost interest in the Latin theme too. During the war years it resurfaced only in **Vengeance Of The West** (Columbia, 1942, directed by Lambert Hillyer), a loose remake of **The Avenger** with Bill Elliott as Joaquin Murietta and Tex Ritter as the Ranger captain on his trail. By gifting this version of Murietta with a Virginian mother, Hillyer relieved Elliott of the need to compete with Buck Jones for worst Mexican accent ever heard in a Western, but of course Elliott didn't sound Southern either.

After the war, and while Gilbert Roland was at Monogram playing Cisco in a six-picture series that will be covered in Chapter Seven, there was a brief flurry of films in more or less the same vein, released by even smaller studios. **Don Ricardo Returns** (PRC, 1946) starred Fred Coby as a Spanish nobleman who comes to California to claim an inheritance only to find that his evil cousin has had him declared legally dead. Ricardo goes into hiding, poses as a peon and, with help from the local padre, sets things to rights. Terry Morse directed from a screenplay by Jack DeWitt and Renault Duncan based on an original story by Zorro creator Johnston McCulley. Renault Duncan was the byline on the quickie scripts ground out between acting jobs by—who else?—Duncan Renaldo.

Bells Of San Fernando (Screen Guild, 1947) was also directed by Morse, scripted by DeWitt and Duncan and set in early California. Despite these facts and its title the film doesn't belong in a chapter on Cisco's rivals since the main character, portrayed by Donald Woods, isn't even Latin but an Irish seaman. A picture from the same period that definitely belongs is **The Adventures Of Don Coyote** (Comet, 1947), directed by Reginald LeBorg from a screenplay by Bob Williams and Harold Tarshis. Don Coyote (Richard Martin) and his sidekick Sancho (Val Carlo) take jobs on a ranch and try to save its lovely owner (Frances Rafferty) from losing her property to schemers who know the railroad is coming through. Soon after wrapping up this forgettable oater, Richard Martin was signed by RKO to join its superb Western series starring Tim Holt. He continued to play Tim's impulsive sidekick Chito José Gonzales Bustamante Rafferty until five years later when the series ended.

While the Cisco TV series with Duncan Renaldo and Leo Carrillo was in its prime, one minor studio and two majors offered features which might have been vaguely inspired by the telefilms. **Bandit Queen** (Lippert, 1950), directed by William Berke from a screenplay by Victor West and Budd Lesser based on West's original story, seems however to owe much more to the screen's other great Latin hero figure. Lola (Barbara Britton) returns to her home in early California, finds her parents murdered, becomes a sort of female Zorro and joins with our old friend Joaquin Murietta (Philip Reed) in her quest for revenge against the men behind the local reign of terror (Willard Parker and Barton MacLane). **Branded** (Paramount, 1951) was directed by Rudolph Maté from a screenplay by Sydney Boehm and Cyril Hume based on *Montana Rides!*, a 1933 novel by Evan Evans, who is much better known as Max Brand. The outlaw Cholla (Alan Ladd) is hired to impersonate the long-lost son of a wealthy rancher (Charles Bickford) but falls in love with the rancher's daughter (Mona Freeman) and redeems himself by bringing back the genuine son from the stronghold of the Mexican bandit (Joseph Calleia) who raised him. Finally came **Apache War Smoke** (MGM, 1952), directed by Harold Kress from a screenplay by Jerry Davis very loosely based on the Ernest Haycox short story "Stage Station" [Collier's, April 22, 1939; collected in *Outlaw* (Little Brown, 1953)]. In his last starring role in a U.S.-made Western feature, Gilbert Roland portrayed Peso, a legendary bandit pursued by Apaches who blame him for the murder of some fellow warriors. When he takes refuge at a way station run by his illegitimate son Tom Herrera (Robert Horton), the Apaches besiege the place and try to make the other trapped whites turn Peso over to them. This film was a remake of **Apache Trail** (MGM, 1942, directed by Richard Thorpe), but the central character of the first version had been an Anglo played by Lloyd Nolan.

The last film we consider here is also one of the strangest. **The Naked Dawn** (Universal, 1955) was set in contemporary Mexico and starred Arthur Kennedy as the bandit Santiago who, fleeing from the law after a botched train robbery, encounters a bewitching young woman (Betta St. John) and her dirt-poor but brutal and greed-racked husband (Eugene Iglesias). With all the

In this scene from **Romance of the Rio Grande** (Fox, 1929) Warner Baxter as Pablo Wharton Cameron is being helped by Mona Maris (Manuelita) while talking with Robert Edeson (Don Fernando) as Antonio Moreno looks on.

philosophic and sometimes mystical dialogue that the script by Nina and Herman Schneider gives him, the role of Santiago would have been perfect for Gilbert Roland, but since he was working steadily in major pictures at the time, he almost certainly would have turned down the lead in this shoestring production. The main reason for the film's reputation is that it was directed by Edgar G. Ulmer (1904-1972), who helmed such cult classics as **The Black Cat** (Universal, 1934), **Bluebeard** (PRC, 1944) and **Detour** (PRC, 1945). Interviewed not long before his death by Peter Bogdanovich, Ulmer included **The Naked Dawn** as one of his favorites among the films he'd made. With a draggy pace, sparse action and all too many signs of its rock-bottom budget, this picture is unlikely to appeal to the hardcore shoot-em-up fan as it did to Ulmer. But its bizarre storyline and characterizations make it a fitting film with which to bring this survey of a quarter century of Latin-themed Westerns to an end.

Before swimming back into the mainstream of the Cisco saga, I'd like to announce the winner of my Celluloid Serape award for the worst imitation-Cisco film ever made. But, faced with what seem to be four equally awful contestants—**Call Of The Coyote, The Pecos Dandy, The Irish Gringo** and **The Tia Juana Kid**—how can I make a single choice among them? Aha! Rather than giving the award to a picture, I shall present it to a man; to the man who somehow contrived to star in two of these four disasters and to direct a third. The serape is hereby awarded to—Patrick Carlyle. If he's still alive and I ever run into him I'll arrange for a ceremony.

A portrait of Warner Baxter, dated 1940.

Five • Cisco Old and New:
Warner Baxter and Cesar Romero

Once the studio heads realized that talking Westerns were feasible in terms of both technology and economics, the genre flourished. During the first half of the Thirties, Columbia offered a fine series starring Buck Jones (1930-34) and another with Tim McCoy (1931-35). Universal presented first a Tom Mix series (1932-33), then a Ken Maynard series (1933-34), and began releasing an offtrail series with Buck Jones (1934-37) after that ace of the saddle had left Columbia. Warner Bros. briefly experimented with a John Wayne series (1932-33) and RKO with an excellent series starring Tom Keene (1930-33). Paramount remade most of its silent films based on Zane Grey novels into talkies, with the spectacular action footage from the silent versions recycled intact. Fox continued its silent-era practice of making a few Westerns a year, with George O'Brien in the leading role and Zane Grey novels or stories as the usual if nominal literary basis. Of the major studios, MGM alone never ventured into Western territory. And of course there were countless Poverty Row outfits that cranked out ultra-cheap oater series and somewhat more respectable and longer-lived studios that made heavy commitments to the genre. Between 1931 and 1935 Monogram for example released five different series respectively starring Bill Cody, Tom Tyler, Rex Bell, Bob Steele and, last and best of all, John Wayne.

In 1935 the Fox corporation merged with another studio but the new entity, 20th Century-Fox, showed little interest in Westerns. Elsewhere it was a watershed year for the genre. Paramount launched the classic Hopalong Cassidy series (1935-44) starring William Boyd. Republic Pictures, a new entity formed from Monogram and several other small studios, offered a short series with John Wayne (1935-36), a much longer series with singing cowboy Gene Autry (1935-42) and, a year later, the excellent Three Mesquiteers series (1936-43), not to mention the oaters with Johnny Mack Brown (1936-37) and Bob Steele

(1936-38) that were released as Republic pictures but were actually made by a smaller outfit with lower standards. Monogram, split off from Republic and reconstituted as a separate entity in 1937, presented series with Jack Randall (1937-40), Tom Keene (1937-38), Tim McCoy (1938) and Tex Ritter (1938-41). Columbia launched the longest-lived Western series of them all with Charles Starrett in the lead (1935-52), plus less successful cycles with Ken Maynard (1935-36), Bob Allen (1936-37) and the unendurable Jack Luden (1938), plus a fine series with Bill Elliott (1938-42). After losing Buck Jones, Universal began a series with Bob Baker (1937-39) and a fine actionful brace of sagebrush sagas with Johnny Mack Brown (1939-42). Republic introduced Roy Rogers (1938-51) at around the same time RKO came back into the Western fold with former Fox star George O'Brien (1938-40). These plus the many low-budget efforts from short-lived outfits like Ambassador and Grand National added up to a total of more than nine hundred feature-length Westerns put on the market between **In Old Arizona** and the beginning of 1939. No wonder the executives at 20th Century-Fox wanted to try the genre again!

The studio still owned the rights to the Cisco Kid character and, in the last year of the decade, decided to reintroduce America's moviegoers to the romantic bandito. The problem they faced was that so many of the people who had worked on the first two Cisco features either weren't under contract or weren't interested. Edmund Lowe was freelancing at Paramount, Universal and elsewhere. Raoul Walsh had left Fox in 1933 and was about to begin a long-term association with Warners that would lead to more than a decade's worth of classic films with Cagney, Flynn and Bogart. Irving Cummings was still with 20th-Fox but by 1939 was specializing almost exclusively in biopics and musicals. Warner Baxter too was under contract but ill health had made him look much older than his forty-six years. Still, he was

Cesar Romero as Lopez, Warner Baxter as Cisco and Chris-Pin Martin as Gordito in a scene from **The Return of The Cisco Kid** (20th Century-Fox, 1939).

the only Cisco anyone knew, and in **The Return Of The Cisco Kid** (1939) he took up the role one more time. But with some differences.

He had dominated **In Old Arizona** and, to a slightly lesser degree, **The Cisco Kid**. In his late forties he couldn't do that again but, thanks to the development of the trio Western concept in the Thirties, he didn't have to try. His third and last outing as Cisco was structured roughly along the lines of the Hopalong Cassidy and Three Mesquiteers series: Cisco as the father or older brother figure, his henchman Lopez from **The Cisco Kid** transformed into a wild young hothead along the lines of Jimmy Ellison from the Cassidys or Bob Livingston from the Mesquiteers films, and the Gordito character from the 1931 feature upgraded (if that's the right word) to traditional comic sidekick. Chris-Pin Martin was at least as fat as he'd been in 1931 and seemed perfect to reprise his role as Gordito, but who should be cast as the young blood Lopez?

"I'm a Latin from Manhattan," Cesar Romero liked to say of himself. His ancestry was Cuban and the island's revolutionary hero Josè Martì was his maternal grandfather but he was born in New York City on February 15, 1907 and grew up on the east coast. His first acting experience came at boarding school when he played four parts in Shakespeare's *The Merchant Of Venice*. The family lost its fortune with the collapse of the sugar market early in the Depression and Cesar went to work in a Wall Street bank. He broke into show business by forming a dance team with a woman friend and soon was both dancing and acting on Broadway. His stage role in *Dinner At Eight* brought him to the attention of MGM, which purchased movie rights to the play but cast Romero in another classic picture, **The Thin Man** (1934), where he appeared as the wealthy decadent Chris Jorgenson. (The movie of *Dinner At Eight* did happen to include former Cisco co-star Edmund Lowe among its distinguished cast.)

Lopez listens as Cisco makes his point to Gordito in this scene from **The Return of The Cisco Kid** (20th Century-Fox, 1939).

For the next three years Romero found work at a variety of studios in more than a dozen featured parts, most notably opposite Marlene Dietrich in Josef von Sternberg's **The Devil Is A Woman** (Paramount, 1935). "They said I was going to be the next Valentino," he recalled in a 1984 interview, but usually he played either gigolos or gangsters. In 1937 he signed an exclusive contract with 20th-Fox and was cast by John Ford as an evil Hindu in the Shirley Temple vehicle **Wee Willie Winkie** (1937). Then, in one of those strange coincidences which make up film history, he was starred in **Dangerously Yours** (1937), a remake of a 1933 Fox feature whose leading man had been Warner Baxter. Two years later Romero and Baxter appeared together for the first time, opposite Loretta Young and Binnie Barnes, in the romantic comedy **Wife, Husband, And Friend** (1939). Shortly after that confection wrapped he was teamed with Baxter again, this time playing Lopez to the older man's Cisco Kid. It was

Romero's first experience in a Western and he came across as a hairy loudmouth with a vicious streak. Maybe the director had seen too many of his gangster pictures.

With Raoul Walsh gone from 20th-Fox and Irving Cummings occupied with lighter fare, a new director had to be found for **The Return Of The Cisco Kid**. The man who wound up with the job was a former film editor still in his twenties with only a year's experience directing. Like most of the small army who made the thousands of movies Hollywood churned out during its golden age, Herbert I. Leeds came and went in modest anonymity, attracting little attention beyond the moment. Reference books will tell you that besides **The Return Of The Cisco Kid** he directed three later Cisco features with Romero, plus entries in most other 20th-Fox series of the late Thirties and early Forties and a number of nonseries pictures. If you are extremely well informed you may know that he also directed two

47

Cesar Romero, Chris-Pin Martin and Warner Baxter are ready for action in this scene from **The Return of The Cisco Kid** (20th Century-Fox, 1939).

episodes of the Cisco TV series of the early Fifties with Duncan Renaldo and Leo Carrillo. But whether you search high or low, you are unlikely to find a word about Leeds himself. Unless, that is, you are lucky enough to have discovered *Realm of Unknowing* (Wesleyan University Press, 1995), a collection by Leeds' nephew, the poet Mark Rudman, whose uncle is the subject of his title essay.

Herbert Levy was born in New York City, around 1910 or 1911. His affluent family sent him overseas to be educated at La Villa Lozanne in Switzerland, where he learned to speak fluent French. Although accepted by Yale, he chose to attend Lehigh University in Pennsylvania so as to be near a favorite cousin. He became a gun enthusiast and often went hunting with his grandfather. Thanks to his family's friendship with Jack Warner, he landed a job at Warner Brothers as an assistant cutter and soon graduated to film editor. Still calling himself Herbert or Bert Levy, he

earned his first screen credits as editor on Warners-First National pictures like **Week-End Marriage** (1932), **Dark Hazard** (1934) and **Side Streets** (1934). In 1936 he moved to 20th-Fox and edited **A Message To Garcia**, **Half Angel** and **Dimples**.

Early in 1938 he changed his name to Leeds and began to direct. Among the four pictures he made that year were **Five Of A Kind**, with the Dionne Quintuplets, shot on location in Quebec, and the crime melodrama **Island In The Sky**, starring Gloria Stuart, Michael Whalen and Paul Kelly, which is considered his finest film by most of those who know Leeds' work at all. In 1939 he turned out six pictures: a Mr. Moto with Peter Lorre, a Charlie Chan with Sidney Toler, the last of the Ciscos with Warner Baxter, the first with Cesar Romero, and two Jane Withers "adorable child" flicks that co-starred the last and greatest Cisco sidekick, Leo Carrillo. Interviewed in 1991 for Mark Rudman's essay on his uncle, Withers

Warner Baxter sings to Lynn Bari (Ann Carver) while Cesar Romero looks bored in a scene from **The Return of The Cisco Kid** (20th Century-Fox, 1939).

described Leeds as "loved by everybody that he worked with. The one word I'd choose to say what he was like is kindness." He sent her a doll for her huge collection every year for the rest of his life.

"My uncle took up a lot of room," Rudman writes. "He was thick-set, bulky, barrel-chested. He wore shades of brown: heavy tweeds. There was something suffocating about him." His sister Marjorie, Rudman's mother, said he was known as "the man who never smiled." He had "brown velvet chocolate eyes" and "a reputation as a difficult man." When the script for one of his Cisco films called for the romantic rogue to pull a guitar from his saddlebag and start to sing, Leeds said the scene was impossible and flatly refused to shoot it.

"Bert always read the crime magazines," an old relative told Rudman. "He was always looking for stories." Apparently there were few he liked, for he directed just one low-budget feature in 1940, the last pair of Romero Ciscos and a Michael

Shayne detective flick with Lloyd Nolan in 1941, three more Shaynes plus a war film with Nolan in 1942. Although a trick knee exempted him from the draft, he volunteered for service and wound up in Europe with the OSS. According to his father, he was one of two Americans on the Remagen bridge across the Rhine when the Germans blew it up with mines. But in the best tradition of Cisco and other Western heroes, he escaped unhurt.

When Leeds returned to Hollywood at the end of the war there seemed no room for him in Westerns or detective films. He directed two comedies for 20th-Fox, one in 1946 and the other in 1948, but seems to have concentrated most of his energy on serving as secretary of the Directors Guild. During the 1949-50 season he migrated into the new medium of television and—along with Leslie Goodwins, who would later become the last director of Cisco TV episodes—cranked out episodes of *The Life Of Riley*, a short-lived sitcom on the ill-fated Dumont network, starring

Warner Baxter charms Lynn Bari in this scene from **The Return of The Cisco Kid** (20th Century-Fox, 1939).

Jackie Gleason and Rosemary DeCamp. (The series fared much better a few years later when it moved to NBC with William Bendix in the lead.) In 1950 Leeds directed a quickie thriller for RKO and a final comedy feature for Monogram. Except for occasional second unit work on large-scale 20th-Fox features like **Broken Arrow** (1950) with Jimmy Stewart and **Diplomatic Courier** (1952) with Tyrone Power, that was the end of his studio career. He went back to Manhattan and, says Rudman, began wandering around "in a fog of depression." The only other TV episodes he is known to have directed are the two 30-minute *Cisco Kid* segments he made in 1953. Whatever stunted his career, it wasn't the blacklist, for according to Rudman his uncle was a "hysterical" anti-Communist. Whatever money he had saved, he spent all too quickly. "Even during his last days he had the newspaper delivered to his [hotel] room..., needing to tip the bellboy a buck, rather than go downstairs and get it for a nickel at a newsstand."

On April 1, 1954, Leeds moved out of the more expensive hotel where he'd been staying and into a $5-a-day room at the Wyndham, between Fifth and Sixth Avenues on 58th Street. On May 15 he underlined a passage in the book he was reading and set the book down on his bathroom floor. "I'm so sorry to do what I'm doing. I'm so ashamed," the passage read. Then he loaded his 20-gauge shotgun with a single shell, sat on his hotel bed, held the gun with its stock in the air and blew out his chest. Jane Withers had no idea that her favorite director had been dead almost forty years when Mark Rudman spoke with her but when told of his suicide she thought she knew the reason. "He was much too kind and sensitive. He couldn't take the world he was living in."

The Return Of The Cisco Kid was clearly influenced by the trio Western vogue but its three compadres were by no means equals. Romero is billed third, after Baxter and female lead Lynn Bari, with poor Chris-Pin Martin relegated to eighth place in the cast. Between Romero and

Lynn Bari and Warner Baxter in a romantic moment from **The Return of The Cisco Kid** (20th Century-Fox, 1939).

Martin were three old reliables and one still young—Henry Hull, Kane Richmond, C. Henry Gordon and an unusually hammy Robert Barrat—while future Western favorites Eddy Waller and Ward Bond wound up at or near the bottom of the credits. The screenplay by Milton Sperling keeps to the quasi-operatic mode of previous Cisco features, with romantic complications at every turn and action nowhere. Baxter looks like a dissipated old man and the way his little mustache turns up at the corners can give a modern viewer the giggles, but Leeds manages to make his star's appearance work for the picture: Baxter may be certain Lynn Bari loves him alone but it's clear to us in the audience that this beautiful young woman would never choose him over virile Kane Richmond. (That Cisco is Hispanic is never made an issue for a moment.) Baxter's Mexican accent had degenerated badly since **In Old Arizona** and Leeds doesn't help by letting his dialogue be saturated with y sounds for him to mangle. ("Why do

jou think I get execute?" "When jou see the stagecoach come, jou know what to do.") But there are some lovely outdoor shots, and the philosophic sadness Baxter projects is not only consistent with his previous renditions of Cisco but eerily prophetic of the shape of what was left of his life.

The year is 1900 and we open outside the ruins of a fort in northern Mexico near the Arizona border with a Mexican captain (C. Henry Gordon) and a firing squad executing The Cisco Kid. As soon as the troops ride off, Cisco climbs out of his open grave and collects his pals Lopez (Cesar Romero) and Gordito (Chris-Pin Martin), who had replaced all the soldiers' bullets the night before with blanks. The three amigos ride north to launch a new wave of thievery with Baxter singing a Spanish love song in English and a flurry of close-ups of the trio riding sawhorses or something.

The first job they plan in Arizona is a stagecoach holdup with Lopez and Gordito pulling the

A publicity still of Warner Baxter for **The Return of The Cisco Kid** (20th Century-Fox, 1939).

actual robbery while Cisco is inside the coach as a passenger. But his plans change when, at the wilderness way station where he's to board the coach, Cisco encounters the alcoholic and slightly larcenous Colonel Joshua Bixby (Henry Hull) and his lovely granddaughter Ann Carver (Lynn Bari), by whom our romantic rogue is smitten on the spot. Cisco bails the colonel out of a financial embarrassment at the way station tavern by cashing a check for him, knowing that he'll shortly be getting his money back in the holdup. As in previous films in the series, Cisco introduces himself as Gonzalo Sebastiano Rodrigo Don Juan Chicuelo, whose father was Portuguese and whose mother came from San Luis Obispo. On the coach, Ann tells Cisco that she's inherited $5,000 and given it to a friend, Alan Davis (Kane Richmond), who is to buy a ranch with it for her and her grandfather outside the town of Fronteras which is their destination. By the time Lopez and Gordito hold up the stage, Cisco is so blindly befuddled by Ann's charms that, to their flabbergastment, he opens fire on them and chases them away.

When the coach reaches Fronteras, Cisco invites Ann to have dinner with him that evening, then finds his amigos and explains that he aborted the holdup because he's fallen in love and decided to stay dead and go straight. Meanwhile Ann and the colonel discover that Alan Davis not only didn't buy the ranch for them but has been in jail for the past week. Alan tells them from his cell that Sheriff McNally (Robert Barrat), who is also the mayor of Fronteras and the saloonkeeper and the chief landowner in the area, simply confiscated the money and threw him into a cell. Cut to McNally's saloon where a local man (Ward Bond) is put on trial—for rustling cattle which McNally had stolen from him—beaten to a pulp by McNally and kicked out of town. A few minutes later Ann and the colonel confront McNally in the saloon and get thrown in

Chris-Pin Martin, Warner Baxter and Cesar Romero in a night scene from **The Return of The Cisco Kid** (20th Century-Fox, 1939).

jail beside Alan Davis.

Cisco meanwhile has made elaborate preparations for his dinner date with Ann including vintage wine, an orchestra and special decorations. When she doesn't come and the hotel clerk finally tells him that she's been locked up, it's too late in the evening for him to visit her legally, so he starts a fire outside the general store which quickly spreads to a large part of town, including the jailhouse, and he has to break in and pistolwhip a deputy in order to save the three prisoners from the blaze he set. Seeing Ann and Davis embrace, he becomes insanely jealous. Davis is wounded as they all flee town, and we must imagine that Cisco takes a special pleasure in the next scene when, on the trail in the middle of the night, he cauterizes his rival's wound. Then he fakes an attack by McNally's men so that he has an excuse to ride off alone with Ann and romance her in the light of "the most beautiful sunrise in the world." Taking her to the top of a

mountain, he demonstrates the echo chamber effect of the place by shouting lines like "Jou are beautiful" and hearing them repeated over and over. Then he tells her of the dream he first told Tonia in **In Old Arizona**—of returning to the Portugal he hasn't seen since childhood with the love of his life—and her reply misleads him into thinking she loves him. Later the reunited group of six cross into Mexico to hide out at the house of old Mama Soledad (Soledad Jimenez). After a hearty meal, Cisco, Lopez and Gordito return north to get the ranch back from McNally, with Cisco still convinced that as soon as her grandfather is secure, Ann will go to Portugal with him.

Back in Fronteras, Cisco poses as a big cattleman from Sonora, offers to buy the property McNally stole from Alan Davis, and agrees to pay McNally's outrageous asking price of $100,000. They agree to close the deal the following Monday evening at McNally's ranch. McNally of

A Lobby Card from **The Return of the Cisco Kid** (20th-Century Fox, 1939). (Courtesy of Boyd Magers.)

course plans to confiscate the money just as he had with Davis before, while Cisco's scheme is to get the money by stealing it from McNally's bank. The three amigos pull the job the next day. In the course of the robbery Cisco has to pistolwhip the teller. The deputy whom he'd pistolwhipped earlier in the fire scene happens to be in the bank and recognizes the technique from before. From this information McNally figures out that Cisco plans to keep his Monday night date to get the deed and sets a trap at his ranch. Meanwhile south of the border, Ann and Alan Davis fall in love.

On Monday night a still love-smitten Cisco sets out to exchange the stolen money for the deed. At the last minute McNally's trap is augmented by the arrival of the Mexican captain who had headed Cisco's firing squad. Cisco of course has slipped into the ranch house early and captures McNally and the captain, whose face drops at sight of what he thinks is a ghost. A simple ruse enables Cisco, Lopez and Gordito to overpower

the deputies who've surrounded the house. As Cisco is about to take off with the deed, McNally challenges him to a fistfight. "Oh, no," Cisco declares. "Thees impossible. No, I do not juse the fists. If I hurt the hand I cannot play the guitar, and if I cannot sing love song I cannot make love, and if I cannot make love, I die." This may have been intended as a dig at **Golden Boy** (1939) with its young boxer hero (William Holden) having to choose between the ring and a classical violinist's career, but its effect is to destroy any hope for action in a film that sorely needs it.

The three amigos return to Mexico just in time to abort the colonel's scheme to sell Mama Soledad some phony gold mine stock. When the colonel reveals that Ann and Alan are going to be married, he breaks Cisco's heart. Furious and bent on revenge, Cisco sends out Gordito to instruct Davis to ride alone, in the dark, through the pass where McNally's men are waiting in ambush, and meet Cisco on the other side. But at the last

This Lobby Card, at the Lone Pine rocks, has Robert Barrat, with gun drawn, on Cesar Romero with Chris-Pin Martin, unable to help, as Ray Teal looks on. (1939). (Courtesy of Boyd Magers.)

minute, when Ann tells Cisco that she and Alan have always been in love and that she never loved Cisco at all, Cisco repents and he and Gordito race like the wind to save Alan's life. After a wild riding sequence intercut with more of those ugly close-ups of Baxter on a sawhorse, Cisco uses the mountain's echo chamber effect to fool McNally and his men into thinking they're surrounded. McNally ultimately agrees to leave the young couple alone if Cisco will stay out of the territory, and we close with the three amigos back in Mexico and Cisco dreaming of another girlfriend, a certain Carmencita. (Not, we hope, the señorita of that name from 1931's **The Cisco Kid**.) "But Carmencita have feet like a duck!" protests Gordito. "I do not have to look at her feet," Cisco tells him. This is the last line Warner Baxter was ever to speak in his role as Cisco. After two more undistinguished films, neither of them Westerns, his twelve-year stint at 20th-Fox limped to an end.

It isn't known whether Romero was tapped to replace him before or after **The Return Of The Cisco Kid** was wrapped, but roughly six months after Baxter's adios, the Latin from Manhattan took over in a six-film series, released between the end of 1939 and the spring of 1941, which Everson in *The Hollywood Western* describes collectively as "strong in casts and elaborate production values, but by their very nature mild in action content." (228) Herbert Leeds smoothed the transition by directing the first of the six, **The Cisco Kid And The Lady** (1939), which might better have been titled **The Cisco Kid And The Baby**. Romero was transformed from a hairy lout to a foppishly dressed, boastful poseur with a somewhat mannered and hyper style but lacking the world-weariness and reflective edge that Baxter brought to the role. The screenplay for Romero's first outing as Cisco was by Frances Hyland from an original story by Stanley Rauh. With Marjorie Weaver and Virginia Field as the ladies in the bandito's life, young George

Cesar Romero has his arm around Virginia Field as Chris-Pin Martin has Robert Barrat covered in this lobby card from 1939. (Courtesy of Boyd Magers.)

Montgomery as Cisco's romantic rival, Robert Barrat reprising the sort of villain part in which Leeds had cast him in **The Return Of The Cisco Kid** and Ward Bond upgraded from his tiny role in the last Cisco film, one can appreciate Everson's remark about the strength of the cast. It's too bad the film itself was rather routine.

After an opening montage showing Cisco perpetrating a crime wave all over Arizona, we cut to our caballero crooning a Spanish love song and riding peacefully with Gordito across lovely barren country. They catch sight of a lone traveler crossing the desert in a covered wagon and decide to steal his horses, but before they can reach the man he's shot from ambush by Jim Harbison (Robert Barrat) and his henchman Stevens (John Beach) and the horses run away with the wagon. In a well-directed action sequence, Cisco stops the horses. Harbison rides up from behind and searches the dying man's pockets as Cisco and Gordito look into the wagon and find, cooing and

googling in the rear of it, a baby boy (Gloria Ann White). The dying man, Drake (J. Anthony Hughes), tells Cisco, Gordito and Harbison that he had discovered a gold mine and was on his way to record his claim—something Harbison was already well aware of—and offers the mine to all three men if they'll swear to give an equal share to the baby. His last act before dying is to tear his map of the mine into three pieces and give one to each man.

No sooner have they buried Drake when Stevens and the rest of Harbison's gang show up, draw their guns on Cisco and Gordito and demand their portions of the map. Too late: Cisco has turned his scrap of paper into a cigarette and burned it up, Gordito has eaten his. Harbison has to keep them alive if he ever wants to locate the mine. They set out with the dead man's wagon and, so they think, with the baby, but Gordito has stupidly left the infant back at its father's gravesite. The child crawls out to the middle of

56

the road and, in a stunningly unfaked-looking shot, is almost run over by a passing stagecoach. When Cisco realizes that the baby isn't with them, he races back to their starting point with Harbison and his men in hot pursuit, then in another swift and well-directed action set-piece, chases after the stagecoach with the baby. They halt the coach and find the infant in the arms of Julie Lawson (Marjorie Weaver), the schoolteacher in the nearby town of Oro Grande. Cisco as usual falls for the woman in two seconds flat but claims the baby as "his."

In Oro Grande, Cisco, Gordito and the baby take a room in Harbison's saloon-cum-hotel and the adult partners in the gold mine share tequila to bind their bargain. Walton (Ward Bond), the town drunk, gets into a loud squabble with dance-hall girl Billie Graham (Virginia Field) which brings Billie into Cisco's ken and sets off a new light of love in his heart. Harbison bribes Billie with a cameo locket to play up to Cisco and wheedle out of him the information on his piece of the map. Gordito amuses the baby by shooting off his pistol and Cisco gives the child a bath. Before the partners go off to hunt for the mine, Cisco spots Harbison sending his men out of town and suspects a double-cross. The baby is dropped off with Julie at the schoolhouse and the gold seekers leave town on the treasure hunt.

A stagecoach arrives in Oro Grande and disgorges Julie's fiancé Tommy Bates (George Montgomery), on an unannounced visit to marry Julie and take her back to Kansas City. When he finds her caring for the baby, he comes instantly to the conclusion that she is, as they used to say, damaged goods, and storms off to get drunk. Meanwhile out on the trail, Cisco pretends to be lost, rides off alone to try to find landmarks, comes upon Harbison's men in ambush, uses the old rope-across-the-road gambit to get the drop on them, and makes Harbison and his gang march behind them for miles, trussed together and shouting "Amigo! Amigo!"

Back in town, Cisco romances Julie—who doesn't bother to mention how "his" baby has cost her a fiancé—filches a photograph of her, drops into Harbison's saloon for a drink, happens to run into the sloshed Tommy Bates and stumbles into his own comedy of errors when Tommy sees Julie's picture in Cisco's pocket and jumps to the conclusion that Cisco is Julie's seducer and the baby's dad. Tommy falls over drunk after taking a swing at Cisco, who puts the young man to bed in the room he's sharing with Gordito, then comes back downstairs for a romantic interlude with Billie.

Harbison trudges into town from his 20-mile

walk just in time to catch them dancing and smooching. Billie tells Cisco that she knows who he is but that she's too smitten with him to turn him over to the law and hints that she'll be only too happy to steal Harbison's portion of the map and form a partnership of her own with the romantic rogue. Cisco sneaks up to the balcony overlooking Harbison's room and watches her take the map from Harbison's pocket while he's taking a bath and hide it inside the locket Harbison had given her. It's the work of a few moments for Cisco to sneak into Billie's room, romance her in the dark, and snatch the locket from her pretty neck. When she finds the brooch gone, she goes back into partnership with Harbison and tells him that "Rodriguez Gonzales Sebastiano Don Juan Chicuelo" is really The Cisco Kid.

Meanwhile back in his own room, Cisco finds a photo of Julie in the pocket of the passed-out Tommy Bates and understands why the drunken youth tried to punch him out. Before Cisco and Gordito can get out of town they're captured by Harbison and his gang and turned over to the sheriff, who wires the nearest military authorities to come pick them up. Tommy is locked up with them, for no better reason than that he was found drunk in their room. When everyone has left the hotel, Billie finds the locket on the floor where Cisco hid it—with the map still inside—and realizes that she made an awful mistake betraying him.

The next morning Julie visits Tommy in his cell and Cisco finally realizes that the two, despite the little misunderstanding over the baby, are in love. That evening Billie pays Cisco a secret visit to ask his forgiveness, which he gladly gives, and to slip him a gun, which he graciously accepts. Before he can use the pistol, Harbison drops by the cell and offers to break out Cisco and Gordito if they'll lead him to the mine. Cisco maneuvers Harbison into agreeing to dress up in a Cisco outfit and hold up that night's stage, so that the sheriff will think he has the wrong men behind bars and let them loose. After Harbison has gone off to pull the robbery, Cisco and Gordito use Billie's pistol to break jail, kidnap the justice of the peace and force him at gunpoint to make Tommy and Julie man and wife—even though they're still at each other's throats. This scene is supposed to be funny but would strike most viewers today as sick.

The last few minutes of the picture pack a bewildering amount of story. The military patrol sent to pick up Cisco and Gordito reach Oro Grande and find the prisoners gone. The night stage comes back into town and the driver reports a robbery attempt by The Cisco Kid. Harbison in his Cisco togs returns with his gang, they find Cisco's and Gordito's horses where Billie has left them, a gun battle breaks out when Cisco and Gordito come for their steeds, and Harbison winds up getting mistaken for Cisco by the burghers of Oro Grande and shot in the back. As dawn breaks, Cisco and Gordito show the location of the mine to the new husband and father Tommy Bates and they ride off with Billie at their side to the strains of another Spanish love song.

The second of the Romero Ciscos was no more an action classic than the first but it boasted an unusual storyline and director. Norman Foster, born Norman Hoeffer in Richmond, Virginia on December 13, 1900, was acting on Broadway opposite his then wife, Claudette Colbert, when both of them were offered movie contracts at Paramount. His first screen role was in the newspaper melodrama **Gentlemen Of The Press** (Paramount, 1929), starring Walter Huston, and he co-starred with Colbert and newcomer Ginger Rogers in **Young Man Of Manhattan** (Paramount, 1930). Later he divorced Colbert and married actress Sally Blane. Foster played the lead in many low-budget early talkies but eventually decided that directing was more to his taste and between 1937 and 1941 was under contract at 20th-Fox, where he worked mainly on whodunits in the studio's Charlie Chan and Mr. Moto series, with occasional ventures into new territory like a Cisco picture. His finest films— **Journey Into Fear** (RKO, 1943) with Joseph Cotten, Dolores Del Rio and Orson Welles, and **Kiss The Blood Off My Hands** (Norma/ Universal, 1948) with Joan Fontaine and Burt Lancaster—are classics of the *noir* thriller, so packed with visual bravura that Welles himself is sometimes credited with ghost-directing them. In the Fifties he went to work for the Disney studio where, among other films, he helmed the Davy Crockett segments of *Disneyland* (1954-55) and thirteen episodes of the first season (1957-58) of the Disney TV series *Zorro*. Near the end of his career he left Disney to direct episodes of series like *The Loner* (1965-66), *The Monroes* (1966-67) and *The Green Hornet* (1966-67). He died in 1976.

The novelty of his single contribution to the Cisco saga, **Viva Cisco Kid** (1940), is the conception of the villain, who is clearly modeled on Charlie Chaplin's rendition of a buffoonish Hitler figure in the same year's **The Great Dictator**. Whether we should credit this to Foster or the authors of the screenplay, Samuel G. Engel and Hal Long, is anyone's guess, but I'll lay my bet on Foster. Lovely Jean Rogers (the original Dale Arden in Universal's Flash Gordon serials) had the female lead, the usually unnotable Stanley Fields cut a fine figure as the frontier fuehrer, and B Western stalwarts like Leroy Mason, Bud Osborne, Tom London, Hank Worden and Eddy Waller had unbilled bit parts.

This adventure begins with a sequence not the least connected with the plot as Cisco discovers that Gordito is about to get married—Foster mercifully never shows us what the woman looks like—and extracts his amigo from disaster by convincing the bride's wealthy brother Don Pancho (Charles Judels) that the dowry he's about to pay will be wasted because, all appearances to the contrary, Gordito is a walking corpse and will soon be dead. The partners ride away together and come upon a stagecoach holdup that went wrong because the $25,000 the bandits wanted had been in the form of $500 bills which the driver had hidden in a tiny envelope under his seat. The leader of the bandits is a masked Leroy Mason, whose name doesn't appear in the film's credits. Coming upon this scene and chasing the thieves off, Cisco meets lovely Joan Allen (Jean Rogers), who has come from the east to live with her father, Jesse Allen (Minor Watson). As we follow Mason and his men back to the town of Towash, we discover that Jesse and saloonkeeper Hank Gunther (Harold Goodwin) are in with the robbers, and that, along with countless other badmen in the region, they all take orders from a mysterious Professor Moriarty-like figure known only as The Boss.

After driving the stage into town, Cisco and Gordito escort Joan to her father's house in the countryside, with Cisco singing a Spanish love song to help pass the time. He also sneaks in a bit of his philosophy. "All my life I have lived for freedom, adventure, laughter and danger. It is the price I must pay for being a little niño." On the road they pass a crazy preacher called Moses (Nigel de Brulier), who is painting THE WAGES OF SIN IS DEATH on a huge rock. Jesse isn't home when they arrive, but they get to meet his Chinese servant Wang (Willie Fung) and Cisco makes a date with Joan for that night. This is the same night Gunther and Jesse plan to steal the $25,000 from the express office safe where it's being kept. Jesse goes home to find his daughter in residence but returns to town almost at once to take part in the robbery. Just as he's leaving, Moses the preacher drops by for a handout. Later when Cisco shows up for his date with Joan, he admits that he's a wanted man and says goodbye to her. "Don't change," she tells him. "Just keep on being a little niño."

Moses rides into town, happens to witness the express office break-in, recognizes one of the

This scene demonstrates how the Fox Cisco's were filled with extras. Here you can pick out Ray Teal (with pipe in hand), Tom London, Hank Worden, Frank Darien, LeRoy Mason, and Frank Ellis (behind man with beard who is) Nigel De Brulier. From **Viva Cisco Kid** (20th Century-Fox,1940). (Courtesy of Boyd Magers.)

thieves as the man who had given him a handout earlier that evening (although, being new in the area, he doesn't know Jesse by name), and leads the sheriff and a posse to the Allen cabin. Catching sight of the posse on his trail, Jesse doesn't return home but goes into hiding. The sheriff and posse search the house for Jesse in vain. When they're gone, Jesse comes back home, arranges to meet Joan later in a shack outside the town of Grande, and takes off. Gunther and Leroy Mason meanwhile catch Moses alone and shoot him in the back so that he can never identify Jesse Allen.

On the way to Grande the next day, Joan is thrown from her horse and stumbles upon Cisco and Gordito again. Then all three stumble upon the sheriff, who arrests them for the express office robbery. The sheriff and posse find Moses' body along the trail and the three prisoners are accused of the murder. Cisco and Gordito break away and ride for their lives. Meanwhile Gunther and Leroy Mason grab Joan and set out to take her to the

headquarters of The Boss so that Jesse will be forced to give them the stolen money to get her back. The excellent chase scene with Cisco and Gordito being pursued by the posse is the only real action sequence in the film.

The headquarters of The Boss is the Sugarloaf Mine, and we soon discover that this fearsome Moriarty of the frontier (Stanley Fields) is nothing but a loudmouthed buffoon who loves to play practical jokes on his underlings and everyone he meets. He locks up Joan in a secret underground room and sends out his men to hunt for Jesse. Meanwhile Cisco and Gordito are captured at a country inn by its bearded proprietor (Francis Ford) but are saved by Jesse, who happened to have chosen the place for his rendezvous with Joan. Cisco, Gordito and Jesse pick up Joan's trail where she was kidnapped and follow it to the Sugarloaf. Leaving Jesse in the rocks overlooking the mine, Cisco and Gordito take the stolen money into the oafish lion's den, identify themselves as the wanted men they in fact are, and ask to join The Boss' organization. The Boss indulges himself in a string of practical jokes like exploding cigars and squirting rings at Gordito's expense, while the gang's black chef (Mantan Moreland) prepares a lavish dinner—and drops a remark that reveals to Cisco that Joan is a prisoner beneath their feet. After another flurry of practical jokes on poor Gordito including a dripping whisky jigger, a water bucket over a door and a rubber turkey, Gunther and Mason return to the Sugarloaf and tell The Boss that it was Cisco and Gordito who broke up their stagecoach robbery and became friends with Joan Allen. Cisco talks his way out of a tight spot by handing over the express money and claiming that he killed Jesse and now wants revenge on Joan. Gordito manages to pick The Boss' pocket and recover the money on the spot. The Boss takes Cisco to where Joan is being held but tells her the lie Cisco told him about having killed her father. That night Cisco sneaks back to the underground room and explains everything to Joan, but meanwhile Gunther and Mason have captured Jesse alive and bring him to The Boss, whose men then capture Cisco, Gordito and Joan just as they're about to escape. The four prisoners are taken to a special mine tunnel that The Boss has rigged like a terror trap in a cliffhanger serial so that when one beam is removed the whole tunnel will cave in. It turns out, however, that this trap is about as well designed as a trap in a Roadrunner cartoon. When the special beam is taken away, the entire mine collapses, killing The Boss and his gang in one fell swoop. The climax of the picture has Cisco desperately hunting for a way out of the tunnel before he, Gordito and the Allens all suffocate. After a *conejito* or little rabbit shows them the way to its hole, they manage to blast their way into daylight. Jesse goes back to Towash to settle his debt with the law and return the express money, while Cisco and Gordito ride off to new adventures.

Next in the series came a routine entry which has earned a tiny niche in film history as perhaps the only movie named for its director. **Lucky Cisco Kid** (1940) was helmed by H. Bruce Humberstone, a man of modest achievements whose career was well profiled in an essay by Jon Tuska included in his anthology *Close-Up: The Contract Director* (Scarecrow Press, 1976). Humberstone was born in Buffalo, New York on November 18, 1903, and won his first movie job at the age of nineteen, as prop boy and assistant cameraman on a Universal silent Western starring Hoot Gibson and directed by the young John Ford. He worked his way up to assistant director, began directing films himself in 1932, and earned

his nickname after he and the legendary action director B. Reeves Eason got blind drunk together at a Hollywood Hills party. On the way home Eason, who was driving, lost control of the car. "We hit a culvert and the car rolled over three times. Breezy and I were thrown clear. When I reported for work the next day, everyone on the lot kept calling me Lucky...." (62) Perhaps the only truly distinguished picture in his career was **I Wake Up Screaming** (20th-Fox, 1941), an early *film noir* starring Betty Grable and Victor Mature, with Laird Cregar literally stealing the show as an obese psychotic cop clearly based on the doom-haunted *noir* suspense novelist Cornell Woolrich. Humberstone died in 1983.

The screenplay for his only contribution to the Cisco saga was by Robert Ellis and Helen Logan from an original story by Julian Johnson. Despite its title and fine cast—Mary Beth Hughes and Evelyn Venable as the love interests, young Dana Andrews in Edmund Lowe's old part as Sergeant Dunn, small parts for cinematic Westerners like Joe Sawyer, Francis Ford and Frank Lackteen— **Lucky Cisco Kid** wasn't a particularly lucky film. Its main interest is in the number of motifs recycled from **In Old Arizona** (the bathtub and vigilante scenes) and **The Cisco Kid** (the widow and small boy trying to keep the economic exploiter played by Willard Robertson from taking over the family ranch) and in the ways this film's storyline is at odds with those of Fox's earliest entries in the series (the Sergeant Dunn of this one, for example, has clearly never laid eyes on Cisco before). This is hardly enough to recommend the film except for those who, like myself, are determined to follow the saga from A to Z with no letters skipped.

As the film opens a horseless Cisco and Gordito are waiting to board a stagecoach for one leg of the journey to Chicago where, I'm not making this up, they have jobs awaiting them with Buffalo Bill's Wild West show. The coach turns out to be full of drunken miners who have struck it rich and are paying the driver (Dick Rich) a bonus for not taking on any other passengers. The miners harass the two Hispanics (without a single ethnic slur passing anyone's lips) and the coach rolls on. Cisco and Gordito decide to rent horses and exact some revenge. That we never see what they do is typical of the actionlessness of 20th-Century Fox's Cisco pictures.

Meanwhile Sergeant Dunn (Dana Andrews), that familiar figure from the first two films in the series, is out on patrol with several troopers, vainly hunting Cisco as usual. The soldiers come upon the miners along the trail, learn that the coach was hijacked by two Mexicans and give chase. Cisco and Gordito elude the cavalrymen by leaping off the empty coach and walking to the next town.

Finding that Dunn and his men have reached the town first and are searching for them, the two split up. Cisco climbs to a hotel balcony, slips into a suite that is clearly a woman's, makes his way to the bathroom—complete with 1940s-style taps!—and treats himself to a hot tub, while Gordito blunders into a temperance meeting and fools the soldiers by belting out anti-liquor songs alongside the ax-faced harridans. The suite where Cisco is scrubbing belongs to Lola (Mary Beth Hughes), a flirtatious dance hall girl and as chance would have it a special favorite of Sergeant Dunn, who barges into the room hunting for Cisco. It's clear from his dialogue with her that he and his quarry have never met, and if you know otherwise from **In Old Arizona** and **The Cisco Kid**, well, as the Brits say, hard cheese. Cisco ducks under the suds in the tub, comes out fully dressed after Dunn has left, and introduces himself by his nickname from previous films, *Conejito* or little rabbit. "You got more nerve than a brass monkey," Lola tells him. Cisco gives her a ring and a gentle rebuke for being too mercenary. "Love is never cheap. It is more valuable than all the gold. Especially when it come from me!" A little later, when he overhears Judge McQuade (Willard Robertson) forming a vigilante committee to track him down, he realizes that an impostor has been using his name to commit crimes and decides to stay around for a while.

That night in the saloon, Cisco and Dunn almost come to blows over Lola's favors. The stage driver identifies Cisco as the man who hijacked his coach and Cisco and Gordito are about to be strung up when young Tommy Lawrence (Johnny Sheffield) comes racing into town with the news that "Cisco" and his gang are raiding his mother's ranch. Cisco and Gordito join the posse that rides to the rescue and actionlessly capture a gang member (Frank Lackteen) who is killed by his confederates before he can talk. Quickly smitten by Tommy's widowed mother, Emily Lawrence (Evelyn Venable), Cisco learns that she's in debt to Judge McQuade and that he's been pressuring her to sell the ranch to him. When the judge offers $5000 for Cisco, Emily's hands quit their jobs to join the hunt. Looking to catch the impostor and pocket the reward, Cisco and Gordito agree to help her run the ranch. When she tells of having had two solid years of hard luck, Cisco's reply is meant to explain the film's title. "I am very lucky fellow. I have horseshoe in both pockets."

The next morning Cisco finds out that the Lawrence ranch controls all the water in the area and concludes that McQuade is behind Emily's troubles. When he rides into town to order supplies for the ranch, storekeeper Ed Stokes (Otto Hoffman) claims that Emily already owes him $386 and refuses to extend more credit. Looking over the account book, Cisco discovers that the store belongs to McQuade and that Emily has been charged twice what anyone else pays for supplies. He distracts Stokes by tossing an apple at a mule on the street so the animal will run amok. Then he sneaks behind the counter, steals the money with which he's just paid Emily's back bill and, a few minutes later, buys fresh supplies for her with the same money.

Sergeant Dunn meanwhile is making sweet talk with Lola until McQuade cuts in and demands a military escort for the night stagecoach, which will be carrying a Wells Fargo strongbox. Cisco takes over the pleasant chore of romancing Lola as soon as Dunn is out of the way. While out buggy-riding with Cisco, she mentions that some of the jewelry she's wearing was given to her by local gunman Bill Stevens (Joseph Sawyer). Cisco jealously rips the jewels from her, cuts her finger in the process, and bandages it with one of his special handkerchiefs which is embroidered with a little rabbit figure.

In the saloon that night, Cisco and Dunn are again on the brink of a fight when Stevens and his men start shooting up the town. Swaggering into the saloon, Stevens sees Lola playing up to Cisco and forces him at gunpoint to down three glasses of tequila. Cisco pretends to have a giggling fit and gets the drop on Stevens. "You make big mistake when you give me tequila. I was raised on it," he boasts, and slaps Stevens' face before he and Gordito ride out of town.

Back at the ranch, Cisco romances Emily and, without revealing who he is, says that his mission in life is to arrange things "so the rich people don't have so much and the poor people have some more." This is as close to the Robin Hood theme as a 20th-Fox Cisco film will venture. Hoping that the impostor will try for the strongbox on the night coach, Cisco and Gordito hit the trail. But Dunn is also expecting the coach to be robbed and both his troops and the vigilantes are waiting in ambush at Big Rock Pass, the likeliest spot for an attack. Lola overhears this news and rides to the ranch to warn Cisco. We now learn what most of us long suspected, that the phony Cisco is Bill Stevens. (We are left to imagine what an Irish mug like Joe Sawyer would do with a Mexican accent.) The outlaws send the coach over a cliff but while taking the Wells Fargo box they're attacked by Gordito and Cisco, who catches a bullet in the shoulder during the fracas. When the troops and vigilantes ride up and a rabbit-embroidered handkerchief is found at the crime scene, Dunn realizes at last that the Hispanic who's stealing Lola from him is Cisco himself.

At the Lawrence ranch, the wounded Cisco admits his identity to Emily but convinces her he's been framed so that she hides him in the attic when the troopers and vigilantes ride up. Just as a thorough search of the house begins, Lola, who's been spying from outside, dashes in and claims she just saw Cisco and Gordito riding away. "Cisco, women are the craziest people," marvels Gordito when the coast is clear. "That is why I love them so much," Cisco says.

The posse stays out all night, accompanied by Lola, who is eager to collect McQuade's reward. When everyone returns to town next morning and Lola goes up to her hotel room, Cisco is waiting to thank her. This is when he learns that the only person who's been in her room since he gave her his special handkerchief was Stevens. The troops and vigilantes spot Cisco on Lola's balcony and a gun battle breaks out but ends in seconds as Cisco singlehandedly gets the drop on McQuade, Stevens and everyone else. He accuses Stevens of being the fake Cisco and the Wells Fargo gold is found in the gunman's saddlebags.

This being the wild and woolly West, Stevens is immediately taken to the saloon, put on trial before Judge McQuade, and convicted on Cisco's and Lola's testimony. Meanwhile Gordito produces some mysterious paperwork he stole from McQuade's safe that proves the judge is behind the raiders. Pulling a gun on McQuade, Cisco makes him mark all Emily Lawrence's IOUs as paid and then forces him to hand over the $5000 reward he offered. Slipping the cash to Lola, he and Gordito once again race out of town. As the film ends we discover that Gordito palmed half the money so our heroes are not broke after all as they ride out of this rather lackluster adventure.

The fourth of Romero's half-dozen Cisco films introduced yet another director into the cycle. Born in Grand Rapids, Michigan in 1895, Otto Brower cut his directorial eyeteeth on seven consecutive late silents and early talkies in Paramount's series inspired by the novels of Zane Grey. During the pit of the Depression, from 1931 through 1935, he bounced from studio to studio on one-shot or short-term arrangements, directing four Hoot Gibson shoot-em-ups for Allied, a Jack Hoxie for Majestic, the 12-chapter cliffhanger serial **The Devil Horse** (1932, starring Harry Carey) for Mascot, two excellent Tom Keenes (**Scarlet River** and **Cross Fire**, both 1933) for

RKO and three Tim McCoys for Columbia, among other jobs. Near the end of the lean years he and Breezy Eason co-directed two well-remembered Mascot serials: **Mystery Mountain** (1934, starring Ken Maynard) and **The Phantom Empire** (1935, starring Gene Autry). In 1936 Brower signed with 20th-Fox, and the next and last decade of his career paralleled Eason's at Warners as he alternated between directing B pictures on his own and helming elaborate action sequences for his studio's big-budget efforts like **Under Two Flags** (1936) and **Suez** (1938). He died in 1946.

The Gay Caballero (1940) is the only Western Brower directed at 20th-Fox and the only one of that studio's Cisco features to be helmed by an action professional. The difference shows. Despite a two month hiatus in mid-production when Romero (depending on which account you believe) either broke a leg or came down with paratyphoid, the picture came out so well that Don Miller in *Hollywood Corral* called it "the best Cisco in the series" and added: "There was nothing new about the plot....but the way Brower sent it humming through the course made it seem better." (183) The screenplay was by Albert Duffy and John Larkin, from an original story by Walter Bullock and Albert Duffy. The nice young couple Cisco brings together were played by rising stars Sheila Ryan and Robert Sterling, with sturdy reliables like C. Montague Shaw and Hooper Atchley in character parts. Since no prints or cassettes of this film seem to be available anywhere, I have no choice but to base my description on existing plot summaries.

If it actually begins as those summaries suggest, **The Gay Caballero** boasts the most dramatic opening of any picture in the series. Cisco and Gordito come upon a woman weeping beside a grave whose headstone reads: HERE LIES THE CISCO KID. The woman is Carmelita (Jacqueline Dalya), a servant working for rancher Kate Brewster (Janet Beecher). Questioned by an understandably curious Cisco, she explains that the grave holds her fiancé Manuel, whom ranch foreman Joe Turner (Edmund MacDonald) accused of being the notorious Cisco Kid and shot down. A little while later Cisco and Gordito happen upon and chase away three outlaws trying to rob the passengers in a wagon and discover that the people they've saved are George Wetherby (C. Montague Shaw) and his daughter Susan (Sheila Ryan), who have come from England to purchase part of the Brewster ranch. Seeing a golden opportunity to find out why Turner falsely accused and shot Manuel, Cisco and Gordito accompany the Wetherbys on the final miles of their journey.

THE GAY CABALLERO

WITH
Cesar ROMERO
AS "THE CISCO KID"

Sheila   Robert   Chris-Pin
RYAN   STERLING   MARTIN

Janet   Edmund   Jacqueline
BEECHER   McDONALD   DALYA

Directed by OTTO BROWER
ASSOCIATE Walter Morosco & Ralph Dietrick
PRODUCED BY
SCREEN PLAY BY ALBERT DUFFY AND JOHN LARKIN
ORIGINAL STORY BY WALTER BULLOCK AND ALBERT DUFFY
BASED ON THE CHARACTER "THE CISCO KID" CREATED BY O. HENRY
A 20th CENTURY

A Title Card from 1940 picturing Janet Beecher and Robert Sterling. (Courtesy of Boyd Magers.)

At the ranch, calling himself Rodriguez Gonzales Sebastiano Don Juan Chicuelo as usual in the 20th-Fox films, Cisco meets Kate and her nephew Billy (Robert Sterling), who has recently been appointed a deputy sheriff. That night at dinner Turner tells the Wetherbys that much of the property they intend to buy had been pillaged by the nefarious Cisco Kid before the foreman had shot the outlaw down. George Wetherby announces that his life's savings, which he plans to invest in the Brewster ranch, will soon be arriving by stagecoach. At this point the three outlaws who had tried to rob the Wetherbys show up at the ranch. Over her other guests' protests Kate allows them to stay, declaring that her late husband's policy had been to offer sanctuary to any visitor. Later when everyone else has gone to bed and Kate berates Turner for sending the three badmen to the ranch, we learn that she and her foreman are plotting to steal the Wetherbys' money and then scare them away.

Eventually Cisco discovers the truth, but by then Kate has caught on that "Chicuelo" is the real Cisco Kid and sends for Sheriff McBride (Hooper Atchley) to arrest him. Cisco claims the same right of sanctuary the three robbers had invoked earlier, and somehow the sheriff lets him get away with it. George Wetherby and deputy Billy Brewster are convinced by now that Cisco is a vicious gunman but Susan defends him.

Kate and Turner launch a new plot: she will lure Cisco away from the ranch on a romantic pretext while the foreman dresses in an outfit like Cisco's and robs the coach bringing in the Wetherbys' money. The plan works and the sheriff arrests Cisco and Gordito. Cisco escapes but goes back to rescue his obese compañero and gets caught. He escapes again, rides back to the Brewster ranch for a showdown and kills Turner in a shootout. Kate is crushed under her wagon while trying to get away. As the sheriff's posse approaches, Cisco tells the Wetherbys not to let Billy learn the truth about his aunt and, with Gordito in tow, rides out of the frame.

Shelia Ryan looks on as Robert Sterling covers Cesar Romero in this Lobby Card from 1940. (Courtesy of Boyd Magers.)

Herbert Leeds was back in the director's chair for Romero's fifth outing as Cisco. The screenplay for **Romance Of The Rio Grande** (1941) was written by Harold Buchman and Samuel G. Engel and nominally based on Katharine Fullerton Gerould's 1923 novel *Conquistador*, the same book that had been the nominal basis for the early Fox talkie **Romance Of The Rio Grande** (1929), starring Warner Baxter but not of course as Cisco. Back in those days, when a studio bought movie rights to a book it had the power of God over the novelist's creation and could even make two or more worlds out of the author's one. Except for a few well-directed moments there was little special about this second version but the cast was fun to watch and, as usual, included both actors who were rarely in Westerns, like Patricia Morison and Ricardo Cortez, and people like Lynne Roberts, Raphael Bennett, Trevor Bardette and Tom London who were rarely in anything else.

During a fiesta at the sprawling Rancho Santa Margarita, in the Arizona territory, we are rapidly introduced to Don Fernando de Vega (Pedro de Cordoba), his nephew Ricardo (Ricardo Cortez), his ward Rosita (Patricia Morison), and to Maria Cordova (Lynne Roberts), the daughter of his best friend. Rustlers have been raiding the property and Ricardo is pressing his elderly uncle to turn over management of the rancho to a younger and more vigorous man, like himself. But Don Fernando has sent to Spain for his estranged grandson Carlos Hernandez (Joseph McDonald), his only direct descendant and his choice both to manage the rancho and to marry Rosita.

The coach bringing Carlos through Arizona is attacked by outlaws Carver (Raphael Bennett) and Manuel (Trevor Bardette), who shoot the driver and Carlos. Cisco and Gordito stop the runaway coach and are about to bury the two dead men in it—"It is better to be buried in the ground than in the stomach of a coyote"—when they discover that one of them, Carlos, is still alive, and an identical double for Cisco to boot. Cisco and Gordito take him to the country inn of Mama

64

Edmund McDonald taunts Cesar Romero with a gun in easy reach in this Lobby Card from 1940. (Courtesy of Boyd Magers.)

Lopez (Inez Palange) to recover. Reading the letters he was carrying from Don Fernando, Cisco sees his chance to come to the rancho as Carlos and steal the de Vega family jewels. On their journey to Santa Margarita, Cisco and Gordito stop to shoot a bullet into the St. Christopher medal Carlos had been wearing.

Cisco makes his triumphal entry during a fiesta in Carlos' honor, is introduced to the lovely Maria and Rosita, displays the medal he says stopped the bullet the stagecoach bandits fired at him, and enjoys a Hollywood Latin-style production number with Maria singing "Ride On Vaquero," also the title of the next and last film in 20th-Fox's Cisco series. Ricardo becomes extremely jealous of the attention "Carlos" is paying to Rosita, who we learn is Ricardo's partner in planning both the rustler raids and the attack on the stagecoach which they now believe to have been a failure.

Gordito, who supposedly rescued "Carlos" from the runaway coach, flirts with the fat cook Marta (Eva Puig) and learns where the family

jewels are kept. Meanwhile, "Carlos" romances Maria—almost giving himself away when he mentions "our rich wine gardens in Portugal" where Cisco in his 20th-Fox incarnations was raised—and learns not only that the notorious Cisco Kid is being blamed for the rustler raids but also that Ricardo claims to have shot at him during one of those raids and describes Cisco as short and "filthy as a pig." The information convinces him that he'll soon be Ricardo's target just as the real Carlos was.

Don Fernando shows "Carlos" around Santa Margarita and so impresses Cisco with his kindness and love that our good-hearted bandito decides not to steal his jewels after all. That night, in a sequence full of the kind of menacing shadows later identified with film *noir*, Ricardo shoots at "Carlos" in his room and, while escaping, clubs Don Fernando in the darkness. The blow turns out to be mortal. On his deathbed the patriarch tells his family that his will laves the rancho to Carlos, but if Carlos should die without

Ricardo Cortez has Cesar Romero covered as Ray Bennett looks on in this Lobby Card from 1941. (Courtesy of Boyd Magers.)

a son the property will pass to Ricardo. His final request is that "Carlos" should look after Maria. "Do you not know that the wish of a dying man is holy?" Cisco admonishes Gordito as he explains why he's now determined to save the rancho for the genuine Carlos. Later both Cisco and Maria overhear Ricardo and Rosita arguing over "Carlos." Rosita thinks she can get the property on her own by marrying him. "After tomorrow," Ricardo proclaims, "I will be the master of Santa Margarita." Cisco knows that another attempt on his life is imminent.

The next morning Ricardo claims that Cisco raided the ranch's herds again and persuades "Carlos" to join the hunt for the raiders. The group from Santa Margarita rides out to where Carver and his gang are waiting in ambush. Cisco gets the drop on Ricardo and Manuel and makes them ride ahead of the others into the trap, where Manuel is shot down and Ricardo escapes to join Carver and his men. Later, as bad luck would have it, Ricardo and Carver stop at the country inn of Mama Lopez for food and drink, find the real Carlos there restored to health and realize that they've been dealing with an impostor.

Leaving Carver to stand guard over Carlos, Ricardo rides to the town of Rio Oro, tells the marshal (Tom London) of the impersonation and claims that the real Carlos is near death. Thanks to having a wanted poster on Cisco, the marshal identifies the impersonator at once. Meanwhile Mama Lopez slips away from Carver, comes to Cisco at the ranch and warns him that the game's up. Just then Ricardo rides up with the marshal and a posse. Mama Lopez creates a diversion while Cisco and Gordito escape. The posse members chase them in a well directed action sequence, climaxing when the fugitives trick their pursuers and leave them without guns or horses and miles from anywhere.

Cisco and Gordito reach the country inn and get the drop on Carver as he's about to kill Carlos. The identical doubles talk to each other for the first time and Cisco explains his impersonation. Then he returns to Santa Margarita, pretending to be the genuine Carlos and claiming that the marshal has Cisco in jail. This second impersonation works as well as the first.

That night Maria visits "Carlos" in his room and warns him of what she learned during the Ricardo-Rosita conversation she overheard with Cisco, namely that Ricardo's out to kill him. Cisco romances her without bothering to tell her who he is. Later, while Ricardo is eavesdropping in Rosita's room, "Carlos" drives a wedge between the conspirators by asking Rosita to marry him the next day. As soon as she agrees and he leaves her room, Ricardo comes out of hiding, gets into another fight with Rosita and they wind up shooting each other to death. Softly singing "La Cucaracha," Cisco returns to his room. The next day he leaves the rancho and sends the genuine Carlos back in his place and into Maria's arms. "When you're about to get married," he advises Gordito as they ride off, "don't."

20th-Fox's involvement with Cisco came to an end with **Ride On Vaquero** (1941), directed by Leeds from a screenplay by Samuel G. Engel. Mary Beth Hughes and Lynne Roberts made their second appearances in a Cisco feature, each of course playing a different role than in her first, and the cast was rounded out by Robert Lowery, William Demarest, Paul Sutton, Don Costello and a long forgotten black actor named Ben Carter who literally steals the picture in a small part as night watchman at the chief villain's bank. Let this be Herbert Leeds' epitaph: at a time when the deck was viciously stacked against people of color, he gave one black man his moment in the sun.

The film opens with the by now familiar sequence of Cisco being betrayed by a predatory señorita (Joan Woodbury) and locked up with Gordito by the soldados Americanos. But Colonel Warren (Paul Harvey) has an ulterior motive for arresting Cisco: in a secret midnight meeting in his office, he explains that he wants Cisco, acting as an undercover agent, to go to the town of Las Tablas and break up a gang that specializes in holding people for ransom. The dialogue stresses what a dirty crime kidnapping is and shows how the snatching of the Lindbergh baby was still echoing in the popular culture almost ten years after it happened. When the colonel reveals that the gang's latest victim is Carlos Martinez (Robert Lowery), son of the family that raised Cisco, an outraged Cisco agrees to take on the job. The colonel then gives Cisco his gun back and helps him and Gordito escape the stockade.

Cisco and Gordito arrive at the Martinez rancho and have a reunion with Carlos' wife Marguerita (Lynne Roberts), who knows her dashing guest only as Gonzales Sebastiano Rodriguez Don Juan de Chicuelo and has no idea that her childhood amigo has grown up to become the notorious Cisco Kid. And it's a good thing she hasn't because the ransom note that she received and now shows her guest, demanding $50,000 for Carlos' return, is signed by, you guessed it, The Cisco Kid himself. Somehow managing to keep his face on straight, Cisco argues that the note must have been written by an impostor because its language is idiomatic English and Cisco as everyone knows is Latino. (Is this a subtle insiders' joke for the few who might remember that Cisco as O. Henry created him was as purebred an Anglo as they come?) Marguerita tells Cisco that in order to raise the ransom money she's had to mortgage the rancho to Las Tablas banker Dan Clark (Edwin Maxwell).

At this point Cisco and Gordito ride into Las Tablas and drop into the local saloon, where in one coincidence-packed scene the plot of this picture is sorted out for us. No sooner has Cisco downed a couple of tequilas than an aggressive dance-hall girl named Sally (Mary Beth Hughes) comes on to him and demands that he buy her a drink. Over wine at a corner table she tells him that she knows he's the infamous Cisco Kid. How can she be sure? Because he romanced her a few years before in another town and has forgotten the affair completely! (Could this be a sly dig at Hughes' role in **Lucky Cisco Kid** as virtually the same character she plays here but with a different name?) While they're talking, Sheriff Johnny Burge (Arthur Hohl) drops into the saloon but Sally doesn't give Cisco away. Then some cavalry troopers hunting the escaped Cisco drop in for a whistle-wetter but again Sally says nothing. The sheriff jokingly orders milk, gets a shock when that's exactly what he's served, and the brainless waiter mumbles something about the milk having been obtained for some mysterious special guest of Redge (Don Costello), the saloon's owner.

Now comes the nightly ritual when Sally "raffles her bustle," which means she auctions off the chance to dance with her, while Redge's silent bouncer Sleepy (Paul Sutton) is posted on the saloon staircase with a shotgun in case the hands of Sally's partner get to wandering. Cisco makes the highest bid, whirls Sally around, and receives a whispered order from her to book a room for the night in the town hotel. Meanwhile the banker Dan Clark drops in for a nightcap, and the conversation he has in private with Redge and the sheriff makes it clear to any moviegoer who might have been napping that these three are behind the kidnap gang and that Redge's mystery guest is Carlos Martinez. Clark tells the others about Marguerita's having mortgaged the rancho and instructs them to set up the swap whereby Carlos, who has refused to eat anything during his confinement and will drink nothing but milk, will be exchanged for the cash. Later that night Sally visits Cisco, whom she too believes to be behind the rash of kidnappings, and demands the release of Carlos, who happens to have been a longtime friend of hers too, in return for her not turning him in. The arrival of a messenger from the Martinez rancho with news that the instructions for Carlos' return have just been received convinces Sally that Cisco is innocent.

The instructions order Marguerita to go out into the countryside and put the ransom money in the bucket at the well on Turkey Creek, ride away, and come back later when she'll find a note in the bucket telling where her husband can be found. Cisco decides to drop off the money for her. En route he and Gordito purchase an old covered wagon which they drive to the well. Cisco keeps his head covered with a serape as he drops off the money. Then he rides back to the covered wagon that Gordito is driving, hides inside, and watches Redge and the sheriff pick up the cash-filled strongbox. The note they leave in the bucket tells Cisco that Carlos can be found in a deserted cabin in San Louis Canyon. Cisco returns to Las Tablas and discovers the identity of the head of the kidnap gang when he sees Redge and the sheriff give the money to Clark to be put in the bank vault.

Meanwhile the muchacho of the peasant family from whom Cisco bought the wagon remembers that the last time he saw the buyer's face it was on a Wanted poster and goes running to the law. That night, while Cisco is dancing with Sally in the saloon, the sheriff tries to arrest him. Cisco and Gordito shoot their way out of the place and race out of town with a posse at their heels, the only genuine action sequence in the picture, halfway decently directed but nothing special. Fleeing from the posse, Cisco and Gordito ride to San Louis Canyon, find Carlos tied up in a closet in the cabin, but before they can get away the posse lays siege to the cabin, sets it afire and forces them to surrender. They are locked up in the local jail and Cisco wrongly believes it was Sally who betrayed them, but when she makes a late-night visit and sweet-talks the idiot deputy into tangoing with her so that Cisco can reach his gun and make him set them free, Cisco knows he's misjudged her. He and Gordito break into the bank and surprise the gleefully larcenous black watchman Bullfinch (Ben Carter), who instantly sees what side his grits are buttered on and becomes Cisco's partner for what's left of the film, stealing the picture in the process. Cisco overpowers Clark, who lives above the bank, and makes him open the vault and disgorge the $50,000 ransom money.

Then with Bullfinch's help he tricks Redge and the sheriff into thinking Clark is about to take off with the loot. When they come to the bank, he gets the drop on them and makes them sign a confession. With the $1500 Cisco has given him in his jeans, Bullfinch says goodbye and heads for Memphis, while Cisco and Gordito lock the evil trio in the bank vault and hit the trail for new adventures—which took four years to materialize.

Ride On Vaquero marked the end of Romero's tenure as Cisco but his acting career lasted for another half-century and more. He remained under contract to 20th-Fox and graced several of the studio's musical romances until mid-1943 when he left to serve in the Coast Guard. From late 1946 through 1950 he was back at 20th-Fox playing major roles in Henry King's **Captain From Castile** (1947), Ernst Lubitsch's **That Lady In Ermine** (1948) and other films. Throughout the Fifties he free-lanced in movies and, to an ever greater extent as time went by, on TV. Two of his best roles during that decade were in Westerns. He appeared opposite Gary Cooper, Burt Lancaster and Denise Darcel in **Vera Cruz** (Flora/United Artists, 1954, directed by Robert Aldrich), and in **The Americano** (Stillman/RKO, 1954), which starred Glenn Ford and Frank Lovejoy, he played a Latin Robin Hood character vaguely reminiscent of Cisco. Romero and the future Cisco star Gilbert Roland had major role together in Henry Hathaway's **The Racers** (20th-Fox, 1955), starring Kirk Douglas and Bella Darvi, and cameos together in **Around The World In 80 Days** (Todd/United Artists, 1956). Most of his movie appearances in later decades were throwaways but he guest-starred in countless TV series episodes and had running parts as The Joker in *Batman* (1966-68) and as Jane Wyman's husband on *Falcon Crest* (1985-87). It was on the latter series that he celebrated his eightieth birthday.

I had wanted to get in touch with Romero and invite him to reminisce about his time as Cisco but kept putting it off. He looked so vigorous and healthy in his promos for the American Movie Classics cable channel that I figured there was no rush. As 1993 drew to an end, I made a resolution: write him care of AMC as soon as the holidays were over. Too late. He had gone into St. John's Hospital and Health Center in Santa Monica with severe bronchitis and pneumonia and, in the last hours of December 31, died there of complications from a blood clot. He was 86 years old. This book is the poorer for my procrastination.

Six • Duncan Renaldo Enters

Cisco left the nation's movie screens about eight months before Pearl Harbor and wouldn't return until a few months before World War II ended. But for one season during the war years he became the hero of a radio series on WOR-Mutual, debuting October 2, 1942. Jackson Beck played "O. Henry's beloved badman who rides the romantic trail that leads sometimes to adventure, often to danger, but always to beautiful señoritas." Louis Sorin portrayed his fat and faithful sidekick Pancho, the first time Cisco's *compadre* was known by that name but hardly the last. Jock MacGregor directed the series, which left the air after a year or so.

Late in 1944, 20th Century-Fox officially said *adios* to Cisco by selling off its rights in the property. The buyers were independent producers Philip N. Krasne and James S. Burkett, who a year earlier had bought from 20th-Fox the rights to carry on the long-running Charlie Chan detective series and then made a deal with Monogram Pictures to release new low-budget Chan features. Burkett was a newcomer to the B-movie game while Krasne had entered the field in 1939 and had formed Criterion Pictures to make half a dozen quickie exploits of Renfrew of the Royal Mounted, starring James Newill, for Monogram release. Now, five years later, Krasne arranged for Monogram to release a new series of Cisco Kid adventures. The original plan called for eight Cisco pictures but the studio then opted to save money by committing only to four, filling the other four slots in its schedule with the first entries in a rock-bottom-budget singing cowboy series starring Jimmy Wakely. As things turned out, the Cisco series in its first incarnation at Monogram lasted for just three films.

Reading what the most knowledgeable commentators on Westerns have to say about the trio, you have to wonder if they were all watching the same pictures. Jon Tuska claims in *The Filming Of The West* that Krasne's financial backing gave the threesome "the best production values of any Western series Monogram made." (441) Don Miller on the other hand writes in *Hollywood Corral* that "Krasne's productions were a long distance from the solid look of 20th Century-Fox. Actually [this] was a blessing in disguise, for the low budgets moved the films closer to the traditional Western. But....[they] were no world beaters....Main trouble with the productions was that they looked about ten years older than they were, even the photography having a sort of mildewed look." (184) William K. Everson in *The Hollywood Western* says just that Monogram's Cisco series "started off rather weakly with....three lackluster entries." (225) I tend to agree with Miller and Everson about the first and third of the trio but the second effort is somewhat better. In any event it's Phil Krasne who deserves the credit for casting the actor still considered the definitive Cisco by most of those who remember the character at all.

Duncan Renaldo was born sometime in the first few years of the century. He himself claimed not to know where or when. One of the six birth certificates in his possession gave his birthdate as April 23, 1904. He never knew his parents or what his ethnic roots were and might have been of Rumanian heritage, or Russian, or Portuguese, or almost anything else. "I had worked aboard a ship as a coal miner," he told Jon Tuska near the end of his life, "and entered the United States on a temporary 90-day seaman's permit." (439) This was apparently in the early 1920s. When the ninety days were up he stayed in the country and got a foot in the door of the movie business in 1925 as producer of a series of silent shorts he sold to Pathè. His Hollywood acting career began at the Tiffany studio in 1928 but his strongest early roles were for MGM, in **The Bridge Of San Luis Rey** (1929) opposite Lily Damita and Ernest Torrence and in **Trader Horn** (1931), which was shot largely in Africa and starred Harry Carey and Edwina Booth. A few years later he was arrested as an illegal immigrant and spent most of the

1934-35 period in prison. The key figure in his release and return to Hollywood was Herbert J. Yates, who owned Republic Pictures and in 1937 signed Renaldo to a seven-year nonexclusive contract.

Renaldo didn't know what nationality he was but proved most convincing playing Mexican roles in several of Republic's classic cliffhanger serials and B Westerns. His first two parts for the studio were as the bandit Zamorro in **The Painted Stallion** (1937), which marked the directorial debut of actionmaster William Witney, and as star John Carroll's confidant and servant in **Zorro Rides Again** (1937), first of the 23 consecutive serials Witney co-directed with his best friend John English. In a later Witney-English cliffhanger, **The Lone Ranger Rides Again** (1939), the directors cast Renaldo as fiery Juan Vasquez in a move to convert the Ranger-Tonto partnership (Bob Livingston and Chief Thundercloud) into a threesome. Next Renaldo found himself alongside Livingston and Raymond Hatton and cast as Rico, the second lead in Republic's Three Mesquiteers trio Western series during its 1939-40 season, while continuing to do Latin parts in Gene Autry features like **South Of The Border** (1939) and **Gaucho Serenade** (1940). His final roles at Republic were in the serials **Secret Service In Darkest Africa** (1943) and **The Tiger Woman** (1944) and the Westerns **Hands Across The Border** (1943, starring Roy Rogers), **The San Antonio Kid** (1944, starring Bill Elliott as Red Ryder), and **Sheriff Of Sundown** (1944, starring Allan Lane). When not acting at Republic or elsewhere, Renaldo moonlighted as a State Department emissary to various countries below the Rio Grande, assigned to help boost support for the Allied cause in World War II among the people, many of whom were of German stock.

If we believe Renaldo's reminiscences of almost thirty years later, Phil Krasne had no clear idea what to do with the Cisco character when he acquired the property from 20th-Fox. Krasne did know that the hero would need a comic sidekick more or less in the mold of Chris-Pin Martin's Gordito, and for that part he signed Martin Garralaga (1895-1981), a former opera singer who'd been playing small and often unbilled Latino parts in Hollywood movies through the Thirties including at least one picture, **Rose Of The Rio Grande** (Monogram, 1938), that also featured Renaldo. Garralaga was a wiry little fellow who couldn't possibly be called Gordito. The new name for Cisco's sidekick was lifted from the 1942-43 radio series and would last, with one interruption, for as long as Cisco films continued to be made. That name of course was Pancho.

With his Republic contract behind him by the end of 1944 and the war in Europe nearly over, Duncan Renaldo was free to accept Krasne's offer of the role of Cisco if he wished. He was willing but only, or so he claimed in conversation with Jon Tuska decades later, on one condition. "I told Phil how much trouble Romero had caused in Latin America playing the Kid as a vicious bandit." (441) Anyone who's seen Romero's Cisco pictures knows this accusation is nonsense: the character he portrayed is certainly an outlaw and something of a boastful poseur in the style of Mr. Toad from *The Wind In The Willows*, but he's never vicious and always ready to abort his own or someone else's criminal schemes for love of a señorita. In any event, Renaldo suggested to Krasne an approach markedly different from Romero's. "Why not base the character on the greatest book in all Spanish literature, *Don Quixote De La Mancha*? Cisco is a modern knight; Pancho is his Sancho Panza, a delicate comedy character—not a buffoon—who always gets his partner in trouble when they try to help people." (441)

Near the end of his life Renaldo still remembered his first sidekick fondly. "Martin was perfect as Pancho....His comedy was very, very human. But he just couldn't stand horses. He was allergic to them." (441) This however is a minority viewpoint, and when most viewers see Garralaga as Pancho what comes to their minds is not Sancho Panza but a weasel. "Every time you open your mouth," Renaldo tells him early in their first picture together, "you fall in it." In the first four Cisco films that followed the Renaldo trio, Garralaga was more appropriately cast in various Latino character parts.

And Renaldo in his first outings as Cisco hardly comes across as a Don Quixote. We never see him being a bandit as we usually did at least in the opening scenes of most of the 20th-Fox Ciscos so it's a bit of a mystery why he's always the prime suspect whenever a crime is committed. He is of Mexican descent, not Portuguese like Romero's Cisco. In the first of the Renaldo trio, which was written by Betty Burbridge, his name is Juan Francisco Hernandez and Cisco is simply a shortened version of his middle name; in the second, also written by Burbridge, his name changes to Juan Carlos Francisco Antonio; and in the third and last he's just Cisco or sometimes, as in his first two exploits, "the Cisco." With his tiny mustache and neat bolero jacket he projects the image of a rogue and *roué* but not at all that of a knight.

70

The millions of us who grew up watching Renaldo as Cisco on the small screen know that he rode a pinto stallion called Diablo, but his horse in the first three Cisco features was a palomino. "He was a fearful horse," Renaldo told Jon Tuska. "He tried to break a double's legs by smashing against trees. I learned to ride very carefully because when I was at Republic working on those Mesquiteers pictures with Bob Livingston, a camera truck skidded into me and pushed both myself and the horse I was on through a barbed-wire fence. Well, they told me about this palomino, but we became good friends and I never had any trouble with him. Later, when we did the television episodes, I bought a paint. I called him Diablo, too, after the palomino." (443)

Besides signing Renaldo as Cisco and creating the original screen version of Pancho, Krasne assembled many of the behind-scenes people who kept working regularly in the series well into its long run on TV, notably assistant director Eddie Davis, film editor Martin G. Cohn, composer Albert Glasser and scriptwriter Betty Burbridge. All four were on the team that made the first of Monogram's Cisco features, **The Cisco Kid Returns** (1945). The film's director, John P. McCarthy (1885-1962), a veteran of low-budget productions since 1919, had spent the first half of the Thirties helming super-cheap Westerns with stars like Bob Steele, Tom Tyler or Rex Bell, often for Monogram release. He was unaccountably out of the business between 1937 and 1943 but came back to direct three more Monogram shoot-em-ups: **Raiders Of The Border** (1944) with Johnny Mack Brown, **Marked Trails** (1945) with Bob Steele and Hoot Gibson, and **The Cisco Kid Returns**, which was the best of an indifferent trio and the last film of his career.

The picture opens with what was supposed to be the marriage of Cisco's former sweetheart Rosita Gonzales (Cecilia Callejo) to businessman John Harris (Roger Pryor), but the ceremony is broken up when Cisco charges in and claims that he's been Rosita's husband for years. Along with Cisco are Pancho and a four-year-old girl who calls the bride Mamacita. At this point Rosita faints—partly no doubt because the child's hair is golden blonde—and Cisco carries her away. The little girl, Nancy Page (Sharon Smith), was borrowed by Pancho from his friend Antonio who's helping her father raise her. Safely away from the Harris ranch, Cisco explains to Rosita that he broke up the wedding because the man was no good for her and vows he'll be faithful to her forevermore. "On my heart I swear it!" he proclaims, the first of many times we'll hear

A Newspaper Ad from 1945. (Courtesy of Charles K. Stumpf.)

Renaldo making this pledge to a señorita.

Cisco rides with Pancho and Rosita to return Nancy to her father but finds both Stephen Page and his servant Antonio lying shot and near death in the living room of Page's ranch house. He sends the others away, explaining the situation to them in Spanish so Nancy won't understand, then goes back inside to investigate. He promises Antonio that he'll take care of Page's child and, in one of the few Catholic touches in the entire Cisco series, helps the dying servant make the sign of the cross. The sheriff (Bud Osborne) and a posse ride up and Cisco from a hiding place in the house overhears enough to know that Harris is trying to pin the murders on him. He dashes out of the house, pausing for no earthly reason to put on a Zorroesque black cloak, and races away with the posse in hot pursuit. Meanwhile we learn from a conversation between Harris and his gunman Jennings (Cy Kendall) that Rosita's jilted fiancé is behind the murders.

Cisco sneaks into his rival's house, gets the drop on Harris and makes him admit having told the sheriff that Cisco was in the area, but Harris swears he didn't give the lawman any physical description of his enemy. (If you're wondering why not, nothing in the film relieves your curiosity.) Cisco takes Harris out to meet the posse on the trail and forces him to describe the bandit to the sheriff as a short, fat, bearded hombre missing a finger. After joining the posse and spending some time hunting for himself, Cisco rejoins Pancho, Rosita and Nancy at the home of Tia Jimenez (Eva Puig), bringing a necklace for the grown woman and a blue dress for the child. Then he and Pancho head for the local mission, where the padre (Fritz Leiber) calls him Francisco and, in another of the film's Catholic touches (director McCarthy's contribution?), asks Pancho how long it's been since his last confession. While they're talking, two women stop at the mission, claim to be Stephen Page's widow (Vicky Lane) and her French maid Jeanette (Jan Wiley), and ask directions to the Page ranch. Cisco agrees to take the women to their destination but for reasons that are never explained he doesn't bother to tell them either that Nancy isn't at the ranch or that he is watching out for her. Instead he focuses on romancing the maid Jeanette. When Julia Page discovers that her daughter is missing she offers a large reward for the child's return but Cisco still says nothing. At this point we learn that the two women are impostors, sent by Page's corrupt business manager Paul Conway (Anthony Warde), who is behind the murders, to get custody of Nancy so he can control the Page fortune.

That night Cisco and Pancho slip away from the home of Tia Jimenez and Rosita, suspecting Cisco's going to make love to another woman, shadows him. Cisco sneaks into Stephen Page's study, finds and pockets a four-year-old letter in the handwriting of the dead man's estranged wife, then makes his presence known and again makes a play for Jeanette. Rosita catches him and throws dishes at the lovebirds until Cisco and Pancho manage to drag her away.

A furious Rosita goes back to Harris and reveals to him that Nancy is with Cisco. Conway arrives on the scene and he and Harris decide they can best trap Cisco and recover Nancy by having the sheriff keep an eye on the Page ranch. Sure enough Cisco and Pancho pay a return visit. Pancho strums a guitar while Cisco once more flings amore at Jeanette. The sheriff and his posse charge into the house and chase Cisco and Pancho through the rooms and out onto the trail. Cisco stops in midflight to pick up Nancy from Tia Jimenez and carry her off in his black cloak.

To force a showdown, Cisco sends Pancho to the sheriff with an offer to lead the lawman to Cisco and Nancy provided that Conway and the two women at the Page ranch are made to come along. Then Cisco goes to the mission and enlists the padre's help. The sheriff and his party arrive and the padre admits that Nancy is staying there but insists that "Mrs. Page" must sign a receipt of sorts before he turns the child over. Cisco and Nancy reveal themselves and Cisco exposes the scheme by showing the difference between the genuine Mrs. Page's signature on the stolen letter and the impostor's signature on the padre's receipt. With all the conspirators except Harris and Jennings actionlessly rounded up, Cisco and the sheriff go on to the Harris ranch where, again without any action to speak of, they round up the last two criminals. With Nancy back in the meaty arms of Tia Jimenez, Cisco carries Rosita away for another interlude of romance as the picture ends.

Soon after completing that picture, the same team started work on the second and by all odds best of the Renaldo trio, **In Old New Mexico** (1945), which far outdid its companion films in both action content and story complexity, so much so that at one point in the Betty Burbridge script Cisco is (not very plausibly) compared by another character to the king of mid-1940s screen sleuths, Sherlock Holmes. Phil Rosen was perhaps a strange choice to direct this adventure but, as events proved, not a bad one. Born in Marienburg, Russia on May 8, 1888, Rosen had emigrated to the U.S. as a child and had begun his film career in 1912, working as a cameraman at Edison, Fox, Universal and other studios and serving as first president of the American Society of Cinematographers, the "A.S.C." frequently found after the cameraman's name in movie credits. He'd been making silent features since 1920, occasionally working with major stars (for example in Paramount's 1922 **The Young Rajah** with Rudolph Valentino) but usually on less prestigious projects. At the end of the Twenties he moved from silents into talkies without missing a beat and picked up his first and only extensive experience making B Westerns in 1931-32 when he directed eight in a row with Ken Maynard at Tiffany and two with Hoot Gibson at Allied, followed by the somewhat higher budgeted **The Vanishing Frontier** (Paramount, 1932) with Johnny Mack Brown. A dozen years later, as luck would have it, Rosen and all three of these cowboy stars were working at Monogram, which was the director's principal employer from 1940 on. Most of Rosen's pictures after 1932 were adventure or detective programmers and he directed Monogram's first four Charlie Chan quickies after Krasne and Burkett bought the property from 20th-Fox. He all but retired at the beginning of 1946 and died five years later.

In Old New Mexico opens most strikingly with an excellent action sequence that runs under the principal credits. Cisco and Pancho chase and stop a stagecoach, rob the male passengers and take away with them the only woman on the coach, Ellen Roth (Gwen Kenyon). Cisco tells her what at one time or another he tells every female in the film—"You are the most beautiful señorita in all this world. On my heart I swear it!"—but anyone who thinks he's kidnapped her for romantic

As Martin Garralaga holds a gun on Bud Osborne, Duncan Renaldo talks to Frank Jaquet and Gwen Kenyon in this Lobby Card from 1945. (Courtesy of Boyd Magers.)

reasons has another think coming. In the nearby town of Gila, Sheriff Clem Petty (Lee "Lasses" White) is waiting to arrest her for murder. It seems that Ellen was nurse to Mrs. Prescott, a wealthy old lady in Denver whose will left her a great deal of money, and that she fled after the old lady was killed by an overdose of sleeping pills. When the stagecoach reaches town and the driver reports Cisco's kidnapping of the female fugitive, the sheriff forms a posse and rides out in pursuit. Cisco and Pancho encounter the posse but escape by hiding in the usual rocks. They leave Ellen at a mission—where Padre Angelo (Pedro de Cordoba) calls Cisco by his full name, Francisco, and describes his father as the most prominent man in the province of Jalisco—and ride into Gila to return the stagecoach loot at the empty sheriff's office, although Cisco catches Pancho trying to hold back a watch he likes. It's clear by now that Cisco knows a lot about the murder of Mrs. Prescott but how he learned it and why he cares is

never revealed to us.

One of the things he mysteriously knows is that the dead woman had often sent letters to Post Office Box 17 in Gila. While watching to see who is renting that box, he bumps into Belle (Donna Dax), a dance hall girl, and instantly starts to flirt with her. Then he observes saloonkeeper Will Hastings (Norman Willis) opening the box and removing a letter, so while Pancho trips Hastings, Cisco picks his pocket. The seemingly innocuous document is signed by someone calling himself Doc and refers to a woman named Dolores. Back at the mission, Ruth tells Cisco her side of the story, claiming that Mrs. Prescott was given the overdose of sleeping pills by a man who called at her house and claimed to be her new doctor. Ruth insists that she fled from Denver to find this man, investigate Mrs. Prescott's letters to Box 17 and clear herself.

Cisco and Pancho visit Hastings' saloon in Gila, where a Broadway-style Latin musical revue is in

Richard Gordon holds a gun on Duncan Renaldo as Martin Garralaga looks on in this Lobby Card from 1945. (Courtesy of Boyd Magers.)

progress, complete with a line of chorus girls in scanty costumes kicking their legs. Cisco learns from Belle that one of the saloon entertainers is named Dolores and that Hastings considers her his property. Dolores (Aurora Roche) comes out and performs a number in the style of Carmen Miranda. No sooner is she done than Cisco takes her aside and starts romancing her and learns that Hastings is the late Mrs. Prescott's nephew, that he claims to have inherited money from her, and that one of his cronies is a man who calls himself Doc Wilson but isn't really a doctor. Hastings, furious at Cisco's playing up to Dolores, accuses him of having taken Ellen Roth from the stage-coach. The fight between them, perhaps the best-directed brawl in any Cisco feature, ends with the sheriff and posse returning to town and Cisco having to make a daredevil escape from the saloon. The chase sequence as the posse goes after Cisco and Pancho is another gem, full of running inserts and tracking shots. After eluding the

pursuers, Cisco returns to Gila, bullwhips a gun from Hastings' hand and, knowing that Ellen must be convicted of murder in order for the saloon-keeper's plot to work, offers to turn her over to the sheriff for ten thousand dollars. When Hastings agrees, Cisco drops in on Sheriff Petty and makes a deal to hand over Ellen in return for the dropping of all charges against himself. Ellen is arrested at the mission and carted off to jail.

Back in Gila, Cisco buys Dolores a fancy gown and the dressmaker's dummy that goes with it. Then he reminds Hastings that if Doc Wilson is ever found and made to talk, Ellen will be cleared. Next he calls on the editor of Gila's newspaper (Edward Earle) and forces him at gunpoint to print a story in the next edition to the effect that Doc Wilson has been arrested in Denver for Mrs. Prescott's murder. Once the paper hits the street, Hastings panics and starts packing his bags. Cisco makes a new proposition: while Ellen is being taken to Denver to identify Doc, why not kill her?

Duncan Renaldo tries to convince Martin Garralaga to relax in scene from **In Old New Mexico** (Monogram, 1945). (Courtesy of Bobby Copeland.)

Hastings agrees, and when a deputy and Ellen leave town in a buckboard, Cisco and Hastings' gunman Al Brady (John Laurenz) get ahead of them. Cisco apparently downs Ellen with a well-aimed rifle shot, the buckboard goes over a cliff, and Brady reports to Hastings that the job is done.

The next stage brings into Gila none other than Doc Wilson (Richard Gordon), who has read the phony story of his arrest. Spying on Hastings' saloon, Pancho sees a man fitting Ellen's description of the fake doctor go in and tells Cisco. The two of them watch Doc go to the newspaper office. Cisco strolls past the window, the editor points him out to Doc as the man who made him run the arrest story, and Doc follows Cisco to a stable where Pancho conks him from behind. While they're taking their prisoner to the mission, Dolores tells Hastings that someone stole her new gown and the dressmaker's dummy it came with, and Hastings suspects that he's been scammed, that it was not Ellen but the dummy that Cisco

shot and sent over the cliff. He and Brady ride out to investigate, are captured by Cisco without a struggle and taken to the mission where, with the sheriff listening from a peephole, Doc is confronted with Ellen and makes a full confession.

The last of Renaldo's first three Cisco films and the only one that looks and sounds like a typical Monogram B Western of its period was **South Of The Rio Grande** (1945). Krasne was still the producer but this time he hired a new slate of production people. William Sickner, veteran of countless B pictures at Universal, served as cinematographer; the script by relative newcomers Victor Hammond and Ralph Bettinson was based on a story by Zorro creator Johnston McCulley; and the uncredited music score consisted of Monogram's standard Frank Sanucci agitato themes, with the studio's other regular composer, Edward J. Kay, billed as music director. The cast included the usual assortment of Latin players

75

THE CISCO KID in *South of the Rio Grande* starring DUNCAN RENALDO A MONOGRAM PICTURE

A mob scene is pictured on this Lobby Card with Duncan Renaldo and Martin Garralaga and maybe Pedro Regas. (Courtesy of Boyd Magers.)

plus some B Western stalwarts like George J. Lewis, Francis McDonald and Charles Stevens, who was a grandson of Geronimo and portrayed Indians, Mexicans and other ethnic primitives in an endless array of Westerns including, as we've seen, Fox's 1931 **The Cisco Kid**.

To direct the picture Krasne brought in a prolific professional who actually had devoted much of his life to making Westerns. Lambert Hillyer was born sometime between 1888 and 1895 (depending on which reference book you consult) in Plymouth, Indiana. After short stints as a newspaperman and actor in summer stock and vaudeville, he moved into the Hollywood community and began writing and directing silent Westerns starring William S. Hart such as **Square Deal Sanderson** (1919), **Wagon Tracks** (1919), **The Toll Gate** (1920), **O'Malley Of The Mounted** (1920) and **Three Word Brand** (1921). He spent most of the Twenties alternating between Tom Mix or Buck Jones Westerns for the

Fox studio and non-Westerns for other companies. As we've seen, his first talkie, **Beau Bandit** (RKO, 1930), was the earliest "imitation Cisco" picture released by a rival of the Fox studio after the success of **In Old Arizona**. From 1931 through 1934 Hillyer wrote and directed most of Columbia's superb series of Buck Jones Westerns including **One Man Law**, **South Of The Rio Grande** (where Buck played a Mexican) and **The Sundown Rider**, all made in 1932. Most of his Columbia features after Jones left the studio were contemporary action pictures but his best known work of the decade was the pair of horror films he directed at Universal: **The Invisible Ray** (1935) with Boris Karloff and Bela Lugosi and **Dracula's Daughter** (1936) with Gloria Holden and Otto Kruger. He began turning out the occasional B feature for Monogram in 1938. From 1940 through late 1942 he was back at Columbia doing Charles Starrett and Bill Elliott shoot-em-ups, perhaps the finest of them being **Prairie**

Duncan Renaldo interrupts Lillian Molieri and George J. Lewis in this Lobby Card from 1945. (Courtesy of Boyd Magers.)

Gunsmoke (1942) in which Elliott co-starred with Tex Ritter.

In 1943 Hillyer moved virtually full-time to Monogram, where he worked almost exclusively on Johnny Mack Brown B Westerns until Krasne tapped him to direct **South Of The Rio Grande**. Afterwards he returned to the Johnny Mack series and later in the Forties to even more routine horse operas starring Jimmy Wakely or Whip Wilson. Anyone who sits through enough of Hillyer's Monogram output will find a huge number of routine yawners and every so often an unsung little gem like the Johnny Mack Brown entries **The Gentleman From Texas** (1946) and **Land Of The Lawless** (1947), both of which are connected with the Cisco saga in a way we'll explore in Chapter Eight. At the end of the decade, like many another B movie directors, Hillyer migrated into series TV. As we'll see in Chapter Nine, he wound up rejoining Renaldo and the Cisco series, contributing more of the character's adventures than anyone else who ever helmed a Cisco feature.

Unfortunately his only full-length Cisco outing was as dreary as the vast majority of his other Monogram oaters. **South Of The Rio Grande** opens with Cisco, dubbed of course by someone with a better voice than Duncan Renaldo, serenading a lovely señorita. The song is interrupted by Pancho with a letter from old Gonzales, who had been kind to Cisco as a child, asking for help in saving him and other rancheros from Miguel Sanchez (George J. Lewis), the corrupt *apoderado* or district governor. Cisco and Pancho arrive in the troubled area just in time to wipe out the squad of *caporales* who were about to execute old Gonzales' son Manuel (Tito Renaldo). The young man tells them that his parents have been murdered and that he's sent his sister Dolores (Armida) to the nearby town for safety, and asks Cisco to lead the rebel group fighting against Sanchez. The next day the rebels

A Title Card from 1945 picturing Duncan Renaldo serenading Armida. (Courtesy of Boyd Magers.)

come upon and wipe out another squad of *caporales* on a murder mission, but are too late to help the victim. Searching the dead man's papers, Cisco learns that he was Dominguez, a new official sent by the government to replace Sanchez as *apoderado*, and decides to take Dominguez' place, with Pancho posing as his servant. Within a few minutes of their triumphal entry into town, Cisco discovers that Dolores Gonzales is singing and dancing at the local *posada*, that Sanchez is making a play for her, and that the *apoderado*'s previous girlfriend, the dancer Pepita (Lillian Molieri), is jealous as only a Mexican spitfire can be. Still passing himself off as the new *apoderado*, Cisco works on Pepita and gets her to talk freely about Sanchez' crimes. Meanwhile Sanchez offers his apparent successor a partnership in his graft, tries to kill him in the middle of the night, gets caught, is made to sign a confession, and gets blown away by Cisco when he makes the mistake of reaching for another gun.

Pancho and the rebel force rout Sanchez' men in about thirty seconds of routine action. If one leaves out all the romance and Mexican songs and wine, that's all there is to this lame excuse for a south-of-the-border Western.

78

Seven • Ride Amigos Ride: Gilbert Roland Takes Over

A revamped version of the Cisco radio series returned to the airwaves in 1946 on the Mutual-Don Lee network, with Jack Mather playing Cisco and Harry Lang as a bullwhip-wielding Pancho. (Had the creators of this series seen some of the PRC Western features with Eddie Dean and Lash LaRue?) According to John Dunning's *Tune In Yesterday: The Ultimate Encyclopedia Of Old-Time Radio* 1925-1976 (Prentice-Hall, 1976), each episode would open with Pancho exclaiming: "Ceesco! The shereef, he ees getting closer!" To which Cisco would reply: "This way, Pancho, vamanos!" Whenever Cisco got up close and personal with a young woman, organ music would accompany the following deathless lines. Woman: "Ohhh, Cisco!" Cisco: "Oooooooh, señorita!" And every adventure would close with the same four bits of dialogue, the first two destined to live forever in the minds of millions of kids hunched in front of their 12" TV sets a few years later.

> "Oh, Pancho!"
> "Oh, Ceesco!"
> "Up, Diablo!"
> "Up, Loco!"

But first came two more cycles of Cisco theatrical features, the earlier produced by a canny veteran of low-budget Westerns whose name will be familiar to many fans of the genre.

Scott R. Dunlap was born in 1891 and, like many young men in Hollywood's pioneer days, started his movie career early. In 1915 he was a location scout for Universal. Four years later, possibly after service in World War I, he moved to Fox and became a director. In 1920 he made his first Western starring the man with whom he forged a permanent bond, Buck Jones. Dunlap directed eight silent features with Buck between 1920 and 1923, then left Fox to free-lance—a period during which he directed six shoot-em-ups starring Harry Carey—then came back to Fox for three final Westerns with Buck in 1926-27. When silent films were made obsolete by talkies, Dunlap gave up directing to work as Buck's manager and agent. In 1937, when Monogram Pictures split from the Republic organization and resumed independent existence, Dunlap was hired as executive in charge of production on the studio's short-lived Tom Keene series (1937-38), the Jack Randall Westerns (1938-39) and the Mr. Wong whodunits with Boris Karloff (1938-39) as well as a few non-series Bs.

In 1941 Dunlap returned to work as an active producer, bringing together Buck Jones, Tim McCoy and Raymond Hatton for the legendary Rough Riders series which ended after only eight films when McCoy, a longtime Army Reserve officer, volunteered for active duty in the second World War. Late in 1942 Dunlap and Buck went east on a war bond sales tour which culminated in the disastrous fire at Boston's Cocoanut Grove nightclub. Dunlap managed to get out of the club without serious injury but Buck was critically burned and died in Massachusetts General Hospital on November 30, two days after the fire which took the lives of almost five hundred people. Returning to Monogram, Dunlap produced about half a dozen of the early entries in the new Western series with Johnny Mack Brown and Raymond Hatton which was devised as a substitute for the Rough Riders pictures. Then, in late 1945 or early 1946, he took over the production reins on Monogram's Ciscos and started hunting for someone to replace Duncan Renaldo in the part.

The actor he settled on was known for more than seventy years as Gilbert Roland but the name his parents gave him was Luis Antonio Damaso Alonso. Exactly when and where he came into the world is a bit of a puzzle. His birth date is usually given as December 11, 1905 but a number of sources leave off the year, which suggests that he may have been born a few years earlier. Every reference I've consulted gives his birthplace as Ciudad Juárez, in the Mexican state of Chihuahua, but in a 1931 interview his father, former bull-fighter Francisco Alonso, claimed that his already

Gilbert Roland

A Postcard used to promote Gilbert Roland's career early on.

famous second son had been born in Bilbao, Spain. All the son had to say was: "I am a Spaniard but Mexico is my second fatherland." The family fled from Ciudad Juárez across the border to El Paso to escape the violence of Pancho Villa's revolution, and when he was fourteen Luis drifted out to Hollywood and quickly got hired for unbilled bit parts in all sorts of movies. By 1923 his parents and five brothers and sisters were also living in the Los Angeles area. More than sixty years later, in an article for Sports Illustrated, Roland described his father as "a brave matador, his mouth always dry on the day of the bulls. Sixteen horn wounds in his body...." Francisco Alonso eventually returned to his native soil and in 1936, during the Spanish Civil War, was machine-gunned to death by a sniper on a church roof.

Choosing a new name in honor of silent stars John Gilbert and Ruth Roland, Luis earned his first screen credit in **The Plastic Age** (Schulberg,

1925), which was directed by Wesley Ruggles and starred Donald Keith and Clara Bow, the first of many famous actresses with whom young Roland enjoyed short and passionate affairs. His big break came two years later when director Fred Niblo cast him as Armand opposite Norma Talmadge in **Camille** (Schenck/First National, 1927). Roland co-starred with Talmadge in several other late silents and one early talkie, **New York Nights** (Schenck/United Artists, 1929), where under the direction of Lewis Milestone he played a gangster. A year later he appeared for the first time as a macho star in the English and Spanish language versions of **Men Of The North** (MGM, 1930), both of which were directed by, of all unlikely people, Hal Roach.

Between 1932 and 1935 Roland was under contract at Fox. If the studio had been making Cisco features during that period, he almost surely would have been in them; as it was, he alternated between starring roles in romances shot in Spanish and thrillers filmed in English. After his time at Fox he free-lanced. His most prestigious parts were opposite Paul Muni and Bette Davis in **Juarez** (Warner Bros., 1939, directed by William Dieterle) and with Errol Flynn in **The Sea Hawk** (Warner Bros., 1940, directed by Michael Curtiz). But his performances were just as intense and his roles far meatier in two Westerns, **Thunder Trail** (Paramount, 1937) and **Rangers Of Fortune** (Paramount, 1940), which were covered in Chapter Four.

In 1941 Roland married actress Constance Bennett, with whom he had co-starred in **Our Betters** (RKO, 1933, directed by George Cukor) and **After Tonight** (RKO, 1934, directed by George Archainbaud). The following year he became a U.S. citizen and, like many another Hollywood personality, joined the military. The day after his discharge from the Army Air Corps he started work in **The Desert Hawk** (Columbia, 1944, directed by B. Reeves Eason), a 15-chapter serial about a sort of Arab Zorro figure. Jimmy Ellison was to have played the title role but had to be hospitalized after a horse fall on the first day of shooting. Roland went on from that cliffhanger to a substantial part opposite Charles Laughton and Randolph Scott in **Captain Kidd** (1945) and from there, after he and Constance Bennett were divorced, to Monogram and the Cisco series.

Duncan Renaldo is reported to have coached Roland in how the part should be played, and one can be pretty certain that Scott Dunlap made suggestions too, but it was Roland himself who called most of the shots. The Cisco he portrays makes Renaldo's version seem light as a feather by comparison. He is a firebrand of anti-establishment ardor, riding at the head of a singing guerrilla band on a magnificent palomino with a flowing white tail that almost touches the ground. (The horse was Don Juan, a national parade champion in 1944 and 1945.) He and his followers roam the countryside, robbing wealthy oppressors and giving to the persecuted poor. But he's also a smoldering sexual volcano who will swagger into a cantina with a cigarette behind his ear, perhaps even a rose in his teeth, and will order tequila, drinking it in the Mexican ritual manner with salt and a slice of lime or lemon, while his eyes burn with desire for every beautiful woman in the room. From an Anglo male perspective it may look absurdly overdone but remember, guys: that seething sexuality isn't being aimed at us. If you doubt it's real, watch a Roland Cisco with a woman you trust and ask her.

Other aspects of characterization and costume were also Roland contributions. The two-inch leather wristband he wore as Cisco was and continued for years to be part of his own wardrobe. Although he never wrote a script for the series, he at times was credited with "additional dialogue" in which, to quote Don Miller in *Hollywood Corral*, he "would declaim lyrically about the beauty of women, or nature, or both, or some such flowery verbiage." (184) It was Roland who suggested that between bouts of thievery and *amour* Cisco should be shown reading Shakespeare by a river bank. "I wanted to be sure the Mexican was not portrayed as an unwashed, uneducated savage clown," he told interviewer Al Martinez. "I refuse roles that picture Mexicans as ridiculous, quaint, or foolish." (The interview is included in Martinez' book *Rising Voices*, New American Library 1974.)

It seems that those who enjoy and write about Western series either love the Roland Ciscos or hate them. In the latter camp is Jon Tuska, who writes in *The Filming Of The West*: "Roland made the Kid a dashing lover, a friend of the poor, an enemy to the rich, a savage killer and robber when necessary, an infidel, a vagabond. His interpretation owed nothing to Duncan [Renaldo], nothing really to O. Henry, and very little to either [Warner] Baxter or [Cesar] Romero. The Latin American market that had been developed by the Renaldo series began to dry up." (443) Among Roland's staunchest champions is William K. Everson, who tells us in *The Hollywood Western* that the involvement of Dunlap and Roland and an increase in the films' budgets "not only salvaged the series but also turned it into an entirely superior one. The Ciscos of Roland had genuine charm, a quality not often found in smaller

Westerns, pictorial qualities were often exceptional and even near-poetic....and action, while never excessive, was often extremely well staged." (225)

Having seen all six of the Ciscos with Roland in the lead, I fall somewhere in the middle. Certainly Roland is the finest actor ever to take the role, surpassing even Warner Baxter thanks to not having to fake a Mexican accent. His characterization is the most unusual and fullest of any of the Ciscos, although the Baxter of **In Old Arizona** perhaps runs him a close second. With 14 to 16 day shooting schedules and considerably higher budgets than any other Monogram Western series of the Forties, these films could have been just as exciting as Roland's personal contribution to them was. By and large, however, they're not. Action is rare and not terribly well directed when it comes, the storylines are routine, most of the dialogue is forgettable except perhaps for Roland's poetic effusions, and the singing guerrillas quickly become laughable because they never do anything but sing.

Ride Amigos Ride
And as we ride we sing a song of victory.
We'll do or die
For those we love
And that is why
The skies above
(Ride, Amigos, Ride)
And fate decide the price we pay for liberty.
The call to arms
Rings far and wide
We ride along.
Amigos Ride!
Ride! Ride! Ride on!

These lyrics were composed by Eddie Cherkose, whose had also written the theme song for the magnificent serial **Zorro's Fighting Legion** (Republic, 1939), and the male chorus belting out the words over the credits of the Roland Ciscos sounds like the group that had sung in the serial. With Edward J. Kay's music the lyrics are much more impressive, almost leading one to expect the same level of action and excitement William Witney and John English brought to that **Citizen Kane** of cliffhangers. Unfortunately the Roland Ciscos were directed by a different William.

William Nigh was born in Berlin, Wisconsin on October 12, 1881 and began directing movies in 1915. In Hollywood's pioneer days he made at least a few relatively prestigious pictures like A **Yellow Streak** (Metro, 1915), starring Lionel Barrymore, and **The Kiss Of Hate** (Columbia, 1916), with Lionel's sister Ethel in the lead. When other leading men were unavailable he liked to cast himself, starring in four silents that he also

Gilbert Roland as Cisco enters the room unconventionally in this Lobby Card from 1946. (Courtesy of Boyd Magers.)

directed. Between 1927 and 1930 he worked at MGM, directing stars like Lon Chaney (in **Mr. Wu**, 1927, and **Thunder**, 1929), John Gilbert and Joan Crawford (in **Four Walls**, 1928), and Tim McCoy (in **The Law Of The Range**, 1928). Once silent pictures had fallen to the onslaught of talkies, Nigh found himself helming bottom-rung pictures for marginal outfits. He squeezed in a shoot-em-up with Ken Maynard at Tiffany (**Fighting Thru**, 1931) and three with Harry Carey at Artclass before carving a niche for himself at Monogram where he stayed for the rest of the Thirties, turning out junk. Perhaps the quintessential William Nigh film is **The Mysterious Mr. Wong** (Monogram, 1935), starring Bela Lugosi as a pigtailed, silk-robed Fu Manchu clone desperate to possess the legendary twelve coins of Confucius. "My name is Vong," he intones. "Vhere is the tvelfth coin?" Or words to that effect. A few year later Nigh directed Lugosi's horror-film partner Boris Karloff as a completely different character with the same last name, James Lee Wong, a grade-Z Monogram version of Charlie Chan. Karloff's Asian makeup and accent were just as ludicrous as Lugosi's. How Nigh got to direct the first four of the Gilbert Roland Cisco features is a mystery more baffling than any that ever faced Mr. Wong.

Except for their casts, the credits of the first four Roland Ciscos are fairly standard. All were photographed by Monogram veteran Harry Neumann and featured background music by regular Monogram composer Edward J. Kay. Many of the actors had little or no experience in Westerns but there were a few familiar faces like Tristram Coffin, John Merton, George J. Lewis, Harry Woods and Terry Frost. Cisco's sidekick is called Baby throughout the quartet but is played by two different actors: Nacho Galindo in the first film, Frank Yaconelli in the next three. All four run between 59 and 65 minutes except the third, **Beauty And The Bandit**, which clocks in at 77 minutes.

The cycle begins with **The Gay Cavalier**

Gilbert Roland, Nacho Galindo and Drew Allen are pictured in this Lobby Card from 1946. (Courtesy of Boyd Magers.)

(Monogram, 1946), which was directed by Nigh from a screenplay by newcomer Charles S. Belden. Everson in *The Hollywood Western* describes its "pictorial qualities" as "exceptional and even near-poetic" (225) while Don Miller in *Hollywood Corral* writes that its "climax was more exciting than usual, but aside from Roland's welcome charm there was little else to merit comment." (184) As usual I find myself somewhere in the middle.

The scene is California in 1850 and we open with some dramatic shots of Cisco carving a notch in the cross on the grave of his father, the greatest bandit of old California, to atone for whose crimes Cisco, in the words of his sidekick Baby (Nacho Galindo), "steals only from the rich who are bad and gives to the poor." Between crimes Cisco has a tendency to philosophize. "Time is a wonderful thing. It ages wine and mellows women." He and Baby and his outlaw band head for the village of El Monte, where a fiesta is under way at the

hacienda of Don Felipe Peralta (Martin Garralaga) to celebrate the expected arrival of Lawton (Tristram Coffin), a wealthy Anglo who is going to pay off Don Felipe's many debts and marry his younger daughter Angela (Helen Gerald). The señorita's true love is Juan (Drew Allen), a sort of Latino Clark Kent, but she's ready to marry Lawton if that's what it will take to save the Peralta property. Her older sister Pepita (Ramsay Ames), who has no man in her life, fantasizes about that romantic rogue The Cisco Kid.

Meanwhile a wagonload of donations from the poor of Monterey to build a mission in El Monte is held up by Lawton and a gang of masked bandits, who kill all but two of the men escorting the wagon and make off with "enough silver to break the backs of the men who lift it." Lawton's henchman Lewis (John Merton) calls him Cisco so that the wounded driver will blame California's Robin Hood for the crime. The one surviving

Tristram Coffin as Lawton and Gilbert Roland are pictured having a sword fight in this Lobby Card from 1946. (Courtesy of Dan Stumpf and Boyd Magers.)

guard (Frank LaRue) they take with them to Don Felipe's hacienda.

Elsewhere on the trail, Cisco and his legion are galloping along and lustily belting out their theme song, including a few stanzas that aren't sung again in later Cisco films. In El Monte, Cisco distributes alms to the poor, enjoys a drink of tequila with lime and salt—the ritual that is repeated over and over during Roland's time in the lead—and stops off on the way out of town to leap onto a balcony and romance the lovely Rosita (Iris Flores), while Baby serenades them. Cisco himself doesn't sing, he explains, because "I have a voice like a frog with a sore throat." As a parting gift he leaves Rosita with a necklace, another little ritual we'll see Roland perform again and again.

Riding across the countryside, the singing legion of good badmen finds the dying wagon driver, who reports with his final breath that the robbers who stole the mission's silver were led by Cisco and that the wounded guard was taken to

Don Felipe's rancho. By this time Lawton has reached the hacienda with his party and also claimed that Cisco was behind the robbery and murders. Pepita, who wants to save her sister from a marriage without love, encourages the spineless Juan to pick a fight with Lawton but gets nowhere.

Cisco comes to the fiesta calling himself Luis Antonio Damaso Alonso Smith, makes a play for Pepita, catches Lawton alone, warns him to be careful what he accuses Cisco of doing, and slips away. While Don Felipe's men search the grounds for the intruder, he hides in Pepita's room, sips her hot chocolate and listens to her sing a romantic song which Ramsay Ames wrote for herself and which is about as Latin as kung pao beef. When he comes out of hiding, Pepita recognizes him as the romantic rogue of whom she's dreamed. Juan disturbs their interlude and is knocked out for his troubles. After Cisco rides into the night, Pepita sends Juan after him, but before he leaves the

The Cisco Kid in "South of Monterey"

starring

GILBERT ROLAND

with

MARTIN GARRALAGA

FRANK YACONELLI   MARJORIE RIORDAN

Produced by SCOTT R. DUNLAP
Directed by WILLIAM NIGH
Original Story and Screenplay by Charles S. Belden
Based upon the character created by O. Henry

A MONOGRAM PICTURE

A Title Card from 1946 picturing Marjorie Riordan, Gilbert Roland and Frank Yaconelli. (Courtesy of Boyd Magers.)

hacienda Juan happens to overhear Lawton and Lewis discussing the robbery they pulled and mentioning that the stolen silver is at their hideout on the Mountain of the Shadows.

Juan somehow manages to follow Cisco to where his men are camped for the night, singing a mournful version of "Ride Amigos Ride." He tells Cisco what he overheard and asks for a chance to help recover the silver. Cisco, Baby and Juan sneak up on the mountain hideout. During the clumsily directed fight between the trio and the gang, Cisco does nothing and Juan proves his manhood. One outlaw (Raphael Bennett) escapes and reports back to Lawton and Lewis at the hacienda. Lawton tells Don Felipe that Cisco stole the money he was going to use to pay the Peralta debts and then unaccountably asks to marry Angela and take over the rancho immediately. Rosita, helping to prepare Angela for the wedding, pays Cisco a glowing compliment that tends to make viewers roll on the floor today: "He

rides like the wind and makes love just as fast. He is the greatest of all *caballeros*!" Pepita tries to persuade Angela not to go through with the ceremony but Angela insists it's the only way to save the family property.

Cisco brings the silver to the padre at El Monte, learns that the wedding is about to take place, rides to the hacienda, accuses Lawton of the robbery and disposes of him in a sword duel that is competently enough directed but can't hold a candle to the sword fights William Witney directed in **Zorro's Fighting Legion**. What no one seems to realize, certainly not the film's director or screenwriter, is that without Lawton's money Don Felipe and his daughters are going to lose their happy hacienda. Cisco leaves Pepita with romantic words and a necklace from his seemingly endless supply and rides out of the picture with his useless guerrillas.

Next in release came **South Of Monterey** (Monogram, 1946), which was also directed by

85

Iris Flores and Marjorie Riordan (in bridal dress) listen as Gilbert Roland confronts Harry Woods and Martin Garralaga holds Harry back in this Lobby Card from 1946. (Courtesy of Boyd Magers.)

Nigh from a pedestrian if socially conscious screenplay by Belden. Don Miller in *Hollywood Corral* says of this picture only that it "moved fairly well." (184) Everson and Tuska don't mention it at all. Its only historic significance is that Frank Yaconelli replaced Nacho Galindo in the sidekick role.

While the legionnaires are singing around the evening campfire and Baby strums a guitar, Cisco philosophizes about what has brought him and his *compañeros* to the area. The Indians and the Latino powerless are being robbed by tax collectors and loan sharks. "The rich get richer and the poor—the poor get children." He sends Baby into town to pose as a blind minstrel and collect information.

Now the situation in the area is presented to us directly. Carlos Madero (George J. Lewis), one of the few ranchers who's been able to pay his taxes, is also the local firebrand. He's in love with Maria Morales (Marjorie Riordan), the lovely sister of

Arturo (Martin Garralaga), the commandante of police, who is in a corrupt alliance with the tax collector Bennet (Harry Woods) and is trying to pressure Maria into becoming Bennet's wife. (The name of Woods' character seems to be an insider joke on action director Spencer Bennet, who had helmed several excellent B Westerns for Monogram while Scott Dunlap was in charge of production.) Maria's heart, however, is with Arturo's and Bennet's victims. "Be sorry for the poor," her brother advises her, "but do not suffer with them. They belong to the lower class, which must always suffer."

Carlos has sold the people's cattle for enough money to pay their taxes and the money is on the way to them by coach, but many coaches have been robbed by a character known as The Silver Bandit who wears a black cape and rides a horse with a silver saddle and who Carlos suspects is a tax collector. When Carlos knocks Bennet down on the street for beating up an old farmer who had

Gilbert Roland and Harry Woods are having a branigan in this Lobby Card from 1946. (Courtesy of Boyd Magers.)

seen his taxes triple overnight, Arturo arrests Carlos for disturbing the peace. The commandante is infatuated with Carmelita (Iris Flores), the local cantina singer, but won't invite her to his house because, as he tells her, "my sister is a lady." Bennet and Arturo conspire to frame Carlos for some crime or other.

While Baby in his blind minstrel guise is picking up this information, Cisco comes swaggering into the cantina and orders a tequila, which he drinks with the usual lemon-and-salt ritual. A local peasant offers to buy him a drink and Cisco accepts. Arturo, curious who this stranger is, offers to buy him a drink and Cisco refuses. "That is an insult to a gentleman," Arturo protests. "Where is he?" Cisco asks. The look on Carmelita's face during this scene suggests that she knows who the stranger is even if Arturo doesn't. Cisco meets with Baby in the plaza and learns most of what we've already seen.

The coach that was carrying the cattle money

comes into town and the driver announces that he was robbed by The Silver Bandit. A posse is formed to go after the thief, stopping at Arturo's hacienda to pick up the commandante and Bennet. Cisco follows the posse but unfortunately he's riding a horse with a silver saddle. The posse spot him, think he's the outlaw they're after, chase him and wound him in the shoulder, but he manages to elude them. A wretched Maria is preparing to move out on her brother when the wounded Cisco sneaks into the Morales hacienda and passes out on her bed. He comes to and is delighted to find himself with his wound bandaged and in the company of a beautiful señorita. He kisses Maria, helps himself to Arturo's tequila, learns that Maria loves the jailed Carlos, hides when Arturo returns from the disbanded posse and overhears him tell Maria that Carlos will stay locked up until she marries Bennet.

That night Cisco pays another visit to the cantina, where Carmelita confronts him and we

An unidentified bartender pours Gilbert Roland and Ramsay Ames a drink in this Lobby Card from 1946. (Courtesy of Boyd Magers.)

learn that he had romanced and jilted her in Monterey but that she's still wild about him. Maria comes to the cantina and tells Arturo that she's going to marry Bennet. The tax collector for no particular reason starts slapping Carmelita, who for no better reason blurts out that the swaggering stranger is, as she persists in calling him, "the Cisco." Arturo arrests Cisco and locks him in the cell next to Carlos, to whom he describes himself as "a prisoner of the government and a friend of the people." Maria comes to the jail to visit Carlos and Carmelita comes to give Cisco to key to the cells, which she stole from Arturo after getting him drunk. Cisco releases Carlos and both men along with Baby gallop out of town and rejoin the legion. Planning to murder both their prisoners, Bennet and Arturo discover them gone.

The climax of this draggy film is at hand, and none too soon. Cisco, Baby and Carlos leave the legion behind and head for the mountain cabin to which Carlos had once followed Arturo. The Silver Bandit, who of course is Arturo himself, robs another coach and makes for the cabin with his loot, followed by Bennet, who shoots down his former partner in crime as he's about to take off with all the money the pair had stolen. Cisco comes on the scene and kills Bennet after a short and stodgily directed fight. Returning to the Morales hacienda, he spares Maria's feelings by telling her that Bennet was The Silver Bandit and that her brother died heroically while struggling with him. With Carlos and Maria reunited, Cisco and Baby rejoin the useless legion and everyone gallops off to the tune of "Ride Amigos Ride."

Beauty And The Bandit (Monogram, 1946), third and, at 77 minutes, by far the longest of the Roland Ciscos, is distinguished by Ramsay Ames, who is definitely a beauty, and by another heaping helping of Thirties-style social consciousness. Everson ranks it on the same level with **The Gay Cavalier**. This may be a bit excessive but it's

Gilbert Roland gets to the seat of the problem with Ramsay Ames in this scene from **Beauty and the Bandit** (1946, Monogram).

certainly one of the more interesting pictures of the six.

The film opens with Cisco at the head of his band of merry *muchachos* riding to a California mountaintop and observing a ship as it approaches the port of San Luis. What he's looking for is a rich newcomer to rob, as becomes clear that night when he visits a sailors' hangout where his old pal Bill (Glenn Strange) in a striped jersey is singing "Blow the Man Down." Bill tells him that the only passenger who left the ship at San Luis was a young Frenchman on his way to the town of San Marino with a strongbox full of silver. Cisco joins the Frenchman on the night coach to San Marino but, when he lights a cigarette for his fellow traveler, he realizes that his companion is a woman (Ramsay Ames). Cisco's men hold up the coach, take the strongbox, shoot it open and remove the pouch of silver from among a bed of rocks. Cisco goes after them, tells them to lock the chest again and returns to the coach with it,

pretending to have driven the bandits off. His disguised traveling companion doesn't bother to open it and see if the silver is still there.

In San Marino, obese Doc Walsh (William Gould), a former medicine show performer who runs the town hotel, is waiting for the coach with his partner in crime, a disgraced doctor named Juan Federico Valegra (Martin Garralaga). We learn from their conversation that Valegra at Walsh's behest has been poisoning the Mexican peasants' crops and that the peasants have sold their land for next to nothing to Walsh, who in turn has sold the property to a Frenchman named Dubois, whose emissary is supposed to be on the night coach with the purchase money. When it arrives, the disguised woman takes a room in Walsh's hotel and has the strongbox deposited in his vault. Cisco, calling himself Luis Antonio Tomas Alonso Gonzales, invites the disguised woman to have a drink with him in the hotel bar. After the usual tequila ceremony Cisco has an unmotivated quarrel with the drunken Dr. Valegra, then enjoys himself playing mind games with the disguised woman, telling her that tequila will put hair on her chest, suggesting that she make a pass at the barmaid Rosita (Vida Aldana). When she finally retires to her room, Walsh is waiting to tell her that he opened the strongbox and found it held nothing but rocks. This is supposed to be a huge surprise to her but she reacts calmly and tells him that the purchase money from Dubois will arrive the next day. Then she lets her hair down for Walsh, identifies herself as Dubois' daughter Jeanne and tells him that her father died recently. Cisco is listening in on this conversation out on Jeanne's balcony. When Walsh has left he slips in, romances Jeanne and invites himself to spend the night in her bed—with her on the couch!—until she pulls a derringer on him and makes him leave.

The next day Cisco encounters a peasant boy with a sick lamb and takes them to Dr. Valegra, who demands an exorbitant fee for a bottle of the antidote to the poison which he himself has been spreading among the farmers, but Cisco takes the medicine from him by force. By this time Baby (Frank Yaconelli) has gotten hired as a cook in Walsh's hotel. Jeanne, now undisguised and beautiful, comes down for breakfast, and Cisco flirts with both her and the barmaid Rosita in the kitchen. Meanwhile the police captain from San Luis (George J. Lewis), who is an idiot, has arrived in San Marino to investigate the coach holdup. He comes close to figuring out that the second passenger on the coach was the notorious Cisco Kid until Walsh covers for Cisco by claiming that he and "Gonzales" are old friends.

Cisco takes Jeanne out for a horseback ride and another spot of romance but the love session is cut short when Baby races up with the news that the captain has arrested two of the merry *muchachos*. This development triggers the only real action sequence in the film as Cisco rides into town and enables his men to escape by getting the troops to chase him, a quite decently directed few minutes of pursuit footage accompanied by Edward J. Kay agitato music from Monogram's Rough Riders series of 1941-42.

That night Cisco rejoins Jeanne and brings her to the location where his men are camped. Instantly she becomes the dominatrix of the entire gang, cowing them with her shooting and knife-throwing prowess, but then she washes Cisco's shirt for him and generally acts like his slave, telling him that she's known all along that he stole her silver but didn't turn him in because he'd also stolen her heart. Claiming to be a cold-blooded businesswoman, she says she doesn't care that the

land her silver was to buy had been stolen from the peasants. "I live only to destroy those who take advantage of the poor people," Cisco tells her, and proceeds to give her a vigorous spanking, after which she bows to him and calls him Master! This is not a film I would recommend to feminists.

The next day Cisco and his men come across a farmer (Felipe Turich) who's been poisoned by eating his own crops. They bring the sick man to town and force Dr. Valegra to treat him, but the man dies in Valegra's office. Cisco finds the incriminating poison in Valegra's closet, substitutes castor oil, makes Valegra drink what he believes will kill him and leaves him to suffer the pangs of conscience. The captain and his troops chase Cisco and his men out of town and Jeanne manages to slip away from the legion, taking the silver with her. Discovering the loss and suspecting that she's planning to buy the peasants' land, Cisco heads for Walsh's hotel. Meanwhile Jeanne has in fact purchased the property, but then she burns the deeds and says she's going to return the land to the farmers, which proves, I suppose, that there's nothing like a spanking to bring out a woman's social consciousness. Walsh grabs her and locks her in one of the hotel rooms, planning to kill Cisco for the price on his head when he comes to rescue her. That spanking Cisco gave her also seems to have taken away all her fighting prowess, for she doesn't resist Walsh in the least. When Cisco arrives, Walsh uses his skill as a medicine show ventriloquist to lure him into the pitch-dark hotel lobby and into a murky gun battle which would have made a marvelous climax with a director like Joseph H. Lewis but which Nigh reduces to a throwaway. Both Walsh and Valegra wind up dead, Jeanne returns their land to the peasants, and Cisco and his legion once again elude the taco-witted police captain and ride off to new adventure.

Riding The California Trail (Monogram, 1947) was directed by Nigh from a screenplay by Clarence Upson Young, who had written a few of Monogram's Johnny Mack Brown B Westerns. Like earlier Roland Ciscos it's marked by strong social consciousness and a few excellent lines of dialogue, but the main virtue is Roland himself. The film opens with Cisco, Baby and the legion galloping pell-mell out of yet another town after Cisco, saying "I do not like angry women," has jilted yet another señorita. Reaching a different part of California he's never seen before, he finds a Wanted poster offering a reward for him of 500 pesos, an amount he considers insultingly small. After stopping off at the mission near the pueblo of San Lorenzo and learning from the padre that

The Cisco Kid in "RIDING THE CALIFORNIA TRAIL"

starring GILBERT ROLAND

with MARTIN GARRALAGA
TEALA LORING   FRANK YACONELLI

Produced by SCOTT R. DUNLAP   Directed by William Nigh   Original Screenplay by Clarence Upson Young   Based upon the character created by O. Henry

A Title Card from 1947 picturing Ted Hecht (bottom left) and Teala Loring with Gilbert Roland. (Courtesy of Boyd Magers.)

the place is a little Eden, with no oppression of the poor or political corruption—"Oh, then this is no place for us," says Baby—Cisco contemplates settling there for good. Riding into the town, he buys a rose from a flower girl in the plaza, and with the rose in his mouth and a cigarette behind his ear, he swaggers into the local cantina and orders tequila and then a meal. The dancer Raquel (Teala Loring) comes out and performs, wiggling up a storm all around him. He ignores her and goes on eating his frijoles, but when she goes back to her dressing room he's waiting for her with the rose and words of romance.

At a knock on her door he hides behind a curtain and listens as she gets rid of her regular suitor, Raoul de la Reyes (Ted Hecht), by claiming to have a headache. Returning to Cisco's embrace, she tells him that though Raoul really loves her, he's going to marry the wealthy and beautiful Dolores Ramirez (Inez Cooper), who loves the poor and is known locally as the Angel

of San Lorenzo. Cisco gives the dancer one of the necklaces he hands out to every attractive woman he meets. A suspicious Raoul barges in on them and finds them kissing. "Oh, so you had a headache," he says to her, then turns to Cisco, demanding: "Who are you?" "I am the headache," he replies. They brawl, Raoul summons help and Cisco is about to be taken to jail when Baby and his men pull their guns and free him. On the way out of town, Cisco catches a glimpse of Dolores in her coach and is entranced. Raoul and his men chase Cisco and the legion to some excellent and unfamiliar Edward J. Kay agitato music.

Deciding that Dolores should get to know him better, Cisco pays a visit to the Ramirez hacienda in a stolen coach, impersonating the wealthy San Francisco playboy and master swordsman Don Luis de Salazar, with Baby posing as his servant. Dolores' uncle, Don José Ramirez (Martin Garralaga), welcomes the guest and introduces his niece. Cisco learns of her great generosity to the

91

The Cisco Kid in

"RIDING THE CALIFORNIA TRAIL"

A Lobby Card from 1947 picturing Gilbert Roland talking with a player while Martin Garralaga looks on. (Courtesy of Boyd Magers.)

poor and of course starts making love to her the first moment they're alone. She resists him, admitting she doesn't love Raoul but is marrying him because Don José told her it was her father's dying wish. The poor come bearing small gifts and hopes for her happiness. "I have the same weakness you have," Cisco tells her. "I cannot see other people suffer." Meanwhile the coachman whose vehicle Cisco hijacked makes it to San Lorenzo and reports the theft to the *policia*.

That night, after Dolores has sung a Latin melody for Cisco, Raoul shows up, is introduced to the newcomer and claims not to have met him before. The two men duel verbally. After some pointed remarks about "the Cisco"—Dolores' comment is "I have heard that he only offends the law helping the poor"—Raoul calls "Luis" an impostor and challenges him to a duel with swords. Cisco's skill with the blade makes Raoul look ridiculous. He and Baby slip away, though no farther than the courtyard of the hacienda,

when the *policia* arrive. In the middle of the night, Dolores' *duenna* Mama Rosita (Marcelle Grandville) tells Cisco that Don José and Raoul are in a conspiracy to get Dolores married to Raoul and split her fortune. Cisco vows to stop the wedding.

Very late, after the cantina has closed, Cisco goes back there and once again romances Raquel, who admits that she's in on the plot and that Raoul and Don José have a secret written agreement proving the conspiracy. He visits Raoul's house, ties him up, rummages through his papers and in five seconds locates an IOU from Don José to Raoul for half a million pesos. Raquel, who's followed Cisco, releases Raoul, who guesses that Cisco's next stop will be the Ramirez hacienda and heads out there to kill him. Cisco slips into the hacienda, breaks into the box containing Don José's secret papers, and discovers a forged will supposedly signed by Dolores' father and providing that her inheritance will pass to Don

A Lobby Card picturing Gilbert Roland fighting with Ted Hecht and Alex Montoya. (Courtesy of Boyd Magers.)

José if she marries Raoul. Caught red-handed by the Ramirez household, Cisco exposes Don José by showing Dolores the false will. When Raoul arrives he and Cisco settle accounts with another stodgily directed swordfight. Dolores helps Cisco escape as the *policia* arrive and he rejoins his warbling amigos.

Riding The California Trail was the last of Scott Dunlap's and William Nigh's contributions to the Cisco saga. Nigh directed two more Monogram quickies—neither of them Westerns, both released in 1948—and then retired. He died in 1955. Dunlap worked very little after the Cisco films, although he did keep his hand in by producing an occasional non-series Western or adventure flick for release by Allied Artists, which bought Monogram in the early Fifties. His last films as a producer—**Johnny Rocco** and **Man From God's Country**, both released in 1958—were directed by Paul Landres, who had helmed more Cisco TV episodes than anyone else. Dunlap

died on March 30, 1970, at age 78.

The production reins on what was left of Monogram's Cisco series were turned over to a newcomer with minimal credentials in the Western genre. Jeffrey Bernerd, born in London around 1892, had worked in the business end of the English movie industry since before the first World War. He became managing director of the Stell film company and later moved to Gaumont-British, where he served as general sales manager and newsreel producer. He came to the United States in 1941 and to Monogram three years later, producing low-budget social problem pictures, weepers, one horror flick. The only film he worked on that is still of some interest today is **Black Gold** (Allied Artists, 1947), a contemporary Western of sorts, directed in Cinecolor by Phil Karlson (with second-unit work by B. Reeves Eason), and starring Anthony Quinn and his then wife Katherine DeMille. Bernerd died in his Beverly Hills home on August 10, 1950.

A Lobby Card from 1947 picturing Martin Garralaga and Gilbert Roland. (Courtesy of Boyd Magers.)

Under his brief regime a number of changes were made in the Cisco films. Thrown on the trash heap were Roland's tequila rituals, most of his swaggering machismo and social consciousness, and the legion of singing guerrillas. His comic sidekick was both rechristened and recast, with obese Chris-Pin Martin from the 20th-Fox Cisco cycle brought in to replace Frank Yaconelli. As in Monogram's earliest Cisco films, the character was again called Pancho. Bernerd unaccountably replaced William Nigh, who had directed more of the Monogram pictures Bernerd had produced than anyone else, but chose another wrong William to take Nigh's place. Born in St. Louis on April 16, 1888, W. Christy Cabanne was established in movies as an actor and assistant director under the legendary D.W. Griffith before he was old enough to vote. Raoul Walsh, the first director of a Cisco feature, knew and worked with Cabanne for a few years around 1910 and makes a dozen references to him in his 1974 auto-

biography *Each Man In His Time*. By 1914 Cabanne was a director in his own right, although Griffith is billed as "supervisor" on a number of his early films. Like William Nigh, Cabanne had the highest-powered stars of his career in some of his first silents. In 1915 and 1916 alone he directed four pictures with Lillian Gish in the lead and another four with Douglas Fairbanks, Sr. Also like Nigh, Cabanne put in a brief stint at MGM during the mid-to-late Twenties and was kicked to the bottom of the directorial ladder with the coming of sound.

Most of his Thirties films are B melodramas with an occasional Western sandwiched among them like **The Dawn Trail** (Columbia, 1930), starring Buck Jones. He made his best known contribution to the genre while a contract director at RKO. **The Last Outlaw** (RKO, 1936) starred Harry Carey and Hoot Gibson in a remake of the 1919 two-reeler of the same name that had been directed by John Ford. To quote Everson's *The*

A Title Card from 1947 picturing Gilbert Roland, Jack LaRue, Evelyn Brent and Chris-Pin Martin. (Courtesy of Bobby Copeland.)

Hollywood Western, the story was "about an old-time outlaw returning from jail to his home in the modern West, encountering prejudice, contemporary racketeers, and....a grown daughter entranced by a singing cowboy in the movies!" (196) As luck would have it, the Autry parody in the movie-within-the-movie was played by Fred Scott, who began starring in his own musical shoot-em-ups that same year. Cabanne, says Everson, "did a competent enough job with it, but totally failed to inject the kind of magic that Ford would have added intuitively." (196) The following year Cabanne directed Preston Foster, Jean Muir and Van Heflin in **The Outcasts Of Poker Flat** (RKO, 1937), another remake of a Ford silent. These are the high spots in Cabanne's meager output of Westerns.

From 1939 till 1942 he worked primarily at Universal cranking out quickies starring Richard Arlen and Andy Devine or, every so often, Andy Devine and future Cisco sidekick Leo Carrillo. By 1945 he was relegated to unprestigious outfits like Monogram, whose final pair of Ciscos, like just about everything else Cabanne directed, were lackluster.

Grizzled B movie scripter Bennett Cohen furnished the screenplay and story and Roland some "additional dialogue" for **Robin Hood Of Monterey** (Monogram, 1947). With a running time of only 55 minutes and the principal villains being played by veterans Evelyn Brent and Jack LaRue, it's understandable that Don Miller in *Hollywood Corral* described the picture as "slight but short and swift....with dependable skull-duggery...." (184) It's tolerable today only because of Roland's performance and a storyline heavily influenced by a type of movie that in 1947 was enjoying its golden age: film *noir*.

We open on Cisco reading Spanish love poetry to Pancho. (No, amigos. Don't say it. Don't even think it.) The interlude is broken up by gunfire and Cisco, riding to the rescue, finds Eduardo

This scene from **Robin Hood of Monterey** (Monogram,1947) pictures Chris-Pin Martin, Gilbert Roland, Donna DeMario and Nestor Paiva along with other players.

Belmonte (Travis Kent) wounded and about to be murdered by the Mexican posse that has been chasing him. Cisco fools the pursuers into thinking their young target is already dead, then he and Pancho patch Eduardo up and take him to the cabin of Pablo (Ernie Adams). As Eduardo tells them his story, which has strong *noir* overtones, the movie shifts into flashback. Although he was running from the law after being charged with the murder of his father, Don Carlos (Pedro de Cordoba), Eduardo claims that the real killers are the Don's scheming second wife Maria (Evelyn Brent) and her lover Ricardo Gonzales (Jack LaRue). Cisco and Pancho leave the young man in Pablo's care and pay a surreptitious visit to the Gonzales hacienda where they run into Eduardo's fianceé Lolita (Donna DeMario). Then Cisco drops in on Maria Belmonte and discovers that she is Maria Sanchez, an avaricious cantina dancer he once knew. Instantly he knows that Eduardo's story was true, and he's even more certain when Maria pulls a derringer on him. As

soon as Cisco is gone, Maria and Gonzales conspire to have him arrested by the local authorities and Gonzales makes tracks for the pueblo of San Blas to tip off the idiot alcalde or mayor (Nestor Paiva) that the notorious Cisco is in the area.

Cisco comes to town, learns from the local doctor that Don Carlos was killed by a very small bullet, but is cornered by the alcalde's troops and forced to make a run for his life with Pancho. The film's only genuine action sequence, and not a bad one either, comes abruptly and not too credibly to an end when Cisco stops along the trail to chat with Lolita. Thanks to this no-brainer he and Pancho are caught by the *soldados* and tossed into the clinko. The next day Cisco is marched out and executed by a firing squad, with Maria and Gonzales as witnesses. Mother of Mercy, is this the end of Cisco? Far from it! We soon learn that he happens to be an old friend of the firing squad leader and paid him to have the men's rifles loaded with blanks.

That night he breaks Pancho out of jail and the

96

Another scene from **Robin Hood of Monterey** (Monogram,1947) picturing Nestor Paiva, Jack LaRue, Evelyn Brent, Travis Kent (curly hair) and Thornton Edwards along with other players.

two of them flee to Pablo's cabin, where they find out that Eduardo, believing naturally enough the reports of Cisco's execution, has gone to the Belmonte hacienda to settle the score on his own. Unfortunately the young man gets himself captured by the troop of soldiers who are hunting for the escaped prisoners, so that Cisco and Pancho have to rescue him from the alcalde's troops all over again. Finally the burrito-witted official understands Cisco's point that if Don Carlos was killed by a derringer the killer must have been Maria and they prepare a rather simple-minded trap, with Cisco returning to the hacienda and getting her to admit her guilt within earshot of the hidden alcalde and his men, who arrest her and Gonzales without a nanosecond of action. With the killers caught and the young lovers reunited, Cisco goes back to reading Spanish love poems to Pancho.

Roland's time as Cisco came to an end with **King Of The Bandits** (Monogram, 1947). Cabanne not only directed but furnished the film's original story (turned into a screenplay by Bennett Cohen, with Roland again credited for additional dialogue) and cast his son Bill in a bit part as an orderly. Visually the picture is dull as dishwater and its plot has more holes than a slab of Swiss *queso*.

The scene is Arizona and the film opens abruptly with Cisco and Pancho being executed by a firing squad just as they had been in Cabanne's **Robin Hood Of Monterey**. They're not really dead this time either: the sequence turns out to be a dream brought on by Pancho's consumption of sixteen enchiladas. On the trail that day, our heroes find a poster nailed to a tree, offering $500 reward for Cisco even though he's never been in Arizona before. (So much for any continuity between this film and the earliest Cisco features.) A few seconds of screen time later they save the life of Pedro Gomez (Pat Goldin), a little saddlemaker who was about to be lynched after being falsely accused of having helped the notorious Cisco Kid and his gang rob a freight

A Lobby Card from 1947 picturing Gilbert Roland holding a gun on Nestor Paiva. (Courtesy of Boyd Magers.)

wagon. Anyone who doesn't have frijoles for brains understands that, as in so many other Cisco films, an impostor has been committing crimes in the *caballero's* name.

Cisco, Pancho and their newfound amigo are riding peacefully along when a runaway stage-coach speeds by. Cisco overtakes and stops the coach (with Roland himself making the transfer from saddle to driver's box in medium close-up) and learns from Alice Mason (Angela Greene) and her injured mother (Laura Treadwell) that the coach was robbed and the women's heirloom jewelry stolen by, you guessed it, the nefarious Cisco Kid and his gang. Cisco prudently declines to identify himself except by his (and Gilbert Roland's) real name, Luis Antonio Damaso Ramon Alonso. Leaving the coach and women at a nearby mission with Pedro to guard them, Cisco and Pancho ride off to summon Alice's brother, Captain Frank Mason (William Bakewell), who is stationed at Fort Roberts.

Stopping off in the town of El Rio for a cigarettes-and-tequila break (though this time he doesn't perform the drinking ritual with lime and salt), Cisco notices a locket around the neck of a dance hall girl (Cathy Carter) and, magically intuiting that it was part of the jewels stolen from Alice, starts to flirt with the dancer. A few minutes of love murmurs and she tells him she was given the locket by Smoke Kirby (Anthony Warde), who's playing poker across the room. Cisco is buying the locket from her for $100 in gold when Kirby sees what's going on, comes over and slaps her face. Cisco knocks him down, finds the rest of the jewels in Kirby's pocket and he and Pancho race out of town in an unexciting chase sequence that ends as usual with them hiding behind some rocks until the pursuers go by.

At Fort Roberts, Colonel Wayne (Boyd Irwin) dispatches Alice's brother and some troopers to search for the overdue coach containing the captain's sister and mother, who at the same time are being escorted to the fort by Cisco, Pancho and Pedro. Cisco by now has fallen deeply in love

A Lobby Card from 1947 picturing Gilbert Roland and Chris-Pin Martin. (Courtesy of Boyd Magers.)

with Alice. "Life is beautiful," he rhapsodizes as he drives the coach with Alice beside him. "There is beauty everywhere. In the trees, in the mountains, in the sky. Do you know how a cloud is born?" That night at their campsite he romances her again but still doesn't reveal who he is except indirectly, talking about a fantasy hero of his, who "hates injustice so he makes his own laws," and saying he'd like to settle down with a woman, "with eyes soft like the sky and hair soft like golden wheatfields." Kirby breaks up this adolescent poetry by riding into their camp and challenging the Mexican who hit him in the saloon to a gun duel. When his adversary identifies himself as Cisco, Kirby tries to cheat in the duel but fails. At this point Captain Mason and his troops come on the scene. Kirby tells the soldiers that his adversary is Cisco and, with the jewels he took back from Kirby found on him, Cisco and Pancho are arrested. This development doesn't make a taco's worth of sense since Alice and her mother are on the spot and can swear that these aren't the

men who robbed them, but logic is not this picture's strong point. (Neither is anything else.)

The troops and their prisoners reach Fort Roberts after dark and Captain Mason is ordered to take Cisco and Pancho to the U.S. marshal in El Rio the next morning. In a cell, Cisco recites a poem about a man condemned to hang. Little Pedro, who had slipped away from the campsite before the troops showed up, sneaks into the fort and steals some guns which he slips to the prisoners in their cell. Just before her brother is to leave for El Rio with the prisoners, Alice begs him to let them escape. When Cisco gets the drop on the captain and forces him at gunpoint to escort them away from the post, Mason concludes that he got the gun from Alice. He tries to protect her by refusing to explain what happened, and Colonel Wayne orders him locked up.

Later in El Rio, Cisco happens to overhear the marshal (Gene Roth) talking in the saloon about the captain's imminent court martial and knows he has to save Alice's brother. He sends Pedro to the

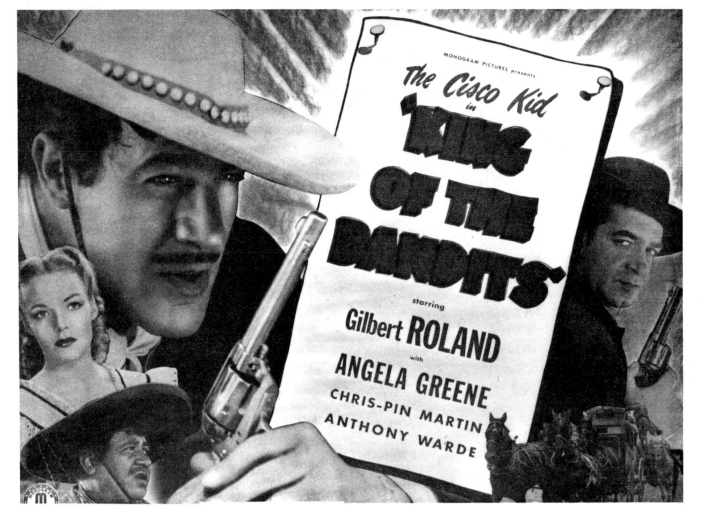

A Title Card from 1947 picturing Gilbert Roland, Angela Greene, Chris-Pin Martin and Anthony Warde. (Courtesy of Boyd Magers.)

saloon with a threatening note for **Kirby**, whose henchman Burl (Rory Mallinson) takes the paper out of town to the gang's hideout cabin, followed of course by Cisco. The minute Cisco and Pancho fire one or two shots at the cabin, two members of the gang run for their lives. That night three others desert. When Burl makes a move in the same direction, a by now drunken Kirby shoots his henchman in the back. Then he comes out of the cabin, shooting wildly into the dark. Cisco stalks him back to town and the deserted saloon, where he collars his quarry actionlessly after Kirby runs out of bullets. With Captain Mason released and the misunderstanding between him and his sister cleared up, Cisco sadly concludes that he will always be "the wanderer, the restless one" and says goodbye to Alice.

After finishing his pair of Ciscos Cabanne once more followed in the career path of his predecessor William Nigh. He directed two mediocre programmers for Monogram that came out in 1948 (**Back Trail** with Johnny Mack Brown and **Silver Trails** with Jimmy Wakely) and then retired. He died soon after he stopped working, on October 15, 1950.

Not long after he'd finished his stint as Cisco, Gilbert Roland's career once again went into orbit, thanks mainly to director John Huston, who gave him a major role opposite Jennifer Jones and John Garfield in **We Were Strangers** (Horizon/ Columbia, 1949). "If Huston hadn't had faith to cast me in his picture," Roland told an interviewer years later, "....I might be back where I started as a kid, selling cushions at the Juárez arena." From that part he went on to appear alongside Spencer Tracy and James Stewart in **Malaya** (MGM, 1950, directed by Richard Thorpe), with Cary Grant and José Ferrer in **Crisis** (MGM, 1950, directed by Richard Brooks), opposite Barbara Stanwyck, Wendell Corey and (in the final role of his life) Walter Huston in **The Furies** (Wallis-Hazen/Paramount, 1950, directed by Anthony Mann), with Robert Stack in **Bullfighter And The Lady** (Republic, 1951, directed by Budd

A Lobby Card from 1947 picturing Gilbert Roland and Anthony Warde ready to duel. (Courtesy of Boyd Magers.)

Boetticher), side by side with a flotilla of stars including Lana Turner, Kirk Douglas, Walter Pidgeon and Dick Powell in **The Bad And The Beautiful** (MGM, 1952, directed by Vincente Minnelli), and opposite James Stewart and Joanne Dru in **Thunder Bay** (Universal, 1953, directed by Anthony Mann).

Roland continued to appear in Westerns and other films through the rest of the Fifties and well into the Sixties while also making guest appearances in a number of TV series episodes of which two in particular stand out. In the fall of 1960 he played El Cuchillo, a more roguish and larcenous offshoot of his version of Cisco, for two 60-minute segments of *Walt Disney Presents* ("El Bandido," October 30, 1960, and "Adios El Cuchillo," November 6, 1960) that brought back Guy Williams as the character he'd played in the Disney TV series of 1957-59: *Zorro*. This virtual movie for the small screen was directed by William Witney, the Hitchcock of the action film, and a succulent stuntfest it is. Five years later

Witney directed and Roland guest-starred in the *Bonanza* episode "The Lonely Runner" (October 10, 1965), a dramatically powerful story of a man who becomes a fugitive rather than surrender his beloved mare to the person the courts have ruled her legal owner.

Roland kept a lower profile after turning sixty or so but still had no trouble finding movie work as and when he wanted. Between 1967 and 1969 he starred in four Westerns shot in Italy and one in Spain. On the sudden death of Frank Silvera, who had been playing Don Francisco de Montoya in *The High Chaparral* (NBC-TV, 1967-1971), Roland came aboard as the don's brother Domingo for the two-hour episode "The New Lion of Sonora" (Feb. 19, 1971) and would surely have stayed on as a continuing character if the series hadn't been canceled. Later in the decade Roland was featured opposite George C. Scott in **Islands In The Stream** (1977, directed by Franklin J. Schaffner), based on the posthumously published Hemingway novel.

A Lobby Card from 1947 picturing Gilbert Roland and Chris-Pin Martin in front of the local saloon. (Courtesy of Boyd Magers.)

His final movie role was in the offbeat Western **Barbarosa** (1982) starring Willie Nelson and Gary Busey. The film's director was Fred Schepisi, a then little-known Australian who went on to helm megahits like **A Cry In The Dark** (1988) and **The Russia House** (1991). When asked by a New York Times reporter what this living legend was like, Schepisi replied: "A friend said to me: 'When you're working with Gilbert Roland, you're like a little boy with a huge white wall, and somebody's given you a box of crayons.' And it's true. As soon as he knows he can trust you, he opens up and offers you all the stuff he's ever learned. He comes prepared. He's gracious to everyone. And when he goes to the set, a man about his age follows him. The man is never in the way, but he gives Gilbert water, or honey and tea, and just before each take, he brings him a mirror. Obviously, Gilbert worked out a long time ago that, in the heat of things, with the best intentions in the world, people forget to give you water or a mirror, so he brings his own." Roland once summed up his philosophy of life by translating his mother's last words: "My son, don't rush yourself, don't worry yourself, goodbye, my soul." He had the words engraved on the gold ring he wore on his left pinky. His great good luck, he said, was to have "the blood of Spain, the heart of Mexico and the freedom of America." He also enjoyed excellent health, continuing to play championship caliber tennis at the Beverly Hills Athletic Club when most men of his age, if alive at all, would be hobbling around on walkers. Early in 1994 I learned his address and sent him a letter, inviting him to look this chapter over, add whatever comments he might wish to make and perhaps write an introduction for the book. As with Cesar Romero, I made my move too late. He was suffering from cancer and died on May 15 at the age of at least 88.

Adios, amigo. If we meet somewhere else and they serve liquor I'll buy you a tequila.

Eight• Duncan Renaldo Returns

During the more than three years when Cisco was being played by Gilbert Roland or no one at all, what was Duncan Renaldo up to? Apparently very little. He had a tiny part opposite Alan Ladd and Brian Donlevy in **Two Years Before The Mast** (Paramount, 1946, directed by John Farrow) and medium-size roles in two forgettable quickies, **Jungle Flight** (Paramount, 1947) and **Sword Of The Avenger** (Eagle-Lion, 1948). Calling himself Renault Duncan, he collaborated with Jack DeWitt on the screenplays for a pair of Latin-themed Westerns, **Don Ricardo Returns** (PRC, 1946) and **Bells Of San Fernando** (Hillcrest/ Screen Guild, 1947), both produced by former Cisco owner James S. Burkett. As far as I can tell, these five pieces of work were all that came Renaldo's way between 1946 and 1948.

His career was pulled out of the doldrums by Phil Krasne, who in partnership with Burkett had bought the Cisco property from 20th Century-Fox in 1944 and sold it to Monogram. With that studio and Roland out of the Cisco business—permanently, as it turned out—Krasne organized a new company called Inter-American Productions, resumed control of the character and closed a distribution deal with United Artists, which had been disappointed with the returns from the Hopalong Cassidy features it had released between 1946 and 1948 but was ready to try again with another Western series. Renaldo, who seems to have been a partner in Inter-American, agreed to play Cisco again as he had in 1945, as a carefree adventurer and righter of wrongs, without Roland's sexuality or tequila rituals or social consciousness, even without the trim mustache that every previous actor in the part including Renaldo himself had worn. His outfit is not the ornate regalia he wore later in the TV series but a functional sombrero and bolero jacket. As for his characterization, he told Jon Tuska late in his life, "When I played Cisco I wanted the world to see....a man of generosity....Cisco was a friend to a better world. That's the way I saw him....But he wasn't above

breaking a señorita's heart." (444)

Cisco's *compañero* in the Inter-American films was again called Pancho as he had been when the part was played by Martin Garralaga in the original Krasne-Renaldo trio and by Chris-Pin Martin in the last two films with Roland. But Krasne wanted someone different for the role, and finally settled on the actor who most of us would say was predestined for it.

Leo Carrillo was a native Californian, born in Los Angeles on August 6, 1881 to one of the state's most distinguished families. His great-grandfather, Carlos Antonio Carrillo, had been California's first provisional governor and his father was the first mayor of Santa Monica. Leo's parents wanted him to be a priest but after studying for a while at Los Angeles' Loyola University the young man joined the Southern Pacific Railway's engineering department and, when not on the job, amused himself drawing cartoons and imitating railroad laborers' accents: Spanish, French, Italian, even Chinese. Then he took an art course, moved to northern California and became a staff cartoonist for the San Francisco Examiner.

What developed into a new career that lasted half a century began one night at the Orpheum Theatre when a scheduled vaudeville act failed to show up and Carrillo suddenly found himself on stage as an instant replacement. He proved so popular that the Orpheum management sent him down to Los Angeles for a three-week engagement and that in turn led to his touring the country in vaudeville for years. His specialty was humorous monologues delivered in foreign accents, and one day in Chicago he happened to take in the act of a young performer named Will Rogers and talked him into supplementing his riding and roping tricks with a monologue of his own.

Carrillo graduated from vaudeville to the legitimate stage with a part in the musical comedy *Fads And Fancies* (1915). His biggest stage hit

Jack Benny, Mary Livingston (Jack's wife) and Leo Carrillo backstage in this candid photo. (Courtesy of Jerry Ohlinger's Movie Material Store.)

was as a good-hearted Italian-American dressmaker in *Lombardi, Ltd.* (1917), which was written expressly for him and in which he barnstormed the country for years. In the New York cast with him, as we've seen, was a young man named Warner Baxter who went on to become the talking movies' first Cisco.

In 1927, at the dawn of talkies, Carrillo came to Hollywood to make a short series of comic monologues as "The Italian Humorist." He played an Italian in his first feature, **Mister Antonio** (Tiffany, 1929), and quickly became stereotyped as a gangster or nightclub owner in early talkies. His first appearance both as a Latin American and in a Western was opposite **In Old Arizona**'s Dorothy Burgess and John (not yet Johnny) Mack Brown in **Lasca Of The Rio Grande** (Universal, 1931), which was discussed in Chapter Four.

Anyone studying the credits of the more than 70 features Carrillo acted in before becoming Pancho must be struck by how many times he

intersected with someone or something else that was to figure in the Cisco saga. In another Latin-themed Western, **Girl Of The Rio** (RKO, 1932, directed by Herbert Brenon), he played opposite Dolores Del Rio and future Cisco director Norman Foster. The film, as it happens, was a remake of **The Dove** (Schenck, 1928), a late silent in which the same roles had been played by Norma Talmadge, Noah Beery and the young Gilbert Roland. When the picture was remade yet again as **The Girl And The Gambler** (RKO, 1939), Carrillo repeated his part—with the other members of the triangle portrayed by Steffi Duna and Tim Holt—for a director who fifteen years later would be helming several episodes of the Cisco TV series, Lew Landers. In **Four Frightened People** (Paramount, 1934, directed by Cecil B. DeMille) Carrillo had a meaty featured part opposite stars Claudette Colbert and Herbert Marshall while the actor he would eventually replace in the role of Cisco's sidekick, Chris-Pin

A generic publicity shot for the Leo Carrillo and Duncan Renaldo movie series based on the Cisco Kid. (Courtesy of Jerry Ohlinger's Movie Material Store.)

Martin, had a bit as a native boatman. In the 15-chapter serial **Riders Of Death Valley** (Universal, 1941) Carrillo can clearly be heard using the single word for which his Pancho is most fondly remembered: "Lezwent!" He actually played a character named Pancho later the same year, in **The Kid From Kansas** (Universal, 1941). And in his twenty years in movies before joining the Cisco team he was directed at one time or another by half a dozen of the men who had helmed or were to helm Ciscos: William Nigh (**Men Are Such Fools**, RKO/Jefferson, 1933, and **The Kid From Kansas** and **Escape From Hongkong**, both Universal, 1941), Herbert I. Leeds (**Arizona Wildcat** and **Chicken Wagon Family**, both 20th Century-Fox, 1939), Lew Landers (**The Girl And The Gambler**, RKO, 1939, and **Crime, Inc.**, PRC, 1945), Irving Cummings (**Lillian Russell**, 20th Century-Fox, 1940), Ford Beebe (**Riders Of Death Valley**, Universal, 1941, and **Frontier Badmen**, Universal, 1943), and Christy

Cabanne (**Top Sergeant** and **Timber**, both Universal, 1942). Carrillo's last role before he became Pancho was one of his most prestigious, opposite Henry Fonda and Dolores Del Rio in John Ford's lavish **The Fugitive** (Argosy, 1947).

Apparently acting in 70-odd pictures wasn't enough to keep him overbusy. He involved himself in California politics and, in 1942, crisscrossed the state with gubernatorial candidate Earl Warren, later to become chief justice of the U.S. Supreme Court. When Warren was elected governor he rewarded Carrillo with an appointment to the State Park Commission, where Leo worked to restore California's old missions and to turn Will Rogers' ranch in Santa Monica into a recreation area. Somehow he also found time to run his own ranch and make it prosper.

Near the end of his life, in conversation with Jon Tuska, Duncan Renaldo took credit for recruiting Carrillo into the Pancho role. "Leo refused. 'The part, amigo, is that of a buffoon,' he

105

Although this publicity photo is from the first TV episode we include it here so you can see the difference in the movie costume on page 105 and the TV costume above of Duncan Renaldo (here pictured with Jane Adams and Leo Carrillo.) (Courtesy of Jane Adams.)

said. 'I am a serious actor, not a buffoon.' I explained to Leo that he wasn't to play it as a buffoon, but rather as a tragic and humane Sancho Panza. Leo said: 'All right. I do it. But only once!'" Carrillo wound up playing the part not once but 161 times, in the five last features and the 156 episodes of the TV series. And, as everyone knows who's seen him, he did play Pancho as a buffoon. "He overdid it," Renaldo admitted to Tuska, "but everyone liked him. His accent was so exaggerated that when we finished a picture no one in the cast or crew could talk normal English anymore." (444) In the features he's often seen smoking but dropped the habit when the series migrated to TV.

Of all the character actors and behind-scenes people from this last sequence of Cisco features who moved into television with Renaldo and Carrillo and the series itself, one who made a special contribution never received adequate credit and therefore deserves some attention here.

Albert Glasser was born in Chicago on January 25, 1916, grew up in southern California, earned a music scholarship to USC and, when he graduated, talked his way into a copyist's job in the music department of Warner Brothers, working under titans like Max Steiner and Erich Wolfgang Korngold, later moving to MGM as an assistant to Dmitri Tiomkin. His first screen credit was for **The Monster Maker** (PRC, 1944), a Grade Z horror pic starring J. Carrol Naish, Ralph Morgan and Tala Birell. "For $250," he told an interviewer for Filmfax (February-March 1991), "I was to compose, orchestrate, copy, conduct, and work with the music cutter! If I didn't want it, they had ten guys waiting." The next year, as mentioned briefly in Chapter Six, he was hired by Phil Krasne to write the scores for Monogram's first two Cisco features with Renaldo, **The Cisco Kid Returns** and **In Old New Mexico**. Four years later, with Krasne and Renaldo back as producer and star after the Gilbert Roland hiatus,

Duncan Renaldo loved kids and would take time to visit with a young fan as in this publicity photo for the movie series. (Courtesy of Jerry Ohlinger's Movie Material Store.)

Glasser was brought in again, this time as both composer and director of the Cisco score. The rousing Latinesque theme under the credits of all five Inter-American features became familiar to a huge audience during the Fifties when it was used—without ever being credited to Glasser—for the opening of each episode of the TV series.

Brought in to direct the first three features was Wallace Fox, who was born March 8, 1896 in Purcell, a settlement in what was then Oklahoma Indian territory. His middle initial was W, and if his full name were something like White Fox or Walking Fox he would be the one and only Native American director of B Westerns, but I haven't been able to confirm this speculation. Fox studied at West Texas Military Academy in San Antonio, served in the Navy during World War I and, in 1919, got a job as prop man at a movie studio in Fort Lee, N.J. After working as an assistant director at First National (1921-25) and FBO (1926-27) he became a full-fledged director,

helming several FBO Westerns that starred Bob Steele. With the coming of talkies and FBO's mutation into RKO, Fox started drifting from one small studio to another and directing whatever came along, which happened to include a hunk of junk called **Trapped In Tiajuana** (Fanchon Royer, 1932), starring Edwina Booth and the young Duncan Renaldo.

Fox spent the middle 1930s at RKO, where he directed two rather dull non-series Westerns that are probably his best known films: **Powdersmoke Range** (1935) with Harry Carey and Hoot Gibson and **Yellow Dust** (1936) with Richard Dix. Between 1938 and 1945 Fox's principal base was Monogram and his chief job was directing East Side Kids flicks. In between times he'd helm a few B Westerns, like **The Mexicali Kid** and **Gun Packer** (both 1938) with Jack Randall and, on loanout to Columbia, **The Lone Star Vigilantes** (1941) and **Bullets For Bandits** (1942) with Bill Elliott and Tex Ritter. Historically perhaps his most important B Western was **The Ghost Rider** (Monogram, 1943), first of the almost endless Johnny Mack Brown series with which the studio replaced the Buck Jones cycle after Buck's tragic death. In 1945-46 Fox produced and directed all seven entries in Universal's short-lived B Western series starring Kirby Grant, then spent a brief stint at Columbia directing yawnful serials like **Jack Armstrong** (1947, starring John Hart) and **The Vigilante** (1947, starring Ralph Byrd). None of his features for Monogram seem to have been produced by Phil Krasne but it was probably the Monogram connection that led to his being hired by Inter-American.

First and best of the three Fox directed was **Valiant Hombre** (1949), a neat little picture with exactly what any good B Western needed: a simple story (scripted this time by Adele Buffington) and plenty of action. The main villain and the female lead were played respectively by John Litel and Barbara Billingsley, neither of whom had appeared in many Westerns, but the cast was filled out by shoot-em-up regulars like Stanley Andrews, Lee "Lasses" White and Gene Roth, with Terry Frost and stunt wizard David Sharpe in unbilled bit parts.

The picture opens with a nice little burst of action as Cisco and Pancho are chased by a posse across the desert landscape to the New Mexico border. Actually the sheriff (Hank Bell, uncredited) just wants to tell this latest and most law-abiding version of Cisco that he's entitled to a reward for capturing an outlaw gang two years before, but our heroes are so used to running from men with badges that they do it by instinct. When they pull up at an unlikely road crossing sign in the middle of the New Mexican wilderness, Cisco determines their next destination by tossing a knife at the various signposts with his eyes shut. This is how they wind up in the town of Brownsville.

On the sidewalk in front of the Red Slipper saloon they encounter Joe Haskins (Guy Beach), an old codger who's vainly trying to coax a despondent little dog called Daisy into taking some meat. When Cisco gets the pooch to eat, Haskins explains that Daisy belongs to Paul Mason, a young mining engineer from Boston who disappeared a week ago after announcing in the Red Slipper that he'd struck gold. On orders from saloonkeeper Lon Lansdell (John Litel), Pete the bartender (Gene Roth) shoots the old man on the street before he can say any more, then claims he saw Cisco commit the murder.

Cisco and Pancho are locked up by Sheriff George Dodge (Stanley Andrews) but stay behind bars only briefly thanks to Daisy, who brings them the keys to their cell in her mouth while Deputy Clay (Ralph Peters) is snoring up a storm. Instead of racing out of town as we might have expected, Cisco and Pancho visit the local undertaker, a genial soul who comes out with one-liners like "It's never too late to be dead." Cisco borrows the bullet that killed Haskins, goes back to the sheriff's office and proves his innocence by showing that the old man was killed not by a .45 like his own guns but by a .38.

While the sheriff arrests Pete the bartender, Cisco learns at Brownsville's land office that no new claims have been filed in the past week and concludes that Paul Mason is still alive and being held prisoner somewhere. When gunman Red (Terry Frost, unbilled) kills the bartender in his cell, Cisco becomes certain that the man behind the two murders and Mason's disappearance is Lansdell. In a sequence that adds nothing to the plot, Pancho manipulates two gamblers in the Red Slipper (one of them ace stuntman David Sharpe, uncredited) into a fierce brawl. Where earlier features in the series tended to avoid action, this one throws it in on every possible occasion.

The next day, while searching Mason's cabin, Cisco discovers the missing man has a sister named Linda. On the trail again, he stops for a chat with Whiskers (Lee "Lasses" White), the driver of a passing stagecoach on the way to Brownsville with a beautiful but imperious female inside. Only when the coach reaches town does Cisco learn that the woman is Linda Mason (Barbara Billingsley), and that she's been sent for by Lansdell. Unfortunately she's too stubborn to believe anything Cisco tells her. Meanwhile Lansdell rides out, crosses a swaying suspension bridge familiar to all lovers of Westerns and serials and enters the shack where his men have been trying to make Paul Mason (John James) reveal the location of his gold strike. Mason refuses to take Lansdell's word that Linda is under his control. Later back in the Red Slipper, Daisy keeps sniffing at Lansdell's trouser legs and Cisco figures the saloonkeeper has seen Mason recently.

Before Lansdell can kidnap Linda, Cisco and Pancho spirit her from the town hotel on a pretext and bring her to Mason's cabin, where all three are then captured by the gang. Lansdell leaves three men to guard Cisco and Pancho while he and the others escort Linda to where they're holding her brother. From this point on the action never stops. Cisco and Pancho overpower the three guards, tie them loosely, wait for them to get free and trail them to the shack on the far side of the suspension bridge. They besiege the place and kill or capture the outlaws, with Cisco tossing Lansdell into the river far below after a decently directed fistfight

A one sheet for **Valiant Hombre** (Monogram,1949).

along the bridge. Later, when Paul offers his rescuers a share in the gold mine, Cisco refuses and explains to Pancho, in words that might have been written by Gilbert Roland: "Pancho, we have the richest mine in the whole world. Every morning and every evening it fills the sky with gold. And no man can take it away from us." On which note they ride out of the frame.

Their next adventure was **The Gay Amigo** (1949), a weaker effort directed by Fox from a screenplay by Doris Schroeder that borrowed two characters (the mercenary dance hall girl and the bumptious cavalry sergeant) and at least one scene from 20th-Fox's 1940 **Lucky Cisco Kid**. The cast included B Western fixtures like Joe Sawyer, Fred Kohler, Jr. and Kenneth MacDonald, with the tiny part of the lieutenant going to Clayton Moore, who later in 1949 began his long and legendary TV career as The Lone Ranger.

This film also opens with a chase but for once Cisco and Pancho aren't the pursued. At the Arizona-Mexico border they see a cavalry troop chasing what seems to be a gang of Mexican bandits who get away across the line but lose one man in the running gun battle. If Captain Lewis (Kenneth MacDonald) had bothered to recover the bandit's body, this picture would have been over in a few minutes. Instead he watches through field glasses, recognizes Cisco as he and Pancho ride up to the fallen outlaw, and jumps to the conclusion that Cisco is the leader of the gang. As they examine the body, Cisco recognizes the dead man as outlaw Vic Harmon, in Mexican disguise, and feels an obligation to help the cavalry capture the bandits who are framing his people for their crimes. At the cavalry post Cisco encounters loud-mouthed Sergeant McNulty (Joe Sawyer) and makes a fool of him by breaking a horse that bucked the sergeant off. Before they can report what they've discovered, a lieutenant (Clayton Moore) recognizes Cisco and sounds the alarm. In the film's second chase Cisco and Pancho escape as usual by hiding in the rocks.

As they enter the nearby town, the cavalrymen once again are on their heels. Cisco takes cover in a deserted cantina, starts flirting at once with the barmaid Rosita (Armida) and, in a sequence more or less borrowed from **Lucky Cisco Kid**, hides in her room while McNulty, who thinks Rosita belongs to him, tries vainly to search the place. Just when Cisco and Pancho think they've tricked the troops into riding out of town, McNulty returns and gets the drop on them. At the post they insist on their innocence to Captain Lewis, who pretends to accept their story and lets them go, but Cisco recognizes that Lewis doesn't believe him and so doesn't bother to report that the Mexican

bandits are gringos. On Lewis' orders, McNulty follows Cisco and Pancho into town.

At the offices of the Arizona <u>Globe</u>, while editor Stoneham (Walter Baldwin) is letting him read back issues of the paper covering the Mexican bandit raids, Cisco overhears Ed Paulsen (Sam Flint) drop in and tell Stoneham he's going to leave on the afternoon coach with a petition for Arizona's statehood that he's taking to Washington. When they see McNulty ineptly shadowing them, Cisco and Pancho decide to make him look ridiculous again and march him to the cantina where Rosita is singing. Cisco notices that she's wearing a belt identical to the distinctive belt worn by the dead Pete Harmon—whether it's the same one or a twin is never explained—and learns that she was given hers by Bill Brack (Fred Kohler, Jr.), the local blacksmith. Leaving McNulty tied up and fuming in the empty cantina, they drop in at the blacksmith shop where Brack lets slip that he knows Harmon is dead. McNulty stops them as they're leaving and challenges Cisco to a fistfight, the only such scene in the film, with Fox relying heavily on long shots to mask Renaldo's double. Cisco and Pancho leave town but come back that night and, while in the barber shop, see a special edition of the <u>Globe</u> reporting that Paulsen was killed in the stagecoach but saying nothing about the statehood petition he was carrying. On this flimsy evidence Cisco concludes that editor Stoneham is behind the fake Mexican bandits.

The next day our *caballeros* launch a complex plan to trap the gang. First they intercept a stagecoach, and while Pancho amuses the passengers with his antics, Cisco sneaks into town and forces Stoneham to print another special edition with the news that the Mexican gang has attacked the coach. He locks the editor in a closet, steals a strongbox from his safe and rides through town distributing the paper, then rejoins Pancho and lets the coach continue on its way. Stoneham refuses to believe that Brack and his fake Mexicans didn't attack the coach and Brack refuses to believe that the strongbox with all the gang's loot was hijacked from Stoneham. The coach reaches town and everyone learns there were only two holdup men. Suddenly the cavalry troop rides in and Cisco and Pancho let themselves be seen and chased away, a well-directed sequence if all too brief. That night Cisco surprises Brack at home, convinces him that Stoneham faked the newspaper office robbery but claims he himself has a new crime set up that will require all of Brack's men. The gullible blacksmith shows him the way to the gang's hideout. Meanwhile in the cantina Pancho pretends to have

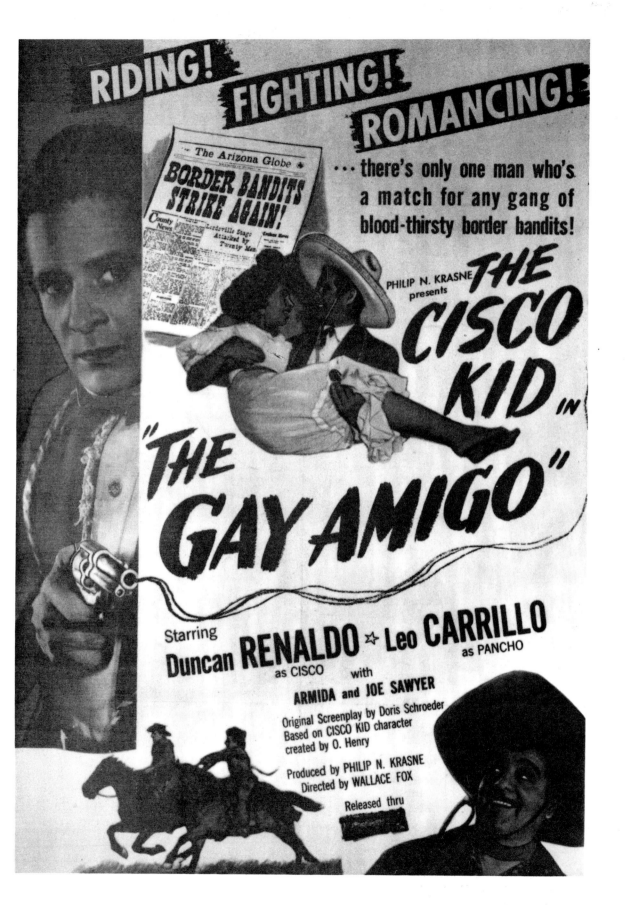

A one sheet from 1949 picturing Duncan Renaldo, Armida and Leo Carrillo.

A Title Card from 1949 picturing Duncan Renaldo fighting with Stephen Chase. (Courtesy of Boyd Magers.)

broken with Cisco and tells Rosita that his former compadre is going to rob the mine wagon at Lopez Rocks the next day at noon. As expected, Rosita tips off McNulty and the cavalry.

In the morning Brack and his men in their Mexican outfits come across the border to pull the job. The driver of the "mine wagon" is Pancho, who pretends to be shot when Cisco fires at him and sends the wagon into a furious runaway with everyone in the gang giving chase. When the wagon is halted, Cisco and the "dead" Pancho get the drop on the outlaws without a scintilla of action. The cavalry troop rides up according to plan and Cisco turns over his prisoners— including Stoneham, whom Pancho had kidnapped and stuffed in the ore wagon—with the mischievous claim that the entire scheme to capture the gang was the brainchild of McNulty.

Third and last of Wallace Fox's contributions to the saga was **The Daring Caballero** (1949), from a screenplay by Betty Burbridge based on an

original story by Frances Kavanaugh. Most of the featured cast members were strangers to the shoot-em-up genre and action took a back seat to plot but, as Don Miller said in *Hollywood Corral* about the Inter-American Ciscos in general, "there were worse Westerns on the market...." (184)

Stopping at a mission as is their custom, Cisco and Pancho find Padre Leonardo (Pedro de Cordoba) worried about Bobby Del Rio (Mickey Little), a young boy who's been staying at the mission but has run away. When they locate the boy, he says he left to find his father and they agree to do the job for him. Back at the mission the padre tells Bobby that his father is going on a long journey he must make alone. Once the boy is safely out of earshot, the priest explains to Cisco and Pancho that Bobby's father, Patrick Del Rio (David Leonard), formerly the town banker, is to hang in the morning for a murder he swears he didn't commit.

Our amigos need to know no more. That

A Lobby Card from 1949 where Duncan Renaldo has George De Normand and friend lassoed. (Courtesy of Boyd Magers.)

evening at suppertime Cisco ties up and then impersonates the waiter bringing the prisoner his last meal. He and Pancho break Del Rio out of jail, elude the posse that chases them, return to the mission, hide Del Rio in the wine cellar and listen to his story. He was convicted of the murder of one of his tellers and the embezzlement of $90,000 on the perjured testimony of E.J. Hodges (Charles Halton), who is now president of the bank, and of Deputy Scott (Edmund Cobb), who is now the town marshal, with the connivance of prosecutor Brady (Stephen Chase), currently the mayor.

Next morning as Marshal Scott is sending out several posses to hunt for Del Rio, Cisco and Pancho ride into town. Pancho goes to buy food for Del Rio and Cisco, dropping in at the mayor's office, recognizes Brady as Barton, an outlaw he used to know. Brady suspects that Cisco was behind Del Rio's escape and orders Marshal Scott to arrest him. While Cisco is at the bank,

exchanging $1000 in gold for paper money he hopes will prove to be part of the missing $90,000, Pancho meets an attractive young woman (Kippee Valez) and tries to impress her by claiming to be the famous Cisco Kid—just at the right moment for Marshal Scott to overhear and throw him in jail. Cisco gets his partner out by forcing Mayor Brady at gunpoint to phone the marshal's office—lucky for him this frontier town has telephone service—and order Scott to release the prisoner. Two of the conspirators' gunmen trail Cisco and Pancho out of town but are caught and left unhorsed and hogtied to each other.

Mayor Brady suspects that Del Rio is hiding at the mission to be near his son and sends out Marshal Scott with a search warrant. In the padre's wine cellar, Del Rio tells Cisco and Pancho that before the $90,000 turned up missing he had made a list of the serial numbers on some of the bills and entrusted it to Kippee Valez, a bank employee and the daughter of his dearest

A Lobby Card from 1949 picturing Duncan Renaldo, Leo Carrillo and Charles Halton. (Courtesy of Boyd Magers.)

friend. He writes a note asking her to give Cisco and Pancho the list, but as they're leaving the cellar they hear the sounds of the marshal's search party approaching and hide behind wine barrels with Del Rio until the danger is past.

Pancho takes the note to Kippee, who of course is the woman to whom he'd passed himself off as Cisco, and learns that she keeps the list at the bank. Meanwhile Cisco burglarizes the mayor's office, finds the key to a bank safe deposit box, and is caught red-handed by Brady himself. After a well-staged brawl between the two, Cisco escapes and rejoins Pancho, with the marshal and a posse hot on their horses' hooves. This neatly directed chase sequence ends as usual with Cisco and Pancho taking cover behind tall rocks as the posse gallops by.

They return to Kippee's house and persuade her to let them into the bank in the middle of the night so they can look at the list of serial numbers, which turns out not to match the numbers on the

bills Cisco got at the bank earlier. Cisco then gets Kippee to open the bank vault so he can use the key he stole and take a peek inside the mayor's safe deposit box, which of course turns out to be the hiding place of the missing $90,000. Mayor Brady, who realizes that Cisco took his key, makes a late-night visit to the bank with Hodges. Cisco, Pancho and Kippee hide behind some furniture and, when the mayor and banker enter the vault to see if their loot is still in the deposit box, lock them in. Then Cisco sends Pancho for Judge Perkins (Frank Jaquet), the obese jurist who presided at Del Rio's trial. The best line in the movie is Pancho's description of this tub of lard as "the circular judge." Marshal Scott returns to town from the earlier chase sequence and is killed shooting it out with Cisco in the street.

In the morning, with the judge and a jury sitting in the bank, Cisco opens the vault, releases the mayor and Hodges, opens Brady's deposit box and finds it empty. It takes him only a moment to

A Lobby Card from 1949 picturing Duncan Renaldo and Stephen Chase. (Courtesy of Boyd Magers.)

figure out that during the night, after Hodges had passed out for lack of air, Brady had taken the key to the banker's own deposit box and hidden the money there. A split-second action flurry leaves the mayor dead and Hodges in custody. With Bobby and his father reunited, Cisco and Pancho gallop away to new adventure elsewhere.

For Wallace Fox that fadeout was the end of the Cisco trail. He returned to Monogram and spent the next two years producing and directing low-budget oaters starring Johnny Mack Brown or Whip Wilson, most of them drearily routine but at least one (**Silver Raiders**, 1951, with Whip Wilson) surprisingly watchable. Then Fox moved to TV and joined the directorial stable at Gene Autry's Flying A Productions, churning out episodes of *The Gene Autry Show* and the Jock Mahoney series *The Range Rider*, then contracting with Poverty Row producer Rudolph C. Flothow to direct the first (and most hackneyed) thirteen episodes of the Jon Hall series *Ramar Of The Jungle.* Fox died on June 30, 1958.

The director of the fourth Inter-American Cisco feature was another old-timer with a long track record. Ford Beebe was born in Grand Rapids, Michigan on November 20, 1888 and, like his contemporary Raoul Walsh, enjoyed a free-wheeling and adventurous young manhood on both sides of the Rio Grande. In 1914 he was hired by Universal as a $25-a-week press agent but soon graduated to writing scenarios for the studio's two-reelers. He spent most of the Twenties writing scripts and, to use his phrase, serving as "director general" for a long string of silent shoot-em-ups starring and nominally directed by Leo Maloney, who died in November 1929 after a booze binge to celebrate the sale of his first talkie. Beebe spent the early years of the Depression and the transition to talking films working as and where he could and wound up at Nat Levine's Mascot Pictures, writing and later

A Title Card from 1949 picturing Duncan Renaldo, Leo Carrillo and Ann Savage. (Courtesy of Boyd Magers.)

directing cliffhanger serials like **Shadow Of The Eagle** (1932), starring John Wayne, and **The Last Of The Mohicans** (1932, co-directed by B. Reeves Eason), starring Harry Carey. Between 1936 and 1945 he was back at Universal, directing ten features (including three B Westerns with Johnny Mack Brown) and co-directing a staggering 23 serials, five of them Westerns. When his Universal contract ran out he started free-lancing at Monogram and other small studios and was hired by Krasne to direct the next Cisco adventure, **Satan's Cradle** (1949).

The screenplay for this one was credited to Jack Benton but the name is a transparent disguise for veteran B Western writer J. Benton Cheney and the script is yet another version of an old Cheney standard in which the tough dance hall girl who heads the town's corrupt element falls in love with the hero trying to bring her down and ends up taking the bullet her jealous male partner-in-crime has fired at his honest rival. This storyline was

first brought to cinematic life in **Hopalong Cassidy Returns** (Paramount, 1936), starring William Boyd (who else?) and directed by Nate Watt from a screenplay by Harrison Jacobs. The dance hall woman attracted to Cassidy was portrayed by Evelyn Brent and the spurned partner who kills her by Stephen Morris, later and better known as Morris Ankrum. Cheney got into the act five years later when he was hired to rework the 1936 script for another Cassidy picture, **Wide Open Town** (Paramount, 1941), directed by Lesley Selander. Evelyn Brent reprised her role as the dance hall woman and Morris Ankrum had a character part but the role of her furious ex-lover went to Victor Jory and this time she survived the climactic gunbattle. Cheney grew so attached to the plot that from here on he treated it as his own and recycled it for at least two of Monogram's Johnny Mack Brown films, both helmed by once and future Cisco director Lambert Hillyer. In **The Gentleman**

116

A Lobby Card from 1949 picturing Leo Carrillo, Duncan Renaldo, Douglas Fowley, George De Normand and others at Pioneertown. (Courtesy of Boyd Magers.)

From Texas (Monogram, 1946), Claudia Drake played the saloon lady and Tristram Coffin her partner. Hillyer gave the role to Coffin again in **Land Of The Lawless** (Monogram, 1947) but the female lead went to June Harrison. Two years later, in **Satan's Cradle**, the dance hall gal was portrayed by Ann Savage, who is best known as the psychotic woman in Edgar G. Ulmer's zero-budget film *noir* classic **Detour** (PRC, 1945), and her spurned lover by B-movie gangster Douglas Fowley. What distinguishes this version is the overtly religious element Cheney added to the basic script and the abundance of action scenes, far more than usual in B Westerns of the late Forties or in any other Cisco feature except perhaps **The Gay Caballero**.

The film opens with Reverend Henry Lane (Byron Foulger) preaching on the main street of Silver City, proclaiming that the town has become a sink of iniquity since being taken over by Lil (Ann Savage), the owner of the Silver Lode Saloon. Gunmen summoned by Lil's lawyer and lover Steve Gentry (Douglas Fowley) beat up the parson and kick him out of town while Gentry in celebration buys drinks for the house.

Cisco and Pancho are heading for Silver City because Cisco has heard that a wealthy widow has moved in. Despite having *amoradas* all over the West, our *caballero* wants to try his luck with this one too. "Just because a man has enjoyed a plum and a few grapes, must he turn his back on a peach when he finds one?" They come upon Lane, beaten and left for dead on the trail, and care for him in a manner recalling the story of the Good Samaritan. (This may be the only Western where two men of Catholic background refer to a Protestant minister as Padre). Lane tells his rescuers how Lil and Gentry took over the town on the basis of Lil's claim to be the widow of Silver City's founder, Jim Mason, who was killed in a supposedly accidental cave-in at his San Miguel mine. A scene back in town, with Lil

A Lobby Card from 1949 picturing Claire Carleton, Leo Carrillo, Duncan Renaldo, bartender extra and Douglas Fowley. (Courtesy of Boyd Magers.)

reminding Gentry that she won't stand for any killings in the course of their scheme, reveals to us that she's a fake with a forged marriage certificate.

Cisco and Pancho accompany the preacher back to Silver City where Lane announces in the saloon that Sunday services will be held as usual. Cisco engages in a long-drawn-out brawl with Idaho (George De Normand), one of the gunmen who beat the parson, and then starts flirting with Lil, telling her: "I shall see you in church—I hope." Lil forbids Gentry to kill Cisco and promises to use her own wiles on him instead. While Cisco and Pancho are helping to rebuild Lane's church, Lil saunters by and swaps romantic banter, with Cisco refusing her invitation to join her and she likewise turning down his offer to reform. A little later Idaho tries to shoot Cisco on the street and winds up dead himself. Lil threatens to expose Gentry's whole scheme unless he lets Cisco alone.

To keep Lane safe until Sunday, Cisco and Pancho camp out with him in a place known as Satan's Saddle. Cisco is convinced that she was never married to Jim Mason but can't prove it and decides to reach her by appealing to the spark of good that both he and Lane believe to be in all of us. (Why this doesn't apply to Gentry and his gunmen is never explained or even explored.) Returning to the saloon, Cisco finds Lil in a revealing black evening gown, plays blackjack with her and catches her in a slip when she claims to have married Mason on a different day of the month than stated in her forged certificate. Gentry gets the drop on Cisco with a concealed pistol but a warning to Pancho in Spanish allows the amigos to get away unscathed.

Some time later, one of the gang locates the camp at Satan's Saddle. In an action sequence that runs close to ten minutes, the outlaws raid the camp but are outgunned and everyone except Gentry and his henchman Rocky (Buck Bailey)

118

A Lobby Card from 1949 picturing Duncan Renaldo in a fight with George De Normand while extras watch. (Courtesy of Boyd Magers.)

are killed. The two survivors trail Cisco and Pancho to the San Miguel mine. Cisco finds a piece of burnt fuse in the tunnel where Jim Mason died, but just then Gentry sets off another dynamite charge like the one he used to kill Mason. Cisco and Pancho of course are unhurt and find another way out of the mine shaft.

Back in town, Gentry boasts that he's killed Cisco and the outraged Lil decides to dump both him and their scheme. That night Cisco and Pancho return for a showdown but are spotted on their way to Lil's house where she's packing her clothes. Lil is so glad to see him alive and so disgusted with Gentry that she agrees to tell the sheriff all she knows. Gentry shoots at her through the window. In the original version of this story, **Hopalong Cassidy Returns**, the woman was killed at this point, and in most of Cheney's subsequent rewrites she was at least wounded. This time she isn't even scratched. Cisco pursues Gentry and shoots him dead after another ten-

minute action sequence with a chase on foot through a nightbound wood. Returning to town, he discovers that Lil is expecting him to turn her over to the law and waiting for him in the church but decides that her repentance is punishment enough and sets off with Pancho for new adventure.

Ford Beebe was in his early sixties when he made this fine little Western but was nowhere near ready to call it quits. He went on to direct the first two entries in a new Don Barry series at Lippert—**The Dalton Gang** and the magnificent **Red Desert** (both 1949)—then returned to Monogram where he made eleven features in the Bomba the Jungle Boy series starring Johnny Sheffield. In the middle Fifties he directed some episodes of the *Adventures Of Champion* TV series (1955-56) for Gene Autry's Flying A Productions. When he was over eighty he came out of retirement to helm a pair of Alaskan wildlife movies, one on his own and the other in

A Lobby Card from 1949 picturing Duncan Renaldo, Douglas Fowley and Ann Savage. (Courtesy of Boyd Magers.)

tandem with Tay Garnett (1894-1977), another old-time action director who didn't know how to stop working. Beebe died in 1978 at the age of eighty-nine.

At the end of **Satan's Cradle** Cisco had told Pancho that their next stop would be a town called San Lorenzo. Beebe knew this because he'd already written and sold the script for what would become the final Cisco feature, **The Girl From San Lorenzo** (1950). But his commitments at Lippert and Monogram made it impossible for him to direct this one himself and the man Krasne hired in his place proved a huge disappointment. Derwin Abrahams was born in 1903 and learned what he knew of the B Western business during the years between 1936 and 1941 when he worked as an assistant director on Paramount's Hopalong Cassidy series. The first films he directed were a pair of lackluster Cassidys, **Border Vigilantes** and **Secret Of The Wastelands** (both 1941), which were as good as his work ever got. He spent most of the Forties at Columbia churning

out four dull serials and nine routine entries in the Durango Kid series starring Charles Starrett, with an occasional detour to Monogram for a yawnful oater with Johnny Mack Brown or Jimmy Wakely. Like everything else he directed, **The Girl From San Lorenzo** is a bore. Its main interest for us is that it became the bridge on which the Cisco series crossed over from the large to the small screen.

The picture opens with a montage of stock footage and newspaper headlines blaming Cisco and Pancho for an epidemic of stagecoach robberies in the Cactus Wells area and the murder of a local resident named Steve McCarger. The next thing we see is Cisco and Pancho being chased across desert scenery, for no reason they can figure out, by a low-budget posse of three men. This sequence, in which they elude their pursuers by hiding behind a huge rock, provided the footage for the opening credits of the Cisco TV series.

Later in the town of San Lorenzo, they receive

A Title Card from 1950 picturing Jane Adams, Duncan Renaldo and Leo Carrillo with Edmund Cobb getting a blow in the upper left. (Courtesy of Boyd Magers.)

a letter in Spanish claiming that Pancho's grandmother is sick in Cactus Wells and needs to see them at once. Cisco recognizes the letter is a fake because the number 7 in the dateline doesn't have a cross-stroke in the Spanish manner and Pancho also spots the message as a phony for the simple reason that his grandmother died years ago. Before they can leave San Lorenzo to investigate the decoy letter, Tom McCarger (Leonard Penn) starts shooting at Cisco on the street. Nora Malloy (Jane Adams) saves Cisco's life by grabbing McCarger's arm and Cisco wounds the man who tried to kill him. While the assailant is being treated by a doctor, Jane tells Cisco that she's on her way to Cactus Wells to marry stagecoach driver Jerry Todd (Bill Lester). When McCarger is well enough to talk, he accuses Cisco of having killed his brother Steve in Cactus Wells and shows a letter from the town's sheriff (Lee Phelps) blaming Cisco for the murder. The *compañeros* head for Cactus Wells to see what's going on.

Not far from their destination, the outlaws Blackie (David Sharpe) and Wooly (Edmund Cobb), dressed in the Cisco and Pancho outfits they've been using for their crime wave, pull yet another stage holdup, killing the guard and seriously wounding the driver, who happens to be Jerry Todd. The real Cisco and Pancho are riding by at just the right time and place to observe the crime. "Cisco, look at us down there holding up the stagecoach!" Pancho exclaims. Instead of going after their impersonators, they chase the runaway coach and bring it to a halt. Blackie and Wooly see them and know that the pair they've framed for their crimes are in the area. The badly wounded Jerry tells Cisco that he's engaged to Nora Malloy and Cisco and Pancho, despite knowing there's a price on their heads, drive the stagecoach into town.

The sheriff rides out to meet the coach, finds Cisco at the reins and tries to arrest him, but Cisco throws a tarpaulin in his face and he and Pancho

The CISCO KID
"THE GIRL FROM
SAN LORENZO"
DUNCAN RENALDO
LEO CARRILLO

Original Screenplay by FORD BEEBE   Directed by DERWIN ABRAHAMS
Produced by PHILIP N. KRASNE   Released thru United Artists

A Lobby Card from 1950 picturing a masked Dave Sharpe, Leo Carrillo and Duncan Renaldo. (Courtesy of Boyd Magers.)

make their getaway. Word goes out over the telegraph wires that Cisco and Pancho have robbed another stage. They stop at Jerry's ranch where Nora is staying and tell her that they had nothing to do with shooting her fiancé. Nora believes him and, when the sheriff and deputies show up with the wounded Jerry, she hides the fugitives in the kitchen, where they later hear a despairing Jerry tell Nora that without an expensive operation he'll never be able to walk again. Cisco and Nora arrange a charade so that Nora will seem to have captured the fugitive pair and earned the reward for them, but the game is interrupted by the sheriff and his deputies, who come back to the ranch and capture them for real.

Cisco and Pancho sit tight in jail until Nora has been paid the reward money, but before they can break out the job is done for them. Three masked men—Blackie, Wooly and their sidekick Rusty (Wes Hudman)—slip into the jailhouse, slug the sheriff, lock him in a cell, release Cisco and

Pancho, take them to their hideout and leave them tied up and guarded by another outlaw called Kansas (Don C. Harvey) while they change into their Cisco and Pancho costumes and go off to commit another stage robbery for which our heroes will be blamed. Kansas, keeping watch over the prisoners, lets slip that the outlaws have secret information about a shipment of gold bullion on the night stage. Pancho wheedles Kansas into giving him a cigarillo to smoke while he's tied up, then drops the smoke and pretends he's on fire, luring Kansas into a position where Cisco can overpower him. They find their horses, intercept the night stage before their impersonators do, and take the express box. When they shoot it open they discover it's empty, while down the trail the fake Cisco and Pancho stop the coach and find they're too late.

Cisco and Pancho slip back into Cactus Wells, release the sheriff from jail and explain the whole situation, convincing him that the empty

122

The CISCO KID
"THE GIRL FROM SAN LORENZO"
DUNCAN RENALDO
LEO CARRILLO

Original Screenplay by FORD BEEBE   Directed by DERWIN ABRAHAMS
Produced by PHILIP N. KRASNE   Released thru United Artists

A Lobby Card from 1950 picturing Jane Adams, Leo Carrillo, Duncan Renaldo and Lee Phelps. (Courtesy of Boyd Magers.)

strongbox proves that the man behind the robberies must be the express agent, Cal Ross (Byron Foulger). The three men set a trap. A rock is tossed through Ross' window with a note from Cisco wrapped around it: "I will come for the loot in your office safe before daylight." Ross and Kansas post themselves in the express office and wait to kill Cisco when he shows up. The person who slips into the office however is Pancho, who pretends to have broken with his partner, tips them off to what he says is Cisco's plan and tricks Ross into opening his safe, at which point Cisco and the sheriff effortlessly get the drop on the thieves. The fake Cisco and Pancho and the rest of the gang ride into town just in time to crash the party and add a few minutes of routine climactic action to the picture, culminating in a one-on-one between Cisco and the man who impersonated him.

The final scene of the last Cisco feature is in the quixotic Robin Hood vein. Nora, who has just married Jerry, comes to town and tries to give back the reward money. Cisco and Pancho conspire with the sheriff to put on another charade so that Nora won't feel guilty about using the money for Jerry's operation. The sheriff pretends to have the pair in custody again and they pretend to get the drop on him and, in a rather nice closing shot, ride off into the rising sun.

To continue their adventures on the small screen.

123

A publicity still for **The Daring Caballero** (Monogram,1949) picturing Kippee Valez in the embrace of Duncan Renaldo. (Courtesy of Boyd Magers.)

Nine • Lezwent!: Cisco on the Small Screen

The Cisco series migrated to TV under the Krasne regime but the person most identified with the move was a shrewd businessman named Frederick Ziv, who founded his own advertising agency in Cincinnati around 1931 and got into the entertainment media by developing a country-Western musical show which he sold to both a local radio station and a local sponsor. He soon became a specialist in the packaging and later in the nationwide syndication of radio entertainment, using the money he made from that venture to buy up other businesses that would make syndication even more profitable. One of his acquisitions for example was the World Library, a huge collection of recorded music which enabled him to add background scores to his syndicated programs without the hassle of squabbling with ASCAP over royalty payments.

By the late Forties Ziv had moved to Chicago and recognized that the syndication of TV shows was the wave of the future. He bought out the General Film Library, a vast assortment of old newsreel and sports footage, and turned the millions of feet of film into *Yesterday's Newsreel* and *Sports Album*, two 15-minute series which he then syndicated around the country as he'd done in the past with his radio programs. The profits from these operations he used to launch his own TV film production company, which took over the Cisco series from Krasne while the earliest episodes were being shot. Ziv sent his salesmen across the country in search of local stations to broadcast the series, reportedly making them wear Cisco sombreros at any out-of-town meetings they attended. Meanwhile he sold the commercial slots built into each Cisco episode's running time to Interstate Bakeries, whose bread products were distributed to firms around the country for resale to the consumer under those firms' brand names. (In the New York City area where I grew up, the original sponsor was Tip Top bread.) The studio and outdoor facilities needed for production were leased on a short-term basis from various studios

until 1955, when Ziv took over the financially troubled Eagle-Lion company with the profits from *Cisco* and other syndicated series like *Boston Blackie* and *I Led Three Lives*. By 1960, having grossed about $11,000,000 from his operations, Ziv sold out to United Artists and retired from TV series production.

Clearly the intent of the Cisco TV series was to continue the movie series seamlessly but on the small screen and at a running time of slightly under thirty minutes per segment rather than slightly over sixty. Not only did Duncan Renaldo and Leo Carrillo carry on their roles as Cisco and Pancho, but all sorts of people out of camera range—director Derwin Abrahams, assistant director Eddie Davis, scriptwriter J. Benton Cheney, cinematographer Kenneth Peach and composer Albert Glasser, just to name a few—moved straight from the last Cisco feature, **The Girl From San Lorenzo**, into the first Cisco TV episode, "Boomerang," taking part of the feature's storyline with them to boot.

Dave Sharpe doubled Renaldo in the earliest episodes of the series but left for a stunting gig in Europe and was replaced by one of the men who contributed hugely to this book. Troy Melton was born in Jackson, Tennessee in 1921, moved with his family to southern California during the Depression, served in the Army Air Corps during World War II, then began a career as an actor and stuntman that lasted several decades. He was one of the founding members of the Stuntmen's Association of Motion Pictures and between 1962 and 1988 he owned the Playboy Restaurant, next door to the Paramount studio on Hollywood's Melrose Avenue. He died of cancer on November 15, 1995, but during the last months of his life we spent several hours on the phone talking about his experiences as Duncan Renaldo's double.

"I was working on a Cisco," Melton told me, "doing a small part and working as a utility double," when Dave Sharpe left for Europe and the job opened up. Krasne and his associates

A publicity photo of Troy Melton. (Courtesy of his widow, Mrs. Jean Melton.)

"tried out two or three guys, trying to get someone who looked like Duncan, who could work with him. I did not look like him. They tried out one or two people who could do the horseback riding, who were good cowboy types, but when it came to fight scenes and the stunts they weren't so good. A couple of others did those things fine but weren't so good with their horseback riding and certain tricks that you needed to do working with horses. I being on the show, they let me try out doing some of the little things like crupper mounts, jumping over the back of the horse, and side mounts and what not. I was quite acrobatic. I don't know how it happened but they informed me that they were going to take me up on location to Pioneertown to do maybe a small part and utility double, but at the same time they were going to test me out in Cisco's outfit. Which they did.

"It happened that my first stunt doubling him was a runaway stagecoach that actually did run away. I was supposed to catch it so I was horse-back-chasing it. At a certain point they wanted to see me transfer to the stagecoach, get up on it and help stop it. They had a tree or a bush as a marker [where filming the scene later was supposed to begin]. Frank Matts was driving and I was trying to catch the coach. When I was finally getting to the point where I could overtake it I saw that bush and decided that as long as I was doing it I might as well get it on film. So I made my jump and came up over the top. I took two of the horses and Frank took the other two and we stopped the coach. When they got the film back they were happy with it and informed me that I was now Cisco's double."

Meanwhile, Texas-born Bill Catching (1926-), who had started out as the horse wrangler for the series, became the double for Carrillo. "They made a body pad for me to double Leo," he remembered when I interviewed him. "I loved it because you'd bounce around in it when you hit the ground." One day early in 1950, Catching and Melton were doing a fight on top of a building when they saw two men watching who turned out to be Fred Ziv and Maurice Unger, the new owners of the production company.

"When Ziv came out here," Melton told me, "he had the rights to a lot of radio. Among his rights was *Boston Blackie*, and Phil Krasne had the rights to *Cisco*. Prior to Ziv coming in here, Phil had made a deal with Jack Gross to do his interiors at California Studios, which used to be Pop [Harry] Sherman's studio. So Krasne and Gross formed a partnership, which later included Ziv when he came out here with *Boston Blackie*. They joined forces and became a unit. As time went by, Ziv took over.

Troy Melton dressed as Cisco relaxes with Leo Carrillo in July 1952.) (Courtesy of Mrs. Jean Melton.)

"We were operating out of an office on Carroll Drive in Beverly Hills, right off Sunset and Doheny. That's where Phil Krasne's office was, that was where the writing was done. The preparations, shooting boards and everything were taken care of there. Then we would go out on location to Chatsworth or wherever and shoot our location shots. When there were some interiors that we had to have, we would rent from some independent studio.

"We would shoot a lot of location stuff up at Pioneertown. They had prop buildings there, like the exterior of the Red Dog cafe or a Chinese restaurant or whatever. Inside was actually a practical setting. In the Chinese restaurant they had a very good place to eat, and the Red Dog was a beer bar. On weekends or even during the week they sold beer to people who were visiting but we also used it as a set.

"Pioneertown was named for the Sons of the Pioneers, Roy Rogers' group. They got the idea of building a location where they could shoot Westerns. Unfortunately they built the street wrong so that you had the sun coming from the wrong direction. Instead of down the street it was coming across, so that you could only shoot certain things in the morning, and then you had to wait and shoot the other things in the afternoon instead of shooting straight down the street with sun. That was a problem we had, but we shot a lot of things on a little insert road below the town."

During production on the first season's episodes, Krasne began looking for a new assistant director to replace the veteran Louis

Bill Catching dressed as Pancho and Troy Melton dressed as Cisco clown around with a visiting executive from Chrysler in 1950. (Courtesy of Bill Catching.)

Bill Catching doubling Leo Carrillo as Pancho in a horse fall. (Courtesy of Bill Catching.)

Germonprez, who had started with the series. The producer asked Troy Melton if he could recommend anyone for the job. "There was a guy named Bob Farfan," Melton told me, "a friend of mine, who was an assistant director. I recommended him and he got an interview. We weren't shooting on that day so I went over to the office. While I was there someone spoke to me and I looked around and it was Eddie Davis. I had worked with him at Monogram. How he came on the interview I don't know.

"A little later Phil called me into the office and said: 'I saw you talking to Eddie Davis out there. How well do you know him?' I said: 'I know him pretty well. I've worked with him.' He said: 'You know the kind of work we're doing here. What kind of an assistant director is he? With the speed and the kind of stuff we have to do, how do you think he fits in with our program?' Well, I asked Bob Farfan to come down on the interview but I told Phil the truth. 'Eddie's a very good assistant director. I've worked with him on those quickies

at Monogram. I've even worked with him on some second units when he's directed on them. He's very good and he would fit in with our program very well.'"

This was how Davis got the job as assistant director, but he soon found himself promoted. "When Ziv took over," Bill Catching explained to me, "Babe Unger was left as the head of the studio, and he didn't know anything about movies and studios. So after they'd been wandering about the sets with stopwatches and talking to people, they realized that the most knowledgeable man in the company was Eddie Davis, so they made him production manager....Eddie's desk was in the front of the room and Babe's desk was behind him. Every transaction that took place went through Eddie Davis. Babe sat behind with a secretary, and all he did was listen and make notes for possibly six months." During that time Davis "ran the studio. That guy could—oh, he did a ten-man job and did it well. Today in films there's ten guys doing what Eddie used to do." The first 26

Karl Davis, Bill Catching, Mickey Simpson and perhaps, Michael Vallon, at the Iverson Ranch in 1952 during the filming of a Cisco episode titled "Robber Crow". (Courtesy of Bill Catching.)

episodes of the series were ready for broadcast by the fall of 1950.

Looking back from almost half a century's distance, most Western enthusiasts would probably agree that the smartest money spent on the series was what it took to shoot every episode in color, even though color TV didn't exist at the time. "It was Kenny Peach's idea," Bill Catching told me. "16mm Cinecolor was cheaper than 35mm black-and-white. You could open the lens up and you got much more light out of 16mm than you could get out of the flat lenses....With the 16mm you could speed the camera up a little and have the people walk slow. We used to do a fight in slow motion." Not so smart was the decision to cut costs by organizing each season's work so that the same director would shoot two, three and occasionally four 30-minute episodes at a time with the same core group of actors who would often have the same character names in each episode even though they were supposed to be different people. This ploy boggled the minds of the youngsters in the audience and was recognized as a cheapskate gimmick by the older kids and adults. But at least the actors who played these multiple parts were welcome friends to viewers who had grown up on theatrical B Westerns. Much less welcome was the decision to use the boring music of Albert Glasser for the sound tracks of the first season's 26 episodes, and the worst move of all was to entrust the initial thirteen segments to Derwin Abrahams, a director whose work never rose above routine competence.

There isn't a single visually exciting moment in the entire six and a half hours' footage Abrahams contributed to the series, and the amount of sloppiness he perpetrated has to be seen to be gaped at. Take the third episode, "Rustling," whose vanishing cattle herd plot was lifted from a Hopalong Cassidy feature, **Twilight On The Trail** (Paramount, 1941), on which Abrahams had served as assistant director. In one scene in a rancher's office he shows us a 1950s lead pencil complete with eraser. Later in an outdoor sequence, a single shot is fired and a character in the distance exclaims: "Those shots came from Hidden Valley!" The showdown between Cisco and the rustlers features several shots being fired without bangs being heard. That the series survived ineptitudes like these is little short of a miracle.

Abrahams, so Bill Catching told me, was "very strict, and knew exactly what he wanted, and had very little patience. If he rehearsed a scene and you did it and you goofed it up, he had very little patience with a person who did that a couple of times, because he was a professional and expected everybody else to be a professional. But he did have a sense of humor. When we were doing one of the first [episodes], I was wrangling on it and we worked at the old Harold Lloyd studio, a little tiny studio, and the stage was not much bigger than somebody's dining room. They had a little old cabin set, with greens and stuff, and Derwin would say: 'Okay now, Duncan and Leo, you guys come charging in and dismount and go in the cabin.' And the horses only had—there was two lengths of horses behind them and there was the wall from the front of the stage. They couldn't even get 'em to lope two jumps, that was all the space they had, and they'd be trotting when they came in. But he'd say: 'Now I want you to come charging in.'"

On the positive side, Abrahams did fill out his casts with fine B Western female leads like Peggy Stewart, Gail Davis and Noel Neill, former stars and stuntmen like Bob Livingston (Renaldo's former partner in Republic's Three Mesquiteers series during the 1939-40 season) and Dave Sharpe, and veteran shoot-em-up character actors like Raymond Hatton, Earle Hodgins, Forrest Taylor and Jack Ingram. Most of the scripts for Abrahams' thirteen segments were by J. Benton Cheney and all of them were drearily routine, if not before then after the director got through with them, but some at least have aspects of historical interest to dedicated Ciscophiles. "Boomerang," the debut episode of the series, overlaps in both cast and storyline with **The Girl From San Lorenzo,** the last Cisco feature and the only one Abrahams directed. In this and other very early episodes Pancho is not just a lovable language-mangling buffoon but also a petty thief, and every so often Cisco gets genuinely angry at him. It was under Abrahams that the "Oh, Pancho!" "Oh, Cisco!" routine, with Renaldo and Carrillo laughing uproariously, evolved from an occasional novelty into the standard closing of every segment. Two of the Abrahams baker's

dozen, "False Marriage" and "Renegade Son," both scripted by Betty Burbridge, are clearly rewrites of Burbridge's screenplays for **The Cisco Kid Returns** and **In Old New Mexico,** the Monogram features in which Renaldo had first played the Robin Hood of the Old West. And one of his episodes, "Cattle Quarantine," is graced by a classic Panchoism: "The she-male of the specimen is more deader than the male." [This one we can trace back to long before Carrillo began playing Pancho. In **History Is Made At Night** (Wanger/United Artists, 1937), directed by Frank Borzage and starring Charles Boyer and Jean Arthur, Carrillo as an Italian chef exclaimed: "The female of the spices is more dead than the male."] Picking up on items like these helps us sit through Abrahams' contributions without nodding off.

Once Abrahams got the Cisco series off the ground (a few inches anyway) he went elsewhere. A few years later he changed his name to Derwin Abbe and, with equal lack of distinction, directed episodes of other early TV Western series like *Hopalong Cassidy* and *Judge Roy Bean*. He died in 1974, totally forgotten. The Cisco series improved hugely when two other directors, one with a long track record and the other new to the game, came aboard to helm the final thirteen segments of the first season.

The experienced hand was Albert Herman, who was born Adam Foelker in Troy, New York sometime (depending on which reference book you consult) between 1887 and 1894 and got his start in the movie business in 1913. During the Twenties he directed dozens of silent two-reel comedies, including more than thirty in the Mickey McGuire series. After talkies put an end to the pie-in-the-face genre, Herman switched to directing ultra-low-budget Westerns with stars like Rex Lease, Big Boy Williams and Bill Cody. In 1937 he joined the short-lived Grand National studio and directed James Newill as a singing, fighting Mountie in **Renfrew Of The Royal Mounted** (1937) and **Renfrew On The Great White Trail** (1938). Then he helmed the studio's last two B Westerns starring Tex Ritter and, when the Ritter series moved to Monogram, he went along. Actionmaster Spencer Bennet, who was directing the rest of Monogram's Ritter pictures, once described Herman to me as a big bull of a man, built like a wrestler. The features with Tex that Herman directed included some routine entries but also some gems like **Sundown On The Prairie** (1939), **The Man From Texas** (1939), **Pals Of The Silver Sage** (1940), **The Golden Trail** (1940) and **Take Me Back To Oklahoma** (1940).

During the war years Herman hung out at PRC,

Bill Catching playing an Indian at Pioneertown for a Cisco episode. (Courtesy of Bill Catching.)

specializing in zero-budget contemporary thrillers and rejoining his former Renfrew, James Newill, for **The Rangers Take Over** (1943) and **Bad Men Of Thunder Gap** (1943), the first features in PRC's Texas Rangers series that co-starred Dave O'Brien and Guy Wilkerson. Herman's last films were released in 1945, which as chance would have it was the year Tex Ritter signed with PRC and took over Newill's role in the Texas Rangers series. It's quite possible, especially if Herman in fact was born in 1887, that at this point he retired. In any event he seems to have done nothing more until the 1950-51 season when he directed half a dozen Cisco segments. "He used to be a fighter," Bill Catching remembered. "And strong! When he'd shake hands with you, whenever he'd grip something tight, it would make his arms pull back, so if you shook hands with him, when he grabbed your hand and squeezed it, that would automatically drag you towards him. We were down in Pioneertown and he was standing across a little ditch and somebody came and said: 'Is that Al Herman?' I said: 'Yes. Come on, I'll introduce you to him.' And he was standing across this little ditch and he stuck out his hand. And before I could cry 'Don't shake hands with him!' they shook hands and he drug the guy right across the ditch."

Herman's segments were filmed in two packages of three episodes apiece, with B Western stalwarts Dennis Moore, Bill Henry, Steve Clark and Ted Adams in one triad and Tristram Coffin, Zon Murray, Hank Patterson and Kenne Duncan in the other. None of the six ranks with the finest Cisco TV episodes but they're a huge improvement on the first thirteen, mainly because Herman took care to invest his action sequences with some visual excitement. It was on his watch that Leo Carrillo perpetrated two of his nuttiest Panchoisms. From "The Old Bum": "Some day, Cisco, you are going to find out that the moon is a mousetrap and you are the green cheese." From "Water Rights": "Cisco, my bones tell me something don't smell so good." Apparently Herman went back into retirement after his month or so on the Cisco series and, as far as I can tell, never worked in TV again. He died on July 2, 1967.

The remaining seven Cisco segments for the first season were the work of a relative newcomer to the director business. Paul Landres was born in New York City on August 21, 1912. After attending California Christian College and UCLA, he found a job as assistant film editor at Universal in 1931. Six years later he was promoted to full-fledged film editor, and B Western fans lucky enough to have prints or cassettes of entries in

Universal's Johnny Mack Brown series like **The Bad Man From Red Butte** (1940), **Pony Post** (1940) and the magnificent **Arizona Cyclone** (1941) will find Landres listed on the credits in that capacity.

His career as a director began with **Grand Canyon** (Lippert, 1949, starring Richard Arlen and Mary Beth Hughes) but he quickly recognized that the theatrical B feature was a dying breed and joined the first wave of directors who began making 30-minute episodes of series for TV. "I was looking around for work," he told me when I interviewed him, "and a friend of mine [Mel Mark] was working as production man for Phil Krasne. He was also related to Krasne, his nephew I think, and prevailed upon him to see **Grand Canyon**. Phil saw it and turned around to Mel and said: 'What the h... am I looking at this for? This guy is a comedy director!' But Mel talked to him and convinced him, and that's the way it happened." Landres turned out a total of 27 Cisco segments and 17 episodes of the Kent Taylor action detective series *Boston Blackie*. Then he hip-hopped from one Western, adventure, comedy or anthology series to another: *Cowboy G-Men, The Lone Ranger, Sky King, Mr. And Mrs. North, Adventures Of Kit Carson, Ramar Of The Jungle, Topper, Waterfront, Brave Eagle, Soldiers Of Fortune,* the list goes on and on. By the late Fifties and early Sixties he had made the transition to prime-time adult Western series like *Bonanza, Law Of The Plainsman, The Life And Legend Of Wyatt Earp, Maverick, The Rifleman, Bronco* and *Cheyenne*, not to mention Warner Bros. PI series like *Hawaiian Eye* and *77 Sunset Strip*. All this in addition to a dozen or so theatrical features! No one so prolific can always be in top form but some of his best early TV work—including some *Cisco* and *Boston Blackie* segments and his three episodes of *Cowboy G-Men*—hold up extremely well more than forty years later, and his *Bonanza* episode "The Paiute War" is simply one of the most powerful Westerns I've ever seen. He is still alive and well in his mid-eighties but in view of all the pictures he made in his prime it's a wonder he didn't drop dead of exhaustion decades ago.

Landres began his association with the Cisco series by one-upping his directorial colleagues. Abrahams and Herman had made two or three segments at the same time with identical or overlapping casts but Landres made first a group of three and then a brace of four. Babe Unger, he recalled during our interview, "would tell me what his plans were and how I should do it. He wanted close shots, close shots, close shots. I said: 'Babe, how close do you want me to get?' He said: 'When

Bill Catching in costume as a townsman at the Iverson Ranch for a Cisco episode. (Courtesy of Bill Catching.)

Bill Catching, Duncan Renaldo and Dale Robertson appearing at the Kiawana's Devonshire Fair in 1950. (Courtesy of Bill Catching.)

I see their tonsils, that'll be close enough.'" Marshall Reed, Lane Chandler and I. Stanford Jolley were featured in Landres' triad and Phyllis Coates, Bill Kennedy, Mike Ragan and Tom Tyler in his quartet. These seven were the best episodes in the first season and one of them, "Pancho Hostage," boasts one of the wackiest aphorisms ever to issue from the mouth of Leo Carrillo: "If a monkey had wings instead of a tail, he could swim in the water like a rabbit."

Whatever Duncan Renaldo owed to others, he clearly owed the most to Leo Carrillo. "In the first year," Bill Catching told me, "Duncan got $320 per week, $160 per episode, and Leo got $1,000 plus a percentage. The second year Leo got Duncan to sign with Leo's agent, William Morris, and Duncan's salary was increased." Without Carrillo's intervention there never would have been a second year for Renaldo in the series, because he was still in the United States illegally. "I was on the set when they came and picked him up," Catching remembered. "I think it was the end of the first year or the beginning of the second year that the immigration department came to the studio and picked him up....Leo Carrillo, who had more important connections in politics than anyone else in Hollywood, pulled strings and helped him to become a legal citizen."

Carrillo, Paul Landres told me, "was one h... of a rider, and he spoke English as well as I did but he was always talking in the Pancho dialect. After the first episodes he started to have fun. I'd have a shot of him coming up over a low hill....He knew I'd be in front of the camera, so when he's coming up the hill, he flicks the horse's head towards the camera, and the horse is coming right for me, and just at the last moment he flicks him away and rides by the camera. It was quite a shot but it was always a scary thing, because if that horse was a fraction of a second later he'd be into me. That was going on constantly."

During the 1951-52 season Landres was

Pictured above is Paul Landres working on **Frontier Gun** (1958). On the back cover of the book is Paul today. (Both courtesy of Paul Landres.)

probably the most overworked director in America, helming twenty of the 26 episodes that made up **The Cisco Kid**'s second season plus 17 segments of the **Boston Blackie** series that Ziv launched that year. That one man could turn out approximately 18 1/2 hours of footage in less than twelve months is amazing enough. Even more astonishing is that the best **Cisco** episodes Landres directed that season were easily the finest in the series and arguably the most exciting exploits of the character ever committed to film. Scads of action, bizarre storylines, excellent supporting casts, Panchoisms galore—these episodes had it all.

One of the luckiest innovations in second-season Cisco was the replacement of Albert Glasser's threadbare background music with a fine new score. Early in the season's first episode, "Phoney Heiress," Cisco and Pancho race after a runaway buckboard with a young woman in it. Every B Western fan has watched hundreds of

scenes very much like it, but what makes this rendition special is the superb agitato score, which continued in use not only for the rest of **Cisco**'s second season but, with additions by other composers, throughout the rest of the program's run. Anyone with ears can tell that the music isn't by Glasser, but since music scores are never mentioned in Ziv credit crawls I can't identify the person who so enriched the rest of the Cisco saga.

The single weakness in the season's output was that too many outdoor scenes were shot indoors, on a cramped soundstage garnished with ugly fake trees and rocks in the manner of **The Lone Ranger**. A case can be made for filming TV Western episodes this way, and veteran director Thomas Carr made it when I taped a conversation with him several years ago. "You'd do your establishing shots [outdoors] and then you'd go into what we called a green set....built inside, on the stage, where you have rocks, you have trees, you have big cycloramas of scenery. You can do

136

Since we do not have any more stills from the TV series we'll use some more from the movie series. A Lobby Card from 1949 picturing Duncan Renaldo, Stanley Andrews and John Litel. (Courtesy of Boyd Magers.)

wagon train scenes or anything in that space....You're restricted, you can't expand, you can't see into the distance, you have a painted cyclorama in the background, not the horizon.... [But] it was easier for me because I had more control. You didn't have to worry about the elements or moving heavy equipment or terrain or anything. You just moved the dirt or moved a rock. In the outdoor pictures, when you wanted to climb up rocks you had to pull the cameras up by ropes. [Shooting indoors,] you just put the camera on a crane and got it up high and shot down." As the Fifties went on and the TV Western grew into a gigantic industry, most series followed the lead of *The Lone Ranger* and second-season *Cisco* when it came to shooting street and trail scenes on a closed set. Directors had more control and saved time and money but deprived us in the audience of what had been one of the central pleasures of watching Westerns: seeing the real outdoors.

Usually the loss of the land's beauty wasn't worth the gains in efficiency, but Paul Landres invested his finest Cisco segments with such visual flair that you hardly notice how much footage was shot on a soundstage. On every criterion by which series Westerns are judged I would rank "Protective Association," "Water Toll" and "Buried Treasure" ahead of almost any Cisco feature, and other segments like "Vigilante Story" and "Sleeping Gas" are almost as good. Perhaps Landres' second-season casts boasted fewer old favorites from theatrical B Westerns but they did include, among a host of less familiar names, stalwarts like Reed Howes, Pierce Lyden, Stanley Andrews, Bud Osborne, Myron Healey, Steve Clark, Terry Frost, John Merton, Earle Hodgins, Edmund Cobb, Milburn Morante, John Cason, Raphael Bennett and Kermit Maynard. First-season workhorse J. Benton Cheney also wrote most of the brace of scripts for 1951-52 but transcended his usual lack of imagination and came up with some memorably weird storylines. In

A Lobby Card from 1949 picturing Ralph Peters, Leo Carrillo, Stanley Andrews and Duncan Renaldo. (Courtesy of Boyd Magers.)

"Jewelry Store Fence" a crazy old man tries to kill Cisco and Pancho with a crossbow built into an ornate clock. "Foreign Agent" dealt with spies from a nameless evil empire (a surprisingly common element in TV Western episodes from the HUAC-Red Menace era) seeking control of a tungsten lode in the old West. "Sleeping Gas" pitted Cisco and Pancho against a family of bank robbers whose modus operandi involved a high-pitched fiddle and an ornamental globe full of the titular gas. "Buried Treasure" with its witchcraft and reincarnation motifs is perhaps the most bizarre episode in the entire series, with Cisco revealed as the living image of pirate Jean Lafitte and trying to save Lafitte's cabin boy, now a very old man, from being tortured by an ancient hag and her sons who are after Lafitte's lost booty. If I had to pick a handful of *Cisco* episodes to be preserved for future generations while the rest were destroyed, this is definitely one I'd save, along with "Protective Association," which is

stagebound but crammed with action, and "Water Toll," which was filmed in the open and includes the single finest sequence in the entire Cisco series as Landres' tracking shots follow Renaldo chasing outlaw leader Michael Whalen into a swamp.

Landres' workload came vividly to life in the course of my conversation with him. "One month we were doing seven shows with Cisco and six with Boston Blackie, the next month we were doing seven with Blackie and six with Cisco." The episodes were organized in groups of two or three, featuring the same character actors and often the same character name for the same actor in different segments. What made this assembly-line method possible was the master scheduling board prepared by production manager Eddie Davis. Babe Unger, says Landres, "was as sharp as they come but he didn't know anything at all about production. As far as he was concerned, that board was sacrosanct....Eddie never came out on

138

A Lobby Card from 1949 picturing Barbara Billingsley, John Litel, Frank Ellis, Terry Frost, Leo Carrillo, Duncan Renaldo and George De Normand. (Courtesy of Boyd Magers.)

location. He stayed in and he was always there with Babe, holding Babe's right hand. Which I didn't like, because I knew d... well he was cutting my throat behind my back." Everything on the scheduling board "was broken down according to locations. They had scenes that were being done outside, up at Pioneertown, and they had stuff that was being done on the sets inside. When we went out on location it was crazy. When we were shooting six or seven episodes we might spend a week up in Pioneertown. The rest we'd do on stage, on the sets." Landres at first had a problem keeping his actors' names straight but he solved it by calling them by their cast names, which were usually the same in each episode within a group. "I started keeping a list of all the actors I ever worked with, and from that I could cast anything, anytime, anywhere. The bad ones I never called back."

Most of the scripts Landres directed were written by J. Benton Cheney. "They were

designed for three action scenes per script, and they were usually impossible to do. They just couldn't be done on our schedule....I would read these things and I'd go screaming in to Joe Cheney and his answer always was: 'Well, that's what Babe wants.' So I'd go in to see Babe, and every time I told him that it was impossible to do what was in the script because of the schedule, he'd look me dead in the eye and say: 'Well, what can you do?' Now the ball was back in my court, so I would really have to extend myself and dream up something that would take the place of this. In effect it was pretty much the same thing but it was in a doable way, and I'd go back and tell Joe what I was going to do and have him write it. It was a very tough situation for me because he had three of these things, one action scene every eight minutes I think it was."

Not all of these action scenes worked out exactly as planned. "One time," Troy Melton recalled, "I had to chase Bill [Catching], jump

139

A Lobby Card from 1949 picturing Barbara Billingsley, Lee "Lasses" White and Duncan Renaldo. (Courtesy of Boyd Magers.)

from my horse, land on the back of his horse, scissor him with my legs, and then catch a limb as we went under it and pull him off the horse. The force of gravity pulled my legs out and we both busted our butts on the ground."

The breakneck pace soon began to affect Landres' health. "I'd come home from a day's shooting and I'd have to prepare. Not the next day's work, because I'd have all seven of them done before I set foot on the stage, but I had to prepare the next group as soon as I was given the scripts. That meant that I'd come home, say at seven o'clock at night, have dinner, work at home until twelve, get up around five or six o'clock in the morning, work for a couple of hours preparing, and get on the set." The demands on him were so great that "I didn't even have time to look at any of the shows as they were edited....But I knew that everything went together because I shot it for the cutting room. That makes a vast difference. My background as an editor

was of tremendous help to me."

How much was Landres being paid for this nonstop work? "I think I was getting $500 a week for directing three episodes a week. Then the Guild was able to get a deal where the director would get $520 per episode and I went from $500 to more than $1500 a week. That was a h... of a bump." But he was pushing himself so hard that eventually "I had to accept Eddie Davis' help."

Davis, as we've seen, had joined the Cisco series as assistant director on its earliest segments after working in that capacity on some of the Monogram Cisco features and countless other B Westerns of the Forties. That he was given a chance to direct in his own right came about largely through the recommendation of Troy Melton. "I said to Babe: 'You've got one guy on the lot right now who would make a fine director and that's Eddie Davis. The guy is very knowledgeable, he knows horses, he knows what you can get done with horses, he knows actors, he

A Lobby Card from 1949 picturing George De Normand, Leo Carrillo, Frank Ellis and Duncan Renaldo. (Courtesy of Boyd Magers.)

knows how to work with actors.' Babe said: 'Well, I'm going to keep that in mind, Troy.'"

In the middle of shooting the superb "Protective Association" episode Landres almost fainted from influenza and had to be sent home. With his permission, Eddie Davis took over as director. "It happened," Troy Melton told me, "that everything we had the rest of that day was action stuff. Bill [Catching] and I had a fight to do on a balcony where I had to come through a rail and swing out on a chandelier. When I saw Eddie come in on the set I said: 'What's doing here?' He said: 'They're going to let me direct the rest of the show, Troy. You'll stick with me, will you?' I said: 'You know that,' because I liked Eddie. I got with Bill and said: 'Bill, this is all action this afternoon. Let's try to do everything in one take, as fast as we can get things done.' Then I talked to some of the crew and said: 'Here's a chance to give one of our guys a break, so let's get in there and pitch.' Which we did.

"A little later, maybe five-thirty or six o'clock, I was outside, the sun was shining down nice, and I ran into Babe. He said: 'What's going on? What's happening?' I said: 'We wrapped. We finished for the day.' He was flabbergasted and asked how we could be finished so early. I said: 'You've got a director.' That's when Eddie Davis was born."

The experience convinced Davis to direct full-time, with Unger taking over as production manager. "I think [Eddie] was a natural-born director or something," Bill Catching told me, "because he'd been an assistant so long, and worked with so many of the good, fast directors. He put quality into the shows. He and Landres I think did some of the best." But Davis had his share of problems with the front office too. As production manager he had been "pretty tight with a dollar." But now that he was directing, "Babe starts using the tactics on Eddie that Eddie had used on the other guys. And Eddie says: 'Wait a minute! You can't do this! I'm the director!' And

A Title Card for **Gay Amigo** (1949) picturing Duncan Renaldo, Armida and Leo Carrillo. (Courtesy of Boyd Magers.)

Babe says: 'Yes? Tell me more!'"

Four of Davis' initial half dozen are rather ordinary but the other two rank with the best in the series. "Hidden Valley," with Cisco and Pancho blundering into and becoming rebel leaders in the Western equivalent of a lost civilization, ruled with an iron hand by a tyrannical ex-sea captain and his terror squads, is so densely packed with action and incident (even a sword duel at the climax) that it might almost have been a condensed version of a 12-chapter cliffhanger serial. And "Ghost Town" with its spooky elements menacing a young woman as she searches through the deserted town for her identity is a fine merger of Western action with the old-dark-house thriller. Studded through Davis' cast lists were fugitives from Monogram B Westerns like Stephen Chase, Dennis Moore, Tristram Coffin, I. Stanford Jolley, Keith Richards, Riley Hill, Denver Pyle and Zon Murray. When not directing Cisco adventures,

Davis spent his 1951-52 workdays turning out half a dozen episodes of *Boston Blackie*.

My own enthusiasm for second-season *Cisco* as a youngster and today was not universally shared. In fact some of the season's most imaginative episodes generated a surprising amount of controversy. TV Guide for February 20, 1953 printed a letter from Sid Kipness of Dumont, N.J. condemning the "Buried Treasure" segment. "My five-year-old daughter was frightened by the old witch. If this is for children, I'll send the makers of Tip Top Bread a broom for an award." Viewers must have written in the same vein about this and other *Cisco* episodes either to the local bread-company sponsors or to Ziv's offices. Before work began on the third season, Unger handed down some rigid new edicts to his staff. There will be no more knife fights as in "Romany Caravan." No more witchcraft or any supernatural elements like the reincarnation motif in "Buried Treasure." Neither Cisco nor Pancho will ever again kill an

142

A Lobby Card from 1949 picturing Leo Carrillo watching Duncan Renaldo knocking out Joe Sawyer (who has on a wristwatch). (Courtesy of Boyd Magers.)

adversary as they had in several episodes from the first and second seasons including "Vigilante Story" and "Romany Caravan." And so on until very little was left except the most simple-minded and juvenile material.

Small wonder that the third season was such a letdown. Most of the outdoor scenes were once again shot outdoors but the front office edicts forced the storylines and direction into standard conventional patterns. Paul Landres had left Ziv to direct 24 of the 52 new episodes of *The Lone Ranger*, with John Hart replacing Clayton Moore as the masked rider of the plains and almost all the action staged on the same sort of excruciating indoor sets Landres had contended with during his Cisco period. Eddie Davis took over as the 1952-53 season's principal director and helmed eleven of the third set of 26 episodes—two simultaneously shot triads, a matched pair, two singletons without companion episodes, and one segment whose companion piece was

unaccountably directed by someone else—but only the old-dark-house thriller "Fear" was in the same league with the best work of the second season. The casts of the Davis episodes were again heavy with veterans of Monogram's B Westerns like Marshall Reed, Zon Murray, Jack Ingram, Gail Davis (soon to star in her own series as Annie Oakley), Keith Richards, Bob Wilke, Kermit Maynard, John Cason, Hank Patterson, Myron Healey, Earle Hodgins, Forrest Taylor and Bill Henry. The taboos laid down by Ziv's front office explain why so many third-season episodes emphasized circus elements: an equestrian clown show in "Monkey Business," a puppet theater in "The Puppeteer," a medicine wagon complete with elephant in "Pancho and the Pachyderm" and, as if to prove that the taste for the weird could not be totally stamped out, a ventriloquist with a living dummy in "Laughing Badman."

In "Pancho and the Pachyderm," Bill Catching told me, "I was doubling Leo on top of the

PHILIP N. KRASNE presents
THE CISCO KID in "THE GAY AMIGO"

Based on
CISCO KID character created by O. Henry
Produced by Philip N. Krasne
Directed by Wallace Fox
Released thru United Artists

A Lobby Card trom 1949 picturing Duncan Renaldo on the side and Leo Carrillo looking in a window. (Courtesy of Boyd Magers.)

elephant. The old gal's name was Emma. She was from the alligator farm up there in Thousand Oaks. I had never ridden an elephant before, and she was shuffling along pretty good and the camera car's in front, and the director told the trainer: 'Make her go faster.' And they speeded up the camera car and the trainer yelled: 'EMMA!!' Man, she shifted gears like a car, and started forward so fast, the leather thing around her neck that I was holding to broke, and I rolled backwards off her. That was the tallest saddle fall I ever did."

Helming three of these circus segments plus four others was George M. Cahan, a novice whose only previous Western experience seems to have been as director of three episodes of the low-budget *Cowboy G-Men* series starring Russell Hayden and Jackie Coogan. "He didn't last very long," Bill Catching says. "He didn't understand action Western shows." But at least he knew enough to cast lots of Monogram B Western veterans like Leonard Penn, Raymond Hatton,

Mike Ragan, Ted Mapes, Tom London, House Peters, Jr., Zon Murray, Jack Ingram and Guy Wilkerson, and he saw the potential in newcomer Sheb Wooley, who near the end of the Fifties would stake out his claim to Western fame opposite Eric Fleming and Clint Eastwood in *Rawhide*. Two of Cahan's septet—scripted, as if you hadn't guessed, by J. Benton Cheney—were as off-trail as anything from the second season. "Face of Death" has Cisco and Pancho joining a murder-plagued archaeological expedition hunting an Aztec high priest's tomb, and in "Lost City" they come upon an Inca community complete with beautiful princess and try to save its treasure from thieves. The budget and time constraints combined with Cahan's inexperience to keep these episodes from living up to the expectations of their premises. After cranking out his seven *Cisco* shows plus four adventures of *Boston Blackie*, Cahan decided that high-speed action stuff was not his forte and switched to directing episodes of

144

A Lobby Card from 1949 picturing Walter Baldwin and Duncan Renaldo. (Courtesy of Boyd Magers.)

sitcoms like *Gilligan's Island* and *The Brady Bunch*. Since he's best known as a comedy director, we shall take leave of him by quoting a Panchoism tossed off by Carrillo during Cahan's "Laughing Badman" which will delight anyone who was forced in high school to memorize gobs of speechifying from *Julius Caesar*: "The evil that men live do after them. The good is oft interrupted in the bones."

Of the third season's other director perhaps more could have been expected. Sobey Martin was born in Leipzig, Germany in 1909 and, after attending the Sorbonne in Paris, emigrated to the United States where he worked in MGM's editorial department between 1936 and 1942. He served in the Army during World War II and began directing documentary films when the war was over. As far as I can tell he was the first person ever to direct a filmed episode of a TV series. The 26-segment series known alternatively as *Your Show Time* and *Story Theater*, broadcast on

NBC during the first half of 1949, offered 30-minute versions of short stories by writers like Stevenson, Conan Doyle, Mark Twain, de Maupassant and Oscar Wilde. The first episode aired was an adaptation of de Maupassant's "The Diamond Necklace," directed by Martin and starring John Beal, which won the first Emmy ever awarded for best film made for television. (Not that there was much competition in this category at the time.) Martin also directed for this series the first telefilm adaptation of a Sherlock Holmes story ("The Adventure of the Speckled Band," with Alan Napier as Holmes), a half-hour version of Mark Twain's "The Celebrated Jumping Frog of Calaveras County," and short films based on tales by Dickens, Stevenson and other greats. Less than three years later he was under contract at Ziv and churning out exploits of *Boston Blackie* and *Cisco*. There's nothing special in his eight *Cisco* segments except for a few featured players—Peggy Stewart, Roscoe Ates, a

145

A Lobby Card from 1949 picturing Duncan Renaldo and Leo Carrillo. (Courtesy of Boyd Magers.)

teen-age Bobby Blake, John Pickard, Bud Osborne, Rand Brooks—and, from "Bell of Santa Margarita," one gorgeous Panchoism: "It will be like hunting for noodles in a smokestack!" Martin kept busy throughout the Fifties and early Sixties directing episodes of *The Millionaire, United States Marshal, Gunsmoke, Rawhide* and other series. In 1964 he became a contract director for Irwin Allen's small-screen fantasy factory and spent the rest of the decade on series like *Voyage To The Bottom Of The Sea, Lost In Space, The Time Tunnel* and *Land Of The Giants*. He seems to have retired around 1970 and died on July 27, 1978.

Neither Cahan nor Martin lasted long on the *Cisco* series. "We put in long days," Troy Melton told me, "usually starting at four-thirty, five, six in the morning, and we never got home before dark, usually seven, eight or nine at night. It was telling on the crew, on the cast, on Leo and Duncan, on everybody. This one particular night I came in on

the lot, and as I walked in the front gate Babe Unger was standing there. He came over to me and said: 'Hey, Troy, how's it going?' I said: 'Well, you can see. The same old thing. Nothing's changed.' He said: 'What's wrong?' I said: 'Well, I don't know where you're getting these directors. Like Sobey Martin, George Cahan. They don't know from nothing. They don't know which end to put the hay in. I don't know where you're finding 'em, Babe, but these are not directors for our kind of show. These guys ask us to do things that you can't do, the wranglers can't handle the stuff. You've got to find some action directors, some guys who have worked around horses, who know what you can do with a horse, who know Westerns.'" Thanks at least in part to this conversation, the people brought in to helm the fourth season's adventures were of a higher caliber.

The 1953-54 quota of 26 episodes was split among five directors. Ten segments went to Eddie

146

Duncan Renaldo seems smitten in this scene from **In Old New Mexico** (Monogram,1945).

Davis and four to the briefly returning Paul Landres. Another four were assigned to old Cisco hand Lambert Hillyer, who had helmed **South Of The Rio Grande** with Renaldo as Cisco back in 1945 and was now under contract to direct episodes of Ziv's new Red Menace series *I Led Three Lives* as well as a few segments of *Cisco*. "Full Load Hillyer they called him," Bill Catching told me. "You could use quarter, half or full loads on the guns. Lambert was a little hard of hearing, and he thought you got better reactions if you used full loads. They finally had to get the SPCA after him, to say that you couldn't fire a full load, you had to use a quarter load if you were riding a horse or close to a horse. Because, man, that noise just made them horses freak out! It just devastated their ears."

A pair of fourth-season episodes were helmed by Herbert Leeds, who had directed 20th-Fox's last Cisco feature with Warner Baxter and four of the sequels with Cesar Romero. "He was determined," says Bill Catching. "He told everybody what to do and he had in his mind that the sky had to drop on Cisco. The bad guy had the gun pointed at Cisco's stomach, and Leeds had in mind that before the guy could cock the gun and fire it, Cisco would knock the gun away. And I said: 'No, God d... it! These blanks will hurt you! I don't want to do it.' And he said: 'Here, I'll show you. Point the gun at me, and before you can cock it and pull the trigger, I can knock it away.' And I said: 'No, Mr. Leeds, I don't want to do that.' He says: 'Do it! Come on!' I cocked the gun and pulled the trigger and shot him right in the stomach. That wad burned the h... out of him. If I'd have been closer...."

The remaining six of the fourth-season segments were directed by Lew Landers (1901-1962), who in an incredibly prolific career as a B picture director had turned out, sandwiched among dozens of mediocre non-Westerns, a few excellent shoot-em-ups like **Back In The Saddle**

147

Armida, Francis McDonald, Lillian Molierri, George J. Lewis, Duncan Renaldo and Martin Garralaga in a scene from **South of Rio Grande** (Monogram,1945).

(Republic, 1941, starring Gene Autry) and **Under The Tonto Rim** (RKO, 1947, with Tim Holt). As Bill Catching remembers it, the Cisco episodes had been on three-day shooting schedules when the Ziv executives summoned Landers and said: "Lew, we want to start making them in two days." To which Landers replied: "Sure! No argument at all!" and left his new employers wondering why the other directors had resisted the change. "But they didn't know Lew," Catching added. "He'd go out to do a show and if an actor read the wrong line he'd say: 'Print! Move the camera over here!'" Much of his slapdash approach must have been repaired by the film editors, because his segments don't look noticeably inferior to others from the fourth season.

Each of the directors organized his episodes in matched pairs with identical or overlapping casts and the work began. At first everything went well. Most rewarding of the early segments was a pair directed by Hillyer and featuring John Doucette, Francis McDonald and former Mesquiteers star Bob Livingston. "Pancho and the Wolf Dog" dealt with a wild dog and skullduggery at the West's first ice house, and "The Faded General" was about a senile ex-officer who locks up Cisco and Pancho in his private stockade. The climax of the latter episode recreated a breathtaking stunt from the Buck Jones feature **One Man Law** (Columbia, 1932) which Hillyer had both written and directed. Herbert Leeds added to the interest of one of his segments, "Bullets and the Booby Trap," by casting Bobby (not yet Robert) Blake as a teen-age inventor living in a ghost town with his shotgun-toting granny. Then disaster struck. A scene in the Lew Landers episode "Battle of Red Rock Pass" went haywire and a flying boulder almost broke Duncan Renaldo's neck.

"That was Duncan's fault," Bill Catching told me. "There was a cute girl on the set, Nan Leslie, a really sweet cute gal, and Duncan really liked her. He was single then and he was kind of

Armida, Duncan Renaldo and Leo Carrillo in a scene from **The Gay Amigo** (Monogram,1949).

pursuing her, and she kept teasing him and Leo that they were two old farts.... So when this scene came up, Troy [Melton] was supposed to do it. He was trailing this guy on foot and looking down at the tracks and Red Morgan, the stuntman actor up in the rocks, rolled this rock at him. It was a big phony rock but it weighed forty pounds or better. They made 'em out of plaster of Paris with wire. And Duncan came walking along, and he insisted on doing this scene because Nan had teased him. Troy and I almost yelled, but he never looked up, and there's nothing Red could do. He rolled the rock off and Duncan---there was a sound made so Duncan would look up and see it and step back. Well, he never even looked up. He had his head down and it hit him in the back of the head and knocked him down. He got up and staggered around and leaned against a rock and started to walk on and then he fell. We rushed over to him and kept him from moving and got him in the— we didn't even have ambulances or anything, we

had a station wagon that had a mattress in the back of it in case somebody got hurt. And we got him in it and took him to the hospital and found out that if he had moved a lot more....The vertebrae in his neck were just a fraction from being severed. He came within a fraction of being killed. He was in the hospital for about six weeks, I think, and in the interim Leo's wife died, and we did either two or three Ciscos without either Cisco or Pancho!"

What would have paralyzed most series seemed to energize the people responsible for this one. While Renaldo was convalescing in the hospital, directors and writers scrambled to concoct new storylines that would keep the star's face out of sight. Where this wasn't possible, the director would cover by photographing Troy Melton from odd angles. "They shot me during the day," Melton recalled during our conversation. "I actually did the dialogue with the other actors, and I did the entire show. At night they would go to

149

Duncan Renaldo enters the saloon ready for anything in this scene from **Satan's Cradle** (Monogram,1949). (Courtesy of Jerry Ohlinger's Movie Material Store.)

the hospital bedside. Duncan would read the dialogue that I had and do it over and they recorded him and put his voice on the soundtrack." When all else failed, the director would recycle footage of Renaldo from pre-accident episodes and later shoot a few extreme close-ups of him against a blue backdrop once he was on the mend. Not only did everyone survive the crisis but, according to Melton, "we hardly lost any time at all."

The segments made while Renaldo was recovering are marked in this book's filmography with an asterisk. Most of them were directed by Eddie Davis and the most ingenious of the lot was "Bandaged Badman." A gunman hired to kill Cisco is blown up in an explosion, and Cisco has a friendly doctor identify the remains as himself and cover his face with bandages so he can pose as the assassin, claim he was burned in the explosion but not killed, and try to connect with whoever paid for the murder. Not having to worry about keeping the double's face concealed, Davis

crammed this episode with more action and stunts than one ever saw in a TV Western series of the time except for *The Range Rider*.

Different coping strategies were devised for other segments. In "The Black Terror," where Cisco invents a masked-bandit persona for himself so he can join a gang of outlaw brothers and break them up from within, Davis cast Reed Howes as the oldest brother so he could recycle Howes' fight scenes with Renaldo from two second-season episodes directed by Paul Landres, "Stolen Bonds" and "Protective Association." But as if to tell the world that he and no one else was in charge, he made sure that in one of the town scenes the camera focused on a sign reading ED DAVIS/FANCY SADDLES. Lew Landers, who clearly wasn't blamed for Renaldo's accident since he continued to work on the series as if nothing had happened, fused these ploys for "The Iron Mask." The outlandish storyline had Cisco replacing a sheriff who's been locked inside the

150

Duncan Renaldo shoots one of the villains on the street of Pioneertown in this scene from **Satan's Cradle** (Monogram,1949). (Courtesy of Jerry Ohlinger's Movie Material Store.)

titular mask by outlaws, and Michael Whalen was cast as the gang leader so the episode could end with Paul Landres' magnificent chase-into-the-swamp sequence from "Water Toll."

The series briefly experimented with a new approach after Renaldo recovered. In a matched pair of episodes directed by Landres, "Not Guilty" and "Horseless Carriage," José Gonzales Gonzales was introduced as Pancho's young nephew José with the evident intent of adding a younger continuing character loosely modeled on Dan Reid, the masked man's nephew in *The Lone Ranger*. The plan fizzled out and Gonzales never again appeared in a Cisco episode. "I couldn't understand him," Landres told me. "It didn't work out too well." Bill Catching however says that Gonzales "got more laughs than Pancho" and Carrillo couldn't tolerate being upstaged.

Of the 26 episodes shot for the 1954-55 season, two were directed by Eddie Davis, one by a newcomer to Westerns who will be formally introduced later in this chapter, and a staggering 23 by Lambert Hillyer, who brought to these fifth-season segments the abundant professional skills he'd acquired in almost forty years at his job but nothing special that made them stand out in a crowd. "Trouble in Tonopah," in which Cisco tries to figure out how someone learned the combination to the Tonopah express office's burglarproof safe and pulled off a series of baffling thefts, is historically interesting because it was the single Cisco script written by that prolific B Western hand Oliver Drake. If you think the storyline sounds familiar even though you've never heard of this episode before, there's a reason: Drake recycled it from his script for the George O'Brien feature **Trouble In Sundown** (RKO, 1939).

Long-memoried viewers who have seen a lot of B Western features may get the same sense of *déjà vu* from other fifth-season episodes. In "Pancho's Niece" Cisco has his *compañero* pose as the uncle of a half-Mexican young woman whose

151

Duncan Renaldo and Leo Carrillo work on the church in this scene from **Satan's Cradle** (Monogram,1949). (Courtesy of Jerry Ohlinger's Movie Material Store.)

banker father apparently killed himself after losing most of the bank's money. The script for this one is credited to Barry Cohon but actually it's a condensed remake of the Buck Jones feature **The Fighting Code** (Columbia, 1933) which Hillyer had both written and directed. He borrowed from himself again in "Juggler's Silver," restaging for the second time in a Cisco episode the spectacular stunt Buck Jones or his double performed in the 1932 **One Man Law**. And in "New Evidence," where Cisco sets out to clear a young man on trial for the murder of his girlfriend's father, Hillyer or scriptwriter Ande Lamb borrowed heavily from the courtroom sequence of John Ford's classic **Young Mr. Lincoln** (20th Century-Fox, 1939).

Aside from historical curiosities like these, fifth-season Cisco segments tended to be solid and reliable without any particular distinction. Most of the scripts were standard issue, Hillyer's casts were about the same as usual—Dennis Moore, Earle Hodgins, Zon Murray, Nan Leslie, John

Cason, Bill Kennedy, Myron Healey, Kenneth MacDonald, Kermit Maynard, I. Stanford Jolley, Leonard Penn, Keith Richards, Lane Bradford, Eddy Waller, Jack Ingram, Raymond Hatton, Marshall Reed, Hank Patterson, Edmund Cobb, Rory Mallinson, Sam Flint, Terry Frost, Glenn Strange—and all in all the Cisco series seemed to be getting a bit stale. In the entire season's output there was only one memorable Panchoism, from "Extradition Papers": "Goodbye, little toes. The next time I see you, I won't be looking at you."

In the fall of 1955 the so-called adult Western began to dominate television with the debuts of **Gunsmoke** and **The Life And Legend Of Wyatt Earp**, and it soon became obvious that the days of the more juvenile oriented series were numbered. The 1955-56 season was the sixth for **The Cisco Kid**, and the weakest, and the last. Hillyer directed 13 of the final 26 episodes but the only one that comes close to his best work for the series was the action-packed "Gold, Death and

Ann Savage and Duncan Renaldo in a publicity photo for **Satan's Cradle** (Monogram,1949). (Courtesy of Jerry Ohlinger's Movie Material Store.)

Dynamite." By the time he completed his sixth-season quota he was well into his sixties, perhaps almost 70, and had put in close to forty years as a director. It was time to retire. He died on July 5, 1969. His best Westerns from all periods—with William S. Hart in the Nineteen Teens and early Twenties, Buck Jones in the Thirties, Bill Elliott in the early Forties, Johnny Mack Brown in the middle and later Forties, and a few at least of his *Cisco* TV episodes with Duncan Renaldo—will continue to be enjoyed as long as there is an audience for the genre.

The sixth season's remaining 13 episodes as well as the final episode from the fifth season were directed by a newcomer to the shoot-em-up. Leslie Goodwins, born in London on September 17, 1889, had cut his professional eyeteeth in the Thirties making comedy shorts at RKO. One of his assistants at that time was later superstar director Robert Aldrich. "You could learn more about comedy assisting Les Goodwins on a two-reel Leon Errol than you could spending two years at film school," Aldrich said near the end of his own life. Goodwins graduated to directing features in 1937. Most of his films from then till 1946 were segments of unpretentious RKO comedy series, like the Mexican Spitfire pictures with Lupe Velez and his two-reeler star Leon Errol, or forgettable low-budget musicals for the same studio. The closest he ever came to directing a Western was **The Singing Sheriff** (RKO, 1944), a croon-em-up with Bob Crosby. The first TV series he worked on was the original version of *The Life Of Riley*, broadcast on the Dumont network during the 1949-50 season and starring the then little known Jackie Gleason. Sharing directorial chores on that series, as we saw a few chapters ago, was Cisco alumnus Herbert Leeds, who had killed himself a year or so before Goodwins unaccountably landed at Ziv.

Why he was asked or agreed to become the last director of Cisco episodes remains a mystery.

Duncan Renaldo introduces Ann Savage to a shy Leo Carrillo in this scene from **Satan's Cradle** (Monogram,1949). (Courtesy of Jerry Ohlinger's Movie Material Store.)

Certainly he wasn't very good at this kind of film: his segments aren't weighted towards comedy as his background might have led one to expect, and in terms of drama and action they're hopelessly inept. But his episodes are graced by the last two Panchoisms worth quoting. From "The Epidemic": "Cisco, we're kind of down the river without water, huh?" And from "Tangled Trails," the 156th and final installment of the series and the only one since early 1953 to be written by the pioneer Cisco TV scripter J. Benton Cheney: "If I had money I would have such a big garden I could be arrested for fragrancy."

Goodwins wasn't much younger than Lambert Hillyer but he continued to direct for many years after the Cisco series came to an end. From 1959 through 1962, under contract to Warner Bros., he helmed episodes of *Maverick, Cheyenne, Bronco, Sugarfoot, The Alaskans* and *Surfside 6.* Will Hutchins, the star of *Sugarfoot,* remembers Goodwins as "a round, bespectacled gent with a

Cockney accent....With a wry smile he referred to those days as the twilight of his career. He was a good bloke; no airs about him. He came to work and did his job. One morning [on a *Sugarfoot* episode] he shot fifteen pages before lunch." From Warners he moved on to direct for a number of well-known Sixties sitcoms like *My Favorite Martian, F Troop* and *Gilligan's Island*. He died on January 8, 1970 at the age of eighty.

When the shooting on *Cisco* stopped, Carrillo looked in his fifties but in fact was approaching his 75th birthday. His wife Edith had died in 1953 after a marriage lasting four decades. Having spent half a century in show business, Carrillo had no need or desire to work any longer. He retired to his Santa Monica ranch, managed his property, rode as grand marshal in civic parades, and spent his spare time writing an informal history of his state, *The California I Love*, which was published by Prentice-Hall in 1961, the year he celebrated his eightieth birthday. A month later, on

154

THE CISCO KID
"THE GIRL FROM SAN LORENZO"
DUNCAN RENALDO
LEO CARRILLO

Original Screenplay by FORD BEEBE   Directed by DERWIN ABRAHAMS
Produced by PHILIP N. KRASNE   Released thru United Artists

A Lobby Card from 1950 picturing Duncan Renaldo, David Sharpe, Don Harvey and Leo Carrillo. (Courtesy of Boyd Magers.) **Below:** A Newspaper Ad from 1945. (Courtesy of Charles K. Stumpf.)

September 10, with his daughter Marie Antoinette and his brother Ottie at the bedside, Leo Carrillo died of cancer.

Duncan Renaldo also retired after the Cisco TV series halted production. He bought a hacienda in Santa Barbara with a view of the Pacific, relaxed, put on some weight, and smoked more than was good for him. Jon Tuska, who interviewed Renaldo in the early and middle 1970s, described him in *The Filming Of The West* as "one of the most charming men I have ever known....White-haired, his lined countenance ruddy with a persistent youthfulness,....at peace with the world...." (438) On September 3, 1980, a week short of nineteen years after the death of his *compañero*, Duncan Renaldo died in Goleta Valley Community Hospital. The cause was lung cancer. His age, if you accept the one birth certificate he had whose date has been published, was seventy-six.

MONOGRAM PICTURES presents
DUNCAN RENALDO
THE CISCO KID RETURNS
MARTIN GARRALAGA (AS PANCHO)   ROGER PRYOR   CECILIA CALLEJO

155

TV's dashing 'Cisco Kid' dies

GOLETA, Calif. (AP) — Duncan Renaldo, who served time in prison for perjury but as the "Cisco Kid" brought law and order to television's Wild West, has died at the age of 76.

He had been suffering from lung cancer and succumbed to heart failure Wednesday in Goleta Valley Community Hospital.

Renaldo, best known to America's first television generation, for his part in 159 episodes of "The Cisco Kid" from 1949-56, also had 164 movies to his credit, including "The Bridge of San Luis Rey," "For Whom the Bell Tolls" and "Zorro Rides Again."

Born Renault Renaldo Duncan, he was stranded in America in 1922 as a merchant marine when his ship burned at dockside in Baltimore. Renaldo went to New York and worked his way up from janitor to scene designer, producer and writer at the old Tec Art movie studio.

He went to Hollywood in 1926. His first leading role was in "Trader Horn," but his life was disrupted just before the movie's premiere in 1931 when he was arrested by immigration authorities for entering the country illegally.

After a sensational trial, he was found guilty of perjury for claiming he'd been born in New Jersey. Renaldo, who thought he'd been born in Spain, served 18 months in prison.

President Franklin D. Roosevelt granted him an unconditional pardon the day before he was to be released. Renaldo later called that episode "the most interesting and tragic time of my life."

By 1940, he was starring in Westerns, and won the lead role in "The Cisco Kid" movies and TV series in 1944.

He and his sidekick, Pancho, played by the late Leo Carrillo, portrayed cowboys who used their wits instead of their guns to bring justice to the Old West.

"'The Cisco Kid' was a cheerful show," he once said. "Pancho and I never killed anyone. The kids that watched our show went to sleep smiling and not with nightmares."

Renaldo always credited "the kids" for his success and said the prayers of 17,000 young fans who sent him get-well cards were responsible for his speedy recovery from a broken neck he received in 1953 during filming of the series.

"It may sound strange to some people," he said then. "But I am convinced that it is the young children who have helped me make a miraculous recovery. There is no other explanation."

Renaldo is survived by his wife, Audrey, daughter Stephanie, and three sons, Richard, Jeremy and Edwin Renaldo.

A funeral Mass will be held Friday night at Santa Barbara's Old Mission, with private burial on Saturday.

Top: Photo of Duncan Renaldo with Diablo in 1973. **Bottom:** The obituary of Duncan Renaldo as it appeared in a September 1976 newspaper. (Both courtesy of Charles K. Stumpf.)

Ten • A Sensitive Nineties Cisco: Jimmy Smits

During the first run of the Ziv TV series, most of America's Ciscophiles were kids. Few if any who followed those 156 episodes were old enough to have seen Cesar Romero, let alone Warner Baxter, in 20th Century-Fox's two cycles of Cisco features; and since the major studios including 20th-Fox were boycotting the new medium and not allowing their old pictures to be shown on the small screen, viewers had no way to compare the TV series with the Cisco movies of previous generations. The three Monogram features with Renaldo and Martin Garralaga and the six with Gilbert Roland were seen on countless local stations, as were the five Inter-American pictures with Renaldo and Carrillo. Usually the titles of these films were changed for TV: **The Cisco Kid Returns** became **The Daring Adventurer, The Gay Amigo** was switched to **The Daring Rogue, The Daring Caballero** got the new name of **Guns And Fury, Satan's Cradle** was altered to **The Devil's Den** and **The Girl From San Lorenzo** found a second life as **Don Amigo.** As if that weren't confusing enough, all references to the Cisco character and even to O. Henry were blacked out of the credits of the TV prints, and whenever "The Cisco Kid," "Cisco" or "Pancho" occurred in the dialogue, either the words were erased so that the actor's lips would move with nothing coming out, or else the new speakers would recite "Chico Villa," "Chico" or "Pablo" onto the soundtrack in voices that even the deaf could tell were not those of the original cast. In **The Gay Amigo,** the alteration resulted in Renaldo explaining that his name Chico was short for Francisco. Why this nonsense was thought necessary I have no idea, but it did cost money: in one feature where a reward poster for Cisco was nailed to a tree, someone actually took the trouble to insert a new shot, showing a poster for that notorious bandit, Chico Villa! Videocassettes copied from these old 16mm prints still exist today and tend to cause giggling fits when a Western fan stumbles upon them. Thanks to the alterations in the Cisco features, and to the use of Renaldo's and Carrillo's images from the TV series both in Dell's Cisco comic book (41 issues, 1950-58) and the daily Cisco comic strip by Rod Reed and José Luis Salinas (1951-68), the millions of us who first discovered the compadres on the small screen find it hard to accept anyone else in the roles—not even Renaldo himself when, as in the features, his looks and outfit are different. Ziv shut down production on the series in 1956 but, having been shot in color, it continued in syndication for decades and can still be seen on local and cable stations today.

The kids who had ridden the TV trails with Hoppy, Gene, Roy, Cisco and The Lone Ranger all too soon grew up. Some looked back on those figures as heroes, others as jokes. It's anyone's guess how they were remembered by the rock group WAR, whose 1973 song about one of them rose to the number two spot on the pop charts.

> Cisco Kid
> He was a friend of mine
> Cisco Kid
> He was a friend of mine.
> He'd drink whiskey
> Pancho drank some wine.
> He'd drink whiskey
> Pancho drank that wine.

Sounds like the WARriors were thinking of Gilbert Roland and his tequila ritual, assuming Cisco really meant anything to them at all. But the makers of *Hill Street Blues* (NBC-TV, 1981-87), the premier TV cop series of the Eighties, left no doubt about their affection for Cisco when they chose for the program's third-season debut (October 13, 1983) a tale about a joyously demented Hispanic, played by Martin Ferrero, who's convinced that he is Cisco and, in an outfit like Duncan Renaldo's and astride a stallion that could be mistaken in dim light for Diablo, rides the mean streets of the city helping its cops keep the peace.

Early in the 1980s screenwriter Michael Kane

made Cisco and Pancho the main characters in a script that borrowed from the period's most spectacular movie success by having the compadres hunt for an old West version of the Lost Ark. The project knocked around for more than a decade and wound up at Turner Pictures, the company formed to produce original features for Ted Turner's TNT cable network. Signed to direct the film and revise Kane's script so as to "kick it into the Nineties" was the foremost Latino playwright-moviemaker north of the Rio Grande.

Luis Valdez (1940-   ) grew up in California's San Joaquin Valley, one of ten children born to a migrant worker couple. "When I was very young," he told a Washington Post reporter, "I was severely scalded and almost died. The local hospital refused to admit me because I was a 'farm labor' child....So for six months I slept on my mother's stomach while the skin on my back came back into place." After Pearl Harbor the Army offered the Valdez family and many other Mexican farm workers the properties that had belonged to California's Japanese-Americans, now forcibly moved into detention camps. "So from 1942 until 1946 we had a ranch, we had land, we had money. I grew up with all that." The family lost the farm after the war and Luis was soon picking cotton for three dollars a day.

In the early 1960s, as a scholarship student at San Jose State College, Valdez discovered his twin careers as playwright and political activist, fusing them in 1965 when he organized El Teatro Campesino, a troupe that rode around the fields performing *actos* (propaganda skits) on the backs of flatbed trucks in support of the United Farm Workers strike to unionize migrant laborers. One of Valdez' sketches from this period was "El Bandido," which was loosely based on his child-hood memories of the late-Forties Cisco features and the TV series. In his version as he described it recently, "Pancho finally asks the operative question: 'Cisco, why the h... are we always helping gringos?'" In 1971 he settled El Teatro Campesino in San Juan Bautista, a tiny farm town 35 miles south of San Jose.

The best known play Valdez wrote during his firebrand years was *Zoot Suit* (1978), a drama-tization of the Sleepy Lagoon case of the 1940s where twelve Chicano street kids were sentenced to life in prison for a murder probably committed by none of them. Co-starring in the play were Valdez' brother Daniel and a young actor named Edward James Olmos who went on to become a movie and TV star and won an Emmy for his role as Lt. Castillo on the *Miami Vice* series. The play won the Los Angeles Drama Critics Circle award and ran in southern California for almost a year.

Valdez then became the first Latino dramatist to have one of his works produced on Broadway but the play closed in New York after five weeks. The movie **Zoot Suit** (Universal, 1981), shot by Valdez on a two-week schedule and a $3,000,000 budget, was a disaster. As one sympathetic observer commented, "They might as well have given him a jar and said, Cross the ocean."

Both critically and commercially Valdez did much better with **La Bamba** (New Visions/ Columbia, 1987), which propelled Lou Diamond Phillips to stardom playing Ritchie Valens, the Chicano rock-n-roll legend who died in a 1959 plane crash at the age of seventeen. "Our attempt now is to reach as large an audience as possible," Valdez said, meaning that he no longer identified himself as a Latino writing and directing for other Latinos but instead would work to balance his ethnic interests with his desire for mainstream commercial success. Former ideological comrades accused him of selling out to the gringos and started calling him Tio Taco, which is the same as calling a black man Uncle Tom. He apparently saw the Cisco project as a golden opportunity to prove he could be as anti-gringo as ever and still make a hit.

"Cisco and Pancho were fun characters," he told TV Guide, "and I was really taken with them [as a child] because they were the only Mexican heroes on the screen." When Turner Pictures hired him to direct and rewrite **The Cisco Kid** (1994), he aimed for it to be two kinds of picture in one: a wild Spielbergesque action flick and a strong assertion of ethnic pride and defiance like "El Bandido" and his earlier features. For the music beneath the credits he chose WAR's 20-year-old Cisco song. As Cisco he cast Jimmy Smits, the handsome young actor of Puerto Rican and Dutch descent who had become a household name playing attorney Victor Sifuentes on the *L.A. Law* series. For the part of Pancho he signed Cheech Marin, best known as the co-star of **Up In Smoke** and other marijuana comedies. The crew and cast were almost all Latino except of course for the Anglo characters, each of whom is a walking cesspool of evil. "If the film is labeled as politically correct," pronounced one of TNT's senior vice-presidents, "that's not a bad brush to be tarred with." If TNT had bothered to season the storyline with some non-political common sense, or had hired a competent second unit director to shoot what passes in the picture for action sequences, **The Cisco Kid** might have turned into a watchable telefilm. As broadcast, it was an unholy mess.

The year is 1867 and, as we learn much later, a dashing young Californio named Francisco

Hernan Sanchez Aguilar de Solares, Cisco for short (Jimmy Smits), has led a grungy assortment of Confederate veterans into Mexico for the purpose of selling a wagonload of Civil War weapons, including a Gatling gun, to the revolutionaries under Benito Juarez who are fighting to overthrow the French-supported puppet emperor Maximilian. Cisco has gotten into some never specified trouble trying to rescue a woman named Libertad from a French army brothel and wound up in a prison cell under sentence of death. In another cell awaiting the same fate is Francisco Rivera, known as Pancho (Cheech Marin), a Juarista with a price on his head, disguised as a priest. (The French think he's a genuine priest and why they're about to kill him is something else Valdez never bothers to explain.) The film opens with its best scene as these two strangers to one another are yoked together with a ball and chain and dragged through the foul prison corridors to the courtyard where a firing squad is at work. Just as they're to be shot, Juaristas raid the prison. How the battle turns out we never learn, but as French general Achille Dupre (Bruce Payne) rides in from out of nowhere with a counterattack force, Cisco and Pancho steal a burro and manage to escape in the confusion.

On their way to the Juaristas' mountain stronghold in Devil's Horns Pass, they go through a town under Dupre's control where tax collector Alain Vitton (Tony Pandolfo) is squeezing pesos from the *campesinos*. Cisco and Pancho kill off the troops guarding Vitton and recover not only a fortune in taxes bled from the people but also Cisco's stallion Diablo, who somehow or other wound up being given to the collector after Cisco's arrest. Stopping off at the town during this encounter is General Dupre's lovely niece Dominique (Sadie Frost), who is traveling to the provincial capital of Chiloquin to marry Delacroix (Ron Perlman), a lieutenant colonel in the army of occupation.

Taken by Pancho to the mountain pass which the rebels must hold against the French at all costs, Cisco is introduced to the local Juarista generals Montano (Pedro Armendariz, Jr.) and Guiterrez (Honorato Magaloni) and to Doña Josefa (Teresa Lagunes), a plain woman with glasses who obviously holds a high rank in the rebel chain of command. "You are not part of us?" she asks. "No," Cisco replies, "I am not political, señora." "Neither are we," she tells him. "We just want our country back." Cisco and the Juaristas agree on a price for the weapons he's brought into Mexico. Meanwhile in Chiloquin his Texan ex-partners Washam (Tony Amendola) and Lundquist (Tim Thomerson) doublecross Cisco

and "that red n..... Indian" Juarez and make their own deal for the guns with Dupre. The general promises them a fortune if they and the other Texans will attack the enemy village of San Miguel de Oro and steal El Niño, a red-gold statue of the infant Jesus cast in the time of Cortez, which is exposed only on Christmas Day and without which the superstitious Juarista peasants will lose their will to fight and cave in to the French. Spookily awesome pseudo-John Williams music on the soundtrack signals to us that the next segment of this film's plot will be borrowed from Spielberg's **Raiders Of The Lost Ark**.

On Christmas morning Cisco is taken into San Miguel and discovers that Pancho is not a priest but a married man with a pregnant wife (Yareli Arizmendi) and six children. The entire Rivera family and Cisco go to church for the ceremony and the exposure of El Niño—which is interrupted when Washam and Lundquist and their gang ride their horses into the building, shoot the altar to pieces and grab the golden statue. Cisco is knocked out in the fight and the church catches fire with Pancho's daughter Linda (Marisol Valdez) trapped in the choir loft. In a scene that reminds younger viewers of the so-called Lash LaRue stunt from **Star Wars** (1977) but actually comes from one of the classic chapter endings of the serial **Zorro's Fighting Legion** (Republic, 1939), Cisco hurls himself and the child on the church bell rope through a stained glass window to the street below.

The next morning over a tequila breakfast Cisco and Pancho make plans to recover the statue. On their way to the governor's palace in Chiloquin where they're convinced El Niño must have been taken, they stop for a meal at a cantina where the old proprietress (Valentina Ponzanneli) and every one of her customers unaccountably sport grotesque facial scars. Van Hoose (Clayton Landey) and several others from the gang that attacked the church happen to drop in at the same cantina and get decimated by our amigos in the film's next shootout.

Once in Chiloquin Cisco and Pancho learn that a rodeo is being held in the municipal arena and that the winner will be a guest at the governor's ball that evening. Seeing a heaven-sent opportunity to search the palace for El Niño, Cisco signs up as a contestant and effortlessly takes top honors in every event. Sharing a box at the games are General Dupre and his niece Dominique, who recognizes Cisco from the tax collector incident but says nothing.

At the lavish ball that night, while Cisco dances sensuously with Dominique under the furious glare of her cigar-chomping fiancé Delacroix,

Pancho slips upstairs and hides in Dupre's office just in time to see Washam and Lundquist arrive and turn over El Niño and to hear the general order an attack on Devil's Horns Pass. He filches the statue but meanwhile downstairs the tax collector Vitton has also recognized Cisco and the compadres have to fight their way out of the palace in a comic action sequence that culminates in their being captured by Washam and Lundquist in the street. The Texans march their prisoners through a stable where a wagon with the U.S. guns is being kept and into the brothel where the rest of the gringo pigs are enjoying themselves. Washam tells his crew that Dupre has refused to pay the fortune promised for El Niño. They search Pancho, find the statue under his shirt and are crowing over their good luck when in yet another played-for-laughs action scene they're set upon by all the women in the brothel (who in fact are patriotic Juarista spies) and El Niño gets tossed around in the air like a golden football until Cisco and Pancho manage to escape with both the statue and the wagonload of guns. Needing something else to make Dupre pay what he's promised, the Texans then kidnap Dominique and hide her in an abandoned mine.

After delivering the weapons and El Niño to Devil's Horns Pass, Cisco demands the money he'd bargained for plus a receipt personally signed by Juarez. "You've been living with the gringos too long," Pancho spits at him. "Screw you, bandido." A fistfight breaks out between them which ends only when Cisco offers an explanation. Seems he'd gotten into some trouble in California and was forced by federal agents to bring the guns into Mexico, or some such gibberish.

A Juarista spy from the governor's palace races into camp with the news that Dupre and the entire French army will attack the next day at dawn. This shouldn't be news at all because Pancho had overheard the general giving the attack order, but if you want a plot with a little common sense, go switch channels to *Inspector Morse*. Pancho rides through the countryside like a Latino Paul Revere, shouting "The Frenchies are coming!" and displaying El Niño so that every farmer drops what he's doing and rushes to join the defense force. The unpolitical Cisco is about to leave with his money when the spy tells him that Dominique has been kidnapped. He runs into several of the Texans in the scarred woman's cantina and, joined at the last moment by Pancho, wipes out all but Van Hoose, who is forced to tell where Dominique is being held. Cisco reaches the mine just in time to save her from a fate-worse-than-death at the hands of her guard Haney (Charles

McCaughan) and, for good measure, from a cave-in. The couple rejoin Pancho and apparently have sex that night.

The French troops attack the Juarista stronghold at dawn. While the battle is raging, Dupre with a small force captures the village of San Miguel. Unable to make anyone tell what happened to El Niño, he orders his Texan accomplices to massacre the women and children with the Gatling gun. (How come they're alongside the general when, the last time we looked, they were holding his niece for ransom? *Quien sabe*?) Cisco and Pancho charge into the town square, seize the gun, lead the villagers in an assault on the French and kill off Washam and Lundquist. As Dupre makes a break for it, Cisco chases him back into the heart of the battle at Devil's Horns Pass and knocks him off his horse. The general is killed when his head hits a rock. Suddenly the battlefield goes silent and Delacroix engages in a flatly directed duel with Cisco that owes a great deal to the one-on-one between Errol Flynn and Basil Rathbone in **The Adventures Of Robin Hood** (Warner Bros., 1938) even to the exchange of insults between sword thrusts. "You fight very well for a Mexican!" "You fight very poorly for a Frenchman." Pancho arrives with San Miguel villagers and the Gatling gun in time to mop up the remnants of the French army. "Viva Benito Juarez!" a suddenly politicized Cisco exclaims.

Juarez himself (Luis Valdez) visits the stronghold to thank Cisco and Pancho and plan for the final battle against Maximilian. At first Cisco wants to go back to California: "I'm thinking I like to be president." "Of what?" Pancho scoffs. "The Gringo States of America? Keep dreaming!" "I will," Cisco tells him. But as the film ends, after saying *au revoir* to Dominique he rides off to rejoin the Juaristas and take part in the good fight with Pancho at his side.

The picture's storyline is a dreadful mess but what does much more harm is a blunder that Valdez shares with many other recent directors: he set out to make an old-fashioned action film and at the same time to show his superiority to a junk genre by making fun of his own work, hedging his bets, playing part of the film straight and the rest as a joke. Right after **The Cisco Kid**'s credits comes a prologue that will remind knowledgeable viewers of the opening of countless B Westerns—until the last line where Valdez tries to make us laugh.

The legend of the Cisco Kid begins in 1867.

The Mexican forces of President Benito Juarez were locked in a life and death struggle with the occupying French armies of Napoleon III and his

A publicity photo of Cheech Marin and Jimmy Smits for TNT's **The Cisco Kid** (Turner Pictures,1993). ©1993 Turner Pictures, Inc. All Rights Reserved.

puppet emperor Maximilian. The fate of Mexico hung in the balance.

Then along came a solitary hero—
Well, maybe two.

On a par with its schizophrenia is the picture's chronic ineptitude, which was so bad that TV critics had a field day making it look ridiculous. Michelle Greppi of the New York Post described the film as "full of hokey dialogue, accents so bad they're actionable,...action sequences that make professional wrestling look real, and hairdos that make Burt Reynolds' toupee look good...[Jimmy Smits] all but counts out loud as he clomps through his big ballroom scene...[In the action scenes] viewers can spot the stand-ins a mile away and count the number of times a punch or butt of a rifle misses its mark by a mile." Gary Danchak of the St. Louis Riverfront Times got a lot of background stuff wrong but almost everything else right. "For once, a TV movie where commercials will make it better....There's plenty

of deliberate bad overacting going on, especially with the secondary players. The fight scenes are straight out of **Batman**, lacking only the BLAMMO! BIFF! KAWHAP! cartoon balloons on the screen....Pepe LePew does a better French accent [than Bruce Payne as Dupre]. Acts better, too....The climactic battle between Cisco and the governor is risibly short, poorly staged, cheesily shot....Oh, Cisco. Oh Pancho. Vaya con queso, boys."

Plans for Valdez to direct a second Cisco telefeature with Smits and Marin were put on hold in the summer of 1994 when David Caruso quit his starring role in ABC's hit series **NYPD Blue** and Smits was signed to replace him. As I put this book to bed, in the fall of 1996, the promised or should I say threatened sequel has not yet surfaced. The Cisco saga may not be quite what we in our middle-to-golden years would have wished for, but chances are it will continue to go on.

Lezwent!

161

A Theatre Broadside from 1947. (Courtesy of Dan Stumpf.)

THE CISCO KID FILMOGRAPHY

1. IN OLD ARIZONA

Copyrighted . . . . .April 4, 1929
Distributor . . . . Fox
Length . . . . 7 reels, 8724 feet
Directors . . . . .Raoul Walsh & Irving Cummings
Producer . . . . None Credited
Adaptation & Dialogue . . . . Tom Barry
Source Story . . . . O. Henry, "The Caballero's Way" (1907)
Cinematographer . . . . Arthur Edeson
Film Editor . . . . Louis Loeffler
Music Director . . . . None Credited

Cast

Warner Baxter . . . . The Cisco Kid
Edmund Lowe . . . . .Sgt. Mickey Dunn
Dorothy Burgess . . . . .Tonia Maria
These three are the only actors who receive screen credit. The rest of the cast consists of **J. Farrell MacDonald** (Tad), **Fred Warren** (Piano Player), **Henry Armetta** (Barber), **Frank Campeau** (Cowpuncher), **Tom Santschi** (Cowpuncher), **Pat Hartigan** (Cowpuncher), **Roy Stewart** (Commandant), **James Bradbury, Jr.** (Soldier), **John Dillon** (Soldier), **Soledad Jiminez** (Cook), **Frank Nelson** (Cowboy), **Duke Martin** (Cowboy), **James Marcus** (Blacksmith), **Alphonse Ethier** (Sheriff), **Helen Lynch** (Woman), **Ivan Linow** (Russian Immigrant), **Joe Brown** (Bartender), **Lola Salvi** (Italian Girl), **Edward Peil, Sr.** (Man).

2. THE CISCO KID

Copyrighted . . . . September 18, 1931
Distributor . . . . Fox
Length . . . . 61 minutes
Director . . . . .Irving Cummings
Producer . . . . .Irving Cummings
Associate Producer . . . . .William Goetz
Screenplay . . . . Alfred A. Cohn
Cinematographer . . . . .Barney McGill
Film Editor . . . . Alex Troffey (uncredited)
Music Score . . . . .George Lipschultz

Cast

Warner Baxter . . . . The Cisco Kid
Edmund Lowe . . . . .Sgt. Mickey Dunn
Conchita Montenegro . . . . Carmencita
Nora Lane . . . . Sally Benton
Frederick Burt . . . . .Sheriff Tex Ransom
Willard Robertson . . . . .Enos Hankins
James Bradbury, Jr. . . . . .Pvt. Dixon
Jack Dillon . . . . .Pvt. Bouse
Charles Stevens . . . . Lopez
Chris (Chris-Pin) Martin . . . . Gordito
Douglas Haig . . . . Billy Benton
Marilyn Knowlden . . . . .Ann Benton

Unbilled Bit Parts

George Irving, Rita Flynn, Consuelo Castillo de Bonzo, Allan Garcia

3. THE RETURN OF THE CISCO KID

Copyrighted . . . . .April 28, 1939
Distributor . . . . 20th Century-Fox
Length . . . . 70 minutes
Director . . . . .Herbert I. Leeds
Associate Producer . . . . Kenneth Macgowan
Screenplay . . . . .Milton Sperling
Cinematographer . . . . .Charles Clarke
Film Editor . . . . .James B. Clark
Music Director . . . . .Cyril J. Mockridge

Cast

Warner Baxter . . . . The Cisco Kid
Lynn Bari . . . . .Ann Carver
Cesar Romero . . . . .Lopez
Henry Hull . . . . .Col. Joshua Bixby
Kane Richmond . . . . Alan Davis
C. Henry Gordon . . . . Mexican Captain
Robert Barrat . . . . .Sheriff McNally
Chris-Pin Martin . . . . .Gordito
Adrian Morris . . . . Deputy Johnson
Soledad Jiminez . . . . Mama Soledad
Harry Strang . . . . .Deputy
Arthur Aylesworth . . . . .Stagecoach Driver
Paul Burns . . . . Hotel Clerk

Cesar Romero and Chris-Pin Martin seem dubious about Warner Baxter taking a bath in this scene from **The Return of the Cisco Kid** (20th Century-Fox, 1939).

Victor Kilian ....Bartender
Eddy Waller ....Guard
Ruth Gillette ....Flora
Ward Bond ....Tough

Unbilled Bit Parts
Ralph Dunn, Gino Corrado, Herbert Heywood, Charles Tannen, Ethan Laidlaw, Max Wagner, Lee Shumway, Harry Debb

4. THE CISCO KID AND THE LADY

Copyrighted ....December 29, 1939
Distributor ....20th Century-Fox
Length ....73 minutes
Director ....Herbert I. Leeds
Associate Producer ....John Stone
Screenplay ....Frances Hyland
Story ....Stanley Rauh
Cinematographer ....Barney McGill
Film Editor ....Nick DeMaggio
Music Director ....Samuel Kaylin

Cast
Cesar Romero ....The Cisco Kid
Marjorie Weaver ....Julie Lawson
Chris-Pin Martin ....Gordito
George Montgomery ....Tommy Bates
Robert Barrat ....Jim Harbison
Virginia Field ....Billie Graham
Harry Green ....Teasdale
Gloria Ann White ....Baby
John Beach ....Stevens
Ward Bond .... Walton
J. Anthony Hughes ....Drake
James Burke ....Pop Saunders
Harry Hayden ....Sheriff
James Flavin ....Sergeant
Ruth Warren ....Ma Saunders

Unbilled Bit Parts
Paul Burns, Virginia Brissac, Adrian Morris, Eddie Dunn, Eddy Waller, Ivan Miller, Lester Dorr, Harry Strang, Arthur Rankin, Paul Sutton, Harold Goodwin, Gladys Blake, William Royle

Warner Baxter sings to Lynn Bari in this Lobby Card from 1939. (Courtesy of Boyd Magers.)

5. VIVA CISCO KID

Copyrighted . . . . .April 12, 1940
Distributor . . . . 20th Century-Fox
Length . . . . 70 minutes
Director . . . . .Norman Foster
Producer . . . . .Sol M. Wurtzel
Screenplay . . . . . . .Samuel G. Engel & Hal Long
Cinematographer . . . . .Charles Clarke
Film Editor . . . . .Norman Colbert
Music Director . . . . Samuel Kaylin
Cast
Cesar Romero . . . . .The Cisco Kid
Jean Rogers .Joan Allen
Chris-Pin Martin . . . . .Gordito
Minor Watson . . . . Jesse Allen
Stanley Fields . . . . .The Boss
Nigel de Brulier . . . . Moses
Harold Goodwin . . . . Hank Gunther
Francis Ford . . . . .Proprietor
Charles Judels . . . . .Don Pancho

Unbilled Bit Parts
LeRoy Mason, Bud Osborne, Paul Sutton, Mantan Moreland, Tom London, Hank Worden, Eddy Waller, Jim Mason, Ray Teal, Paul Kruger, Willie Fung, Frank Darien, Jacqueline Dalya, Margaret Martin, Inez Palange

6. LUCKY CISCO KID

Copyrighted . . . . June 28, 1940
Distributor . . . . 20th Century-Fox
Length . . . . 68 minutes
Director . . . . H. Bruce Humberstone
Associate Producer . . . . .John Stone
Screenplay . . . . Robert Ellis & Helen Logan
Story . . . . .Julian Johnson
Cinematographer . . . . .Lucien Andriot
Film Editor . . . . Fred Allen
Music Director . . . . .Cyril J. Mockridge

Cesar Romero seems to agree that we will get even in this scene from **Viva Cisco Kid** (20th Century Fox, 1940) as a player shakes his fist.

Cast
Cesar Romero . . . . The Cisco Kid
Mary Beth Hughes . . . . Lola
Dana Andrews . . . . Sergeant Dunn
Evelyn Venable . . . . Emily Lawrence
Chris-Pin Martin . . . . .Gordito
Willard Robertson . . . . Judge McQuade
Joseph Sawyer . . . . .Bill Stevens
Johnny Sheffield . . . . .Tommy Lawrence
William Royle . . . . Sheriff
Francis Ford . . . . Court Clerk
Otto Hoffman .Ed Stokes
Dick Rich . . . . .Stagecoach Driver
Unbilled Bit Parts
Harry Strang, Gloria Roy, Frank Lackteen, Spencer Charters, Bob Hoffman, Boyd Morgan, Adrian Morris, Jimmie Dundee, William Pagan, Lillian Yarbo, Lew Kelly, Milton Kibbee, Sarah Edwards, Ethan Laidlaw, Thornton Edwards, James Flavin, Henry Roquemore, Syd Saylor, Charles Tannen, Pat O'Malley, Sid Jordan

7. THE GAY CABALLERO

Copyrighted . . . . October 4, 1940
Distributor . . . . 20th Century-Fox
Length . . . . 57 minutes
Director . . . . .Otto Brower
Associate Producers . . . . .Walter Morosco &
Ralph Dietrich
Screenplay . . . . Albert Duffy & John Larkin
Story . . . . Walter Bullock & Albert Duffy
Cinematographer . . . . Edward Cronjager
Film Editor . . . . Harry Reynolds
Music Director . . . . Emil Newman
Cast
Cesar Romero . . . . .The Cisco Kid
Sheila Ryan . . . . .Susan Wetherby
Robert Sterling . . . . Billy Brewster
Chris-Pin Martin . . . . .Gordito
Janet Beecher . . . . Kate Brewster

Stanley Fields, Cesar Romero and Chris-Pin Martin in a scene from **Viva Cisco Kid** (20th Century-Fox). (Courtesy of Bobby Copeland.)

Edmund MacDonald . . . . Joe Turner
Jacqueline Dalya . . . . .Carmelita
C. Montague Shaw . . . . George Wetherby
Hooper Atchley . . . . Sheriff McBride
Unbilled Bit Parts
George Magrill, Jim Pierce, Ethan Laidlaw, John Byron, Tom London, Dave Morris, Jack Stoney, Lee Shumway, LeRoy Mason, Frank Lackteen

8. ROMANCE OF THE RIO GRANDE

Copyrighted . . . . .January 17, 1941
Distributor . . . . 20th Century-Fox
Length . . . . 73 minutes
Director .Herbert I. Leeds
Producer .Sol M. Wurtzel
Screenplay .Harold Buchman & Samuel G. Engel
Source Novel . . . . . Katharine Fullerton Gerould,
Conquistador (Scribner, 1923)
Cinematographer . . . . .Charles Clarke

Film Editor . . . . Fred Allen
Music Director . . . . Emil Newman
Cast
Cesar Romero . . . . .The Cisco Kid
Patricia Morison . . . . Rosita
Lynne Roberts . . . . Maria Cordova
Ricardo Cortez . . . . Ricardo de Vega
Chris-Pin Martin . . . . .Gordito
Aldrich Bowker . . . . Padre Martinez
Joseph McDonald . . . . Carlos Hernandez
Pedro de Cordoba . . . . . .Don Fernando de Vega
Inez Palange . . . . Mama Lopez
Raphael Bennett . . . . Carver
Trevor Bardette . . . . .Manuel
Tom London . . . . Marshal
Eva Puig . . . . .Marta
Unbilled Bit Parts
Richard Lane

Chris-Pin Martin, Johnny Sheffield, Mary Beth Hughes and Cesar Romero in a scene from **Lucky Cisco Kid** (20th Century-Fox).

9. RIDE ON VAQUERO

Copyrighted . . . . .April 18, 1941
Distributor . . . . 20th Century-Fox
Length . . . . 64 minutes
Director . . . . .Herbert I. Leeds
Producer . . . . .Sol M. Wurtzel
Screenplay . . . . .Samuel G. Engel
Cinematographer . . . . .Lucien Andriot
Film Editor . . . . Louis Loeffler
Music Director . . . . Emil Newman

Cast

Cesar Romero . . . . .The Cisco Kid
Mary Beth Hughes . . . . .Sally
Lynne Roberts . . . . .Marguerita Martinez
Chris-Pin Martin . . . . .Gordito
Robert Lowery . . . . Carlos Martinez
Ben Carter . . . . .Bullfinch
William Demarest . . . . .Barney
Robert Shaw . . . . Cavalry Officer
Edwin Maxwell . . . . Dan Clark

Paul Sutton . . . . .Sleepy
Don Costello . . . . .Redge
Arthur Hohl . . . . .Sheriff Johnny Burge
Irving Bacon . . . . Baldy
Dick Rich . . . . .Curly
Paul Harvey . . . . Colonel Warren
Joan Woodbury . . . . .Dolores

10. THE CISCO KID RETURNS

Copyrighted . . . . .March 19, 1945
Distributor . . . . Monogram
Length . . . . 64 minutes
Director . . . . John P. McCarthy
Producer . . . . .Philip N. Krasne
Associate Producer . . . . .Dick L'Estrange
Screenplay . . . . .Betty Burbridge
Cinematographer . . . . .Harry Neumann
Film Editor . . . . Martin G. Cohn
Music Score . . . . .Albert Glasser
Music Director . . . . .David Chudnow

Johnny Sheffield and Cesar Romero in a publicity photo for **Lucky Cisco Kid** (20th Century-Fox).

Cast

Duncan Renaldo . . . . The Cisco Kid
Martin Garralaga . . . . .Pancho
Roger Pryor . . . . John Harris
Cecilia Callejo . . . . Rosita Gonzales
Fritz Leiber . . . . Padre
Jan Wiley . . . . .Jeanette
Sharon Smith . . . . .Nancy Page
Vicky Lane . . . . Julia
Anthony Warde . . . . Paul Conway
Bud Osborne . . . . Sheriff
Eva Puig . . . . .Tia Jimenez
Cy Kendall . . . . Jennings

Unbilled Bit Parts

Bob Duncan, Elmer Napier, Carl Mathews,
Jerry Fields, Neyle Marx, Cedric Stevens,
Walter Clinton

11. IN OLD NEW MEXICO

Copyrighted . . . . .March 26, 1945

Distributor . . . . Monogram
Length . . . . .62 minutes
Director . . . . Phil Rosen
Producer .Philip N. Krasne
Screenplay . . . . .Betty Burbridge
Cinematographer . . . . .Arthur Martinelli
Film Editor . . . . Martin G. Cohn
Music Score . . . . .Albert Glasser
Music Director . . . . .David Chudnow

Cast

Duncan Renaldo . . . . The Cisco Kid
Martin Garralaga . . . . .Pancho
Gwen Kenyon . . . . Ellen Roth
Pedro de Cordoba . . . . Padre Angelo
Aurora Roche . . . . .Dolores
Lee "Lasses" White . . . . .Sheriff Clem Petty
Norman Willis . . . . Will Hastings
Edward Earle . . . . Newspaper Editor
Donna Dax . . . . Belle
John Laurenz .Al Brady
Richard Gordon . . . . Doc Wilson

A tense Chris-Pin Martin is calmed down by a relaxed Cesar Romero in a scene from **Romance of the Rio Grande** (20th Century-Fox, 1941). (Courtesy of Bobby Copeland.)

Frank Jaquet . . . . .Stagecoach Passenger
James Farley . . . . .Deputy
The Car-Bert Dancers . . . . .Dance Troupe
Unbilled Bit Parts
Ken Terrell, Harry Depps, Bud Osborne, Artie Ortego

12. SOUTH OF THE RIO GRANDE

Copyrighted . . . . .August 25, 1945
Distributor . . . . Monogram
Length . . . . 62 minutes
Director . . . . .Lambert Hillyer
Producer . . . . .Philip N. Krasne
Screenplay . Victor Hammond & Ralph Bettinson
Story . . . . .Johnston McCulley
Cinematographer . . . . .William Sickner
Film Editor . . . . .William Austin
Music Score . . . . .Frank Sanucci (uncredited)

Music Director . . . . .Edward J. Kay
Cast
Duncan Renaldo . . . . The Cisco Kid
Martin Garralaga . . . . .Pancho
Armida . . . . Pepita
George J. Lewis . . . .Apoderado Miguel Sanchez
Lillian Molieri . . . . .Dolores Gonzales
Francis McDonald . . . . .Torres
Charles Stevens . . . . .Sebastian
Pedro Regas . . . . .Luis
Soledad Jimenez . . . . Mama Maria
Tito Renaldo . . . . .Manuel Gonzales
With **The Guadalajara Trio**

13. THE GAY CAVALIER

Copyrighted . . . . .March 15, 1946
Distributor . . . . Monogram
Length . . . . 65 minutes
Director . . . . .William Nigh
Producer . . . . Scott R. Dunlap
Screenplay . . . . .Charles S. Belden
Story . . . . .Charles S. Belden
Cinematographer . . . . .Harry Neumann
Film Editor . . . . Earl Maguire
Music Director . . . . .Edward J. Kay
Cast
Gilbert Roland . . . . .The Cisco Kid
Martin Garralaga . . . . .Don Felipe Peralta
Nacho Galindo .Baby
Ramsay Ames . . . . .Pepita Peralta
Helen Gerald . . . . .Angela Peralta
Tristram Coffin . . . . Lawton
Drew Allen . . . . .Juan
Iris Flores . . . . Rosita
John Merton .Lewis
Frank LaRue . . . . .Graham
Unbilled Bit Parts
Gabriel Peralta, Pierre Andre, Iris Becigon, Raphael Bennett, Artie Ortego, Terry Frost, Ernie Adams

14. SOUTH OF MONTEREY

Copyrighted . . . . June 29, 1946
Distributor . . . . Monogram
Length . . . . 63 minutes
Director . . . . .William Nigh
Producer . . . . Scott R. Dunlap
Screenplay . . . . .Charles S. Belden
Story . . . . .Charles S. Belden
Cinematographer . . . . .Harry Neumann
Film Editor . . . . Richard Heermance
Music Director . . . . .Edward J. Kay
Cast
Gilbert Roland . . . . The Cisco Kid
Martin GarralagaCommandante Arturo Morales

Cesar Romero and Mary Beth Hughes examine a letter in this scene from **Ride On Vaquero** (20th Century-Fox, 1941).

Frank Yaconelli . . . . .Baby
Marjorie Riordan . . . . .Maria Morales
Iris Flores . . . . Carmelita
George J. Lewis . . . . Carlos Madero
Harry Woods . . . . .Bennet
Terry Frost . . . . .Morgan
Rosa Turich . . . . .Lola
Unbilled Bit Parts
Wheaton Chambers

15. BEAUTY AND THE BANDIT

Copyrighted . . . . October 28, 1946
Distributor . . . . Monogram
Length . . . . .77 minutes
Director .William Nigh
Producer . . . . Scott R. Dunlap
Screenplay & Story . . . . Charles S. Belden
Cinematographer . . . . .Harry Neumann
Film Editor . . . . Fred Maguire
Music Director . . . . Edward J. Kay

Cast
Gilbert Roland . . . . The Cisco Kid
Martin Garralaga . . . Dr. Juan Federico Valegra
Frank Yaconelli . . . . .Baby
Ramsay Ames . . . . Jeanne Dubois
Vida Aldana . . . . Rosita
George J. Lewis. . . . . .Captain
William Gould. . . . . .Doc Walsh
Dimas Sotello. . . . . Farmer
Felipe Turich. . . . . Sick Farmer
Unbilled Bit Parts
Glenn Strange, Alex Montoya, Artie Ortego

16. RIDING THE CALIFORNIA TRAIL

Copyrighted . . . . January 27, 1947
Distributor . . . . Monogram
Length . . . . 59 minutes
Director. William Nigh
Producer. . . . . .Scott R. Dunlap
Screenplay. . . . . Clarence Upson Young

Arthur Hohl, Don Costello, Robert Shaw, Irving Bacon, Mary Beth Hughes and Cesar Romero are pictured in this Lobby Card from 1941. (Courtesy of Phil Loy.)

Story . . . . .Clarence Upson Young
Cinematographer. . . . . Harry Neumann
Film Editor . . . . Fred Maguire
Music Director. . . . . .Edward J. Kay

The Cast

Gilbert Roland . . . . The Cisco Kid
Martin Garralaga . . . . .Don Jose Ramirez
Frank Yaconelli .Baby
Teala Loring . . . . Raquel
Inez Cooper . . . . .Dolores Ramirez
Ted Hecht . . . . .Raoul de la Reyes
Marcelle Grandville . . . . Mama Rosita

Unbilled Bit Parts

Eve Whitney, Frank Marlowe, Alex Montoya, Rosa Turich, Julia Kent, Gerald Echevarria

17. ROBIN HOOD OF MONTEREY

Copyrighted . . . . September 11, 1947
Distributor . . . . Monogram
Length . . . . .55 minutes

Director . . . . Christy Cabanne
Producer . . . . .Jeffrey Bernerd
Screenplay . . . . .Bennett Cohen
Additional Dialogue . . . . .Gilbert Roland
Story . . . . Bennett Cohen
Cinematographer . . . . .William Sickner
Film Editor . . . . Roy Livingston
Music Director . . . . Edward J. Kay

The Cast

Gilbert Roland . . . . The Cisco Kid
Chris-Pin Martin . . . . Pancho
Evelyn Brent . . . . .Maria Sanchez Belmonte
Jack LaRue . . . . Ricardo Gonzales
Pedro de Cordoba . . . . . . .Don Carlos Belmonte
Donna de Mario . . . . Lolita
Travis Kent . . . . .Eduardo Belmonte
Thornton Edwards . . . . Unknown Role
Nestor Paiva . . . . .Alcalde
Ernie Adams . . . . Pablo

Unbilled Bit Parts

Julian Rivero, Alex Montoya, Fred Cordova,

Gilbert Roland listens to Chris-Pin Martin in this scene from **King of the Bandits** (Monogram, 1947).

Felipe Turich

18. KING OF THE BANDITS

Copyrighted . . . . November 8, 1947
Distributor . . . . Monogram
Length . . . . 66 minutes
Director . . . . Christy Cabanne
Producer . . . . .Jeffrey Bernerd
Screenplay . . . . .Bennett Cohen
Additional Dialogue . . . . .Gilbert Roland
Story . . . . .Christy Cabanne
Cinematographer . . . . .William Sickner
Film Editor . . . . Roy Livingston
Music Director . . . . Edward J. Kay
The Cast
Gilbert Roland . . . . The Cisco Kid
Angela Greene . . . . Alice Mason
Chris-Pin Martin . . . . Pancho
Anthony Warde . . . . Smoke Kirby
Laura Treadwell . . . . .Mrs. Mason

William Bakewell . . . . .Captain Frank Mason
Rory Mallinson . . . . Burl
Pat Goldin . . . . .Pedro Gomez
Cathy Carter . . . . .Connie
Boyd Irwin . . . . .Colonel Wayne
Antonio Filauri . . . . Padre
Jasper Palmer . . . . U.S. Marshal
Bill Cabanne . . . . .Orderly
Gene Roth . . . . Unbilled Bit Part

19. VALIANT HOMBRE

Copyrighted . . . . .January 21, 1949
Distributor . . . . . . Inter-American/United Artists
Length . . . . 60 minutes
Director .Wallace W. Fox
Producer . . . . .Philip N. Krasne
Associate Producer . . . . Duncan Renaldo
Screenplay . . . . .Adele Buffington
Cinematographer . . . . Ernest Miller

173

Gilbert Roland and Chris-Pin Martin are in the hands of the military in this scene from an unidentified film.

Film Editor . . . . Martin G. Cohn
Music Score . . . . .Albert Glasser
Music Director . . . . Albert Glasser
The Cast
Duncan Renaldo . . . . The Cisco Kid
Leo Carrillo . . . . .Pancho
John Litel .Lon Lansdell
Barbara Billingsley . . . . .Linda Mason
Guy Beach . . . . Joe Haskins
Stanley Andrews . . . . . . .Sheriff George Dodge
Lee "Lasses" White . . . . Whiskers
John James . . . . Paul Mason
Eugene (Gene) Roth . . . . Pete
Ralph Peters . . . . .Deputy Clay
Frank Ellis . . . . Outlaw
Herman Hack . . . . .Outlaw
George De Normand . . . . Outlaw
With Daisy the Wonder Dog
Unbilled Bit Parts
Terry Frost, David Sharpe, Frank McCarroll, Hank Bell

20. THE GAY AMIGO

Copyrighted . . . . May 13, 1949
Distributor . . . . . . Inter-American/United Artists
Length . . . . 60 minutes
Director . . . . .Wallace W. Fox
Producer . . . . .Philip N. Krasne
Associate Producer . . . . Duncan Renaldo
Screenplay . . . . .Doris Schroeder
Cinematographer . . . . Ernest Miller
Film Editor . . . . Martin G. Cohn
Music Score . . . . .Albert Glasser
Music Director . . . . Albert Glasser
Cast
Duncan Renaldo . . . . The Cisco Kid
Leo Carrillo . . . . .Pancho
Armida . . . . Rosita
Joe Sawyer . . . . .Sergeant McNulty
Walter Baldwin . . . . Stoneham
Fred Kohler, Jr. . . . . .Bill Brack
Kenneth MacDonald . . . . .Captain Lewis

174

Evelyn Brent is charmed by Gilbert Roland in this scene from **Robin Hood of Monterey** (Monogram, 1947).

George De Normand . . . . Corporal
Clayton Moore . . . . .Lieutenant
Fred Crane . . . . .Duke
Helen Servis . . . . .Old Maid
Beverly Jons . . . . .Girl
Bud Osborne . . . . Stage Driver
Sam Flint . . . . .Ed Paulsen

21. THE DARING CABALLERO

Copyrighted . . . . June 24, 1949
Distributor . . . . . . Inter-American/United Artists
Length . . . . 60 minutes
Director .Wallace W. Fox
Producer .Philip N. Krasne
Associate Producer . . . . Duncan Renaldo
Screenplay . . . . .Betty Burbridge
Story . . . . .Frances Kavanaugh
Cinematographer . . . . Lester White
Film Editor . . . . Martin G. Cohn
Music Score . . . . .Albert Glasser

Music Director . . . . Albert Glasser
The Cast
Duncan Renaldo . . . . The Cisco Kid
Leo Carrillo . . . . .Pancho
Kippee Valez . . . . .Kippee Valez
Charles Halton . . . . E.J. Hodges
Pedro de Cordoba . . . . .Padre Leonardo
Stephen Chase . . . . .Barton/Mayor Brady
David Leonard . . . . .Patrick Del Rio
Edmund Cobb . . . . Marshal Scott
Frank Jaquet . . . . Judge Perkins
Mickey Little . . . . Bobby Del Rio

22. SATAN'S CRADLE

Copyright Date . . . . None
Distributor . . . . . . Inter-American/United Artists
Length . . . . 60 minutes
Director . . . . .Ford Beebe
Producer .Philip N. Krasne
Associate Producer . . . . Duncan Renaldo

Kippee Valez, Charles Halton, Stephen Chase and Duncan Renaldo in this scene from **The Daring Caballero** (Monogram, 1949). (Courtesy of Buck Rainey.)

Screenplay . . . . .Jack Benton (J. Benton Cheney)
Cinematographer . . . . Jack Greenhalgh
Film Editor . . . . Martin G. Cohn
Music Score . . . . .Albert Glasser
Music Director . . . . Albert Glasser

Cast

Duncan Renaldo . . . . The Cisco Kid
Leo Carrillo . . . . .Pancho
Ann Savage Lil
Douglas Fowley . . . . Steve Gentry
Byron Foulger . . . . .Rev. Henry Lane
Claire Carleton . . . . Belle
Buck Bailey . . . . .Rocky
George De Normand . . . . .Idaho
Wes Hudman . . . . Peters

23. THE GIRL FROM SAN LORENZO

Copyrighted . . . . .February 21, 1950
Distributor . . . . . . Inter-American/United Artists
Length . . . . 59 minutes

Director . . . . Derwin Abrahams
Producer . . . . .Philip N. Krasne
Screenplay . . . . Ford Beebe
Cinematographer . . . . .Kenneth Peach
Film Editor . . . . Martin G. Cohn
Music Score . . . . .Albert Glasser
Music Director . . . . Albert Glasser

Cast

Duncan Renaldo . . . . The Cisco Kid
Leo Carrillo . . . . .Pancho
Jane Adams . . . . Nora Malloy
Bill Lester . . . . Jerry Todd
Byron Foulger . . . . Cal Ross
Don C. Harvey . . . . Kansas
Lee Phelps . . . . .Sheriff Ed Morrison
Edmund Cobb . . . . .Wooly
Leonard Penn . . . . Tom McCarger
David Sharpe . . . . Blackie
Wes Hudman . . . . .Rusty

176

Duncan Renaldo has found something in the safe in this scene from **The Daring Caballero** (Monogram, 1949). (Courtesy of Buck Rainey.)

24. THE CISCO KID

Broadcast Debut	February 6, 1994
Distributors	Turner Pictures
Length	100 minutes
Director	Luis Valdez
Producers	Gary Goodman & Barry Rosen
Associate Producers	Moctezuma Esparza & Robert Katz
Screenplay	Michael Kane & Luis Valdez
Story	Michael Kane
Cinematographer	Guillermo Navarro
Film Editor	Zach Staenberg
Music Score	Joseph Julian Gonzales

Cast

Jimmy Smits	Francisco Hernan Sanchez Aguilar de Solares (The Cisco Kid)
Cheech Marin	Francisco Rivera (Pancho)
Sadie Frost	Dominique
Bruce Payne	General Achille Dupre
Ron Perlman	Lt. Col. Delacroix
Tony Amendola	Washam
Tim Thomerson	Lundquist
Pedro Armendariz, Jr.	General Montano
Phil Esparza	Kessler
Clayton Landey	Van Hoose
Charles McGaughan	Haney
Tony Pandolfo	Alain Vitton
Roger Cudney	Alcott
Joaquin Garrido	Lopez
Guillermo Rios	Hernandez
Miguel Sandoval	Hidalgo
Tomas Goros	Trevino
Rufino Echegoyen	Aparicio
Teresa Lagunes	Dona Josefa
Honorato Magaloni	General Guiterrez
Luis Valdez	Benito Juarez
Yareli Arizmendi	Rosa Rivera
Marisol Valdez	Linda Rivera
Julius Jansland	Antonio Rivera
Mario Ecatl Zapata	Juanito Rivera
Mario Alberto	Hector Rivera

Above: Duncan Renaldo with Clyde Beatty and a friend from the Clyde Beatty Circus. Duncan is in his TV costume so this should be in the early 50's. (Courtesy of Buck Rainey.) **Below:** A drawing of Leo Carrillo as Pancho Villa. (Courtesy of Charles K. Stumpf.)

Boris Peguero . . . . Eduardo Rivera
Maya Zapata . . . . .Alicia Rivera
Gerardo Zepeda . . . . .Guerrero
Lorena Victoria . . . . .Libertad
Valentina Ponzanneli . . . . Old Cantina Lady
Pedro Altamirano . . . . .Prison Guard
Gerardo Martinez . . . . .Dungeon Soldier
Rojo Grau . . . . Firing Squad Lieutenant
Guido Bolanos . . . . .Vitton's Guard
Roberto Olivo, Roberto Antunez . . . . . .Farmers
Pablo Zuak . . . . French Officer
Lakin Valdez . . . . Little Boy
Mario Valdez . . . . .San Miguel Man
Luisa Coronel, Emilia Zapata, Alexandra
Vicencio . . . . Women
Moctezuma Esparza . . . . .Bishop
Susan Benedict, Patricia Brown, Carolyn
Caldera, Corrina Duran, Claire Lewin,
Herendia Silva . . . . .Spies for the Cause

178

The Cisco Kid TV Series

Starring DUNCAN RENALDO

and LEO CARRILLO

FIRST SEASON, 1950-51

BOOMERANG

Copyrighted . . . . September 5, 1950
Director . . . . .Derwin Abrahams
Teleplay . . . . J. Benton Cheney (?)
Cast
Duncan Renaldo . . . . The Cisco Kid
Leo Carrillo . . . . .Pancho
Jane Adams . . . . .Miss Harley
Byron Foulger . . . . .Mr. Harley
Stephen Chase . . . . .Jim Brent
Edmund Cobb . . . . .Martin
Lee Phelps . . . . Sheriff
David Sharpe . . . . Fake Cisco
George De Normand . . . . Deputy
Story: The Cisco Kid and his companion Pancho find themselves wanted by the law after a prominent real estate broker has two gunmen impersonate them and rob the Mesa Verde bank.
Notes: Companion episode: *Chain Lightning*. There is considerable overlap between the cast and storyline of this debut episode and that of the last Cisco feature, **The Girl From San Lorenzo** (InterAmerican/United Artists, 1950).

COUNTERFEIT MONEY

Copyrighted . . . . September 12, 1950
Director . . . . Derwin Abrahams
Teleplay . . . . J. Benton Cheney
Cast
Duncan Renaldo . . . . The Cisco Kid
Leo Carrillo . . . . .Pancho
Peggy Stewart . . . . Jane
Forrest Taylor .Hale
Luther Crockett. . . . . .Tom Henderson
Riley Hill . . . . Terry

Robert Livingston. . . . . .Red Saunders
George De Normand . . . . George
Art Dupuis . . . . .Marshal Ben Lane
Fred Kohler, Jr. Sheriff
Story: Cisco and Pancho hunt a brother-sister team of counterfeiters who are using a secret room in a bank as their headquarters and forcing the banker to pass their phony money.
Notes: Companion episodes: *Oil Land, Cattle Quarantine*.

RUSTLING

Copyrighted . . . . September 19, 1950
Director . . . . Derwin Abrahams
Teleplay . . . . .J. Benton Cheney
Cast
Duncan Renaldo . . . . .The Cisco Kid
Leo Carrillo . . . . .Pancho
Christine Larson . . . . Mary Austin
Raymond Hatton . . . . .Sheriff
Jonathan Hale . . . . .Barry Owens
Douglas Evans . . . . .Joe Dawson
Frank Matts . . . . .Jud Morgan
George De Normand . . . . .Henchman
Story: Cisco and Pancho are charged with murder when a rancher who secretly heads a rustling ring kills a suspicious neighbor and frames Cisco for the crime.
Notes: Companion episode: *Medicine Flats*. J. Benton Cheney recycled the rustling gimmick in this episode from his screenplay for the Hopalong Cassidy feature **Twilight On The Trail** (Paramount, 1941), starring William Boyd.

BIG SWITCH

Copyrighted . . . . September 26, 1950
Director . . . . Derwin Abrahams
Teleplay .Royal Cole
Cast
Duncan Renaldo . . . . The Cisco Kid
Leo Carrillo . . . . .Pancho

CAST

CISCO KID TELEVISION PICTURES

CHAPTERS 22-23-24-26

CISCO	DUNCAN RENALDO................	STate 4-2885
PANCHO	LEO CARRILLO.................	EXbrook 5-9345
MARG #22-23) PAULA #24-26)	PHYLLIS COATES................	CHarlstn 8-0406
	(Agent: Jessie Wadsworth-CR 6-0698)	
FOSTER #22-23) RED #24) KELLY)	BILL KENNEDY................. 8576 Telfair, Sun Valley	
JASON #22-23) SHELBY #24-26)	MICHAEL RAGAN (HOLLY BANE)....	SUnset 3-9255
	(Agent: Antrim Short-CR 5-0626)	
BILL #22-23) BLACKIE #24-26)	DAVID BRUCE..................	SUnset 2-1251
	(Agent: Gus Dembling-CR 1-2161)	
SHERIFF #22-23) SHERIFF #23-26)	TOM TYLER....................	HIllside 4126
	(Agent: Art Meyers-CR 5-7865)	
DEPUTY #22	TROY MELTON.................	ARizona 3-6812

RIDERS

HEAVY A

HEAVY B

HEAVY C

DAY PLAYERS

U.S. MARSHALL #24-26

MANAGER #24-26

LACEY #22

LACEY #23

BANKER BARTON #23

PHOTO DOUBLES

CROECEREDCONC CISCO	TROY MELTON.................	ARizona 3-6812
PANCHO	FRANK URTAN.................	Beaumont 2871

Director Paul Landres' cast sheets for **The Cisco Kid** episodes "Wedding Blackmail," " Haven for Heavies," "Phoney Sheriff" and "Uncle Disinherits Niece." Landres shot all four simultaneously with overlapping casts. (Courtesy of Paul Landres.)

Pamela Blake . . . . .Margie Murdock
Sarah Padden . . . . Sarah
Nelson Leigh . . . . .Jim Holbrook
Fred Kohler, Jr. . . . . Henchman
Carol Henry . . . . Deputy
Jack Ingram. . . . . . . .Jim Hardy/Henry Murdock
Pierre Watkin . . . . Sheriff
Story: Cisco and Pancho help the niece of a secretly murdered cattleman outwit a clever forger who closely resembles the woman's uncle.
Notes: Companion episodes: *Railroad Land Rush, Renegade Son*. This is the first episode to end with the familiar "Oh, Pancho!" "Oh, Cisco!" exchange between Renaldo and Carrillo.

CONVICT STORY

Copyrighted . . . . October 3, 1950
Director . . . . Derwin Abrahams
Teleplay . . . . Sherman L. Lowe
Cast
Duncan Renaldo . . . . The Cisco Kid
Leo Carrillo . . . . .Pancho
Gail Davis . . . . .Ruth Drake
Riley Hill . . . . Bob Drake
Robert Livingston . . . . Cantwell
Fred Kohler, Jr. . . . . .Lefty
Forrest Taylor . . . . .Sheriff
Story: Cisco and Pancho try to help an escaped convict who stole Pancho's clothes and horse while Pancho was swimming and then tried to kill the mine owner he says framed him.
Notes: Companion episodes: *The Will, False Marriage*. This is the second episode with the "Oh, Pancho!" "Oh, Cisco!" ending.

OIL LAND

Copyrighted . . . . October 10, 1950
Director . . . . Derwin Abrahams
Teleplay . . . . .J. Benton Cheney
Cast
Duncan Renaldo . . . . The Cisco Kid
Leo Carrillo . . . . .Pancho
Peggy Stewart . . . . .Peggy Williams
Fred Kohler, Jr. . . . . .Hank
Forrest Taylor (listed but not in cast)
Robert Livingston . . . . .Walter Stuart
Luther Crockett . . . . Sheriff
Earle Hodgins . . . . Idaho
Story: When a rancher who's just discovered oil on his property is murdered by one of his hands, suspicion falls on Cisco and Pancho.
Notes: Companion episodes: *Counterfeit Money, Cattle Quarantine*. This is the first of several episodes that give credit to an actor who didn't appear on screen. Usually the reason is that he did

appear in a companion episode and, to save money, the production company used the same cast list for the credits of both.

CHAIN LIGHTNING

Copyrighted . . . . October 14, 1950
Director . . . . Derwin Abrahams
Teleplay . . . . .J. Benton Cheney
Cast
Duncan Renaldo . . . . The Cisco Kid
Leo Carrillo . . . . .Pancho
Noel Neill . . . . .Rita Shannon
Don C. Harvey . . . . Jim Brent
Edmund Cobb . . . . Larry Martin
David Sharpe . . . . .Bill Shannon
Lee Phelps . . . . Sheriff
Story: After being sent to prison by Cisco and Pancho with the help of stage line owner Bill Shannon, gunfighter Jim Brent is released and sets out for revenge on all three.
Notes: Companion episode: *Boomerang*.

MEDICINE FLATS

Copyrighted . . . . October 17, 1950
Director . . . . Derwin Abrahams
Teleplay . . . . .Unknown
Cast
Duncan Renaldo . . . . The Cisco Kid
Leo Carrillo . . . . .Pancho
Christine Larson . . . . .Judy Summers
Raymond Hatton . . . . .Sheriff
Jonathan Hale . . . . .Barry Owens
Douglas Evans . . . . .Curt Reynolds
Frank Matts . . . . .Parker
George De Normand . . . . .Jack
Story: Suspecting a gambling-house owner of being behind the gang of rustlers that framed them for murder, Cisco and Pancho convince him that they're wanted for killing a sheriff and try to break up the gang from within.
Notes: Companion episode: *Rustling*

RAILROAD LAND RUSH

Copyrighted . . . . October 28, 1950
Director . . . . Derwin Abrahams
Teleplay . . . . .Unknown
Cast
Duncan Renaldo . . . . The Cisco Kid
Leo Carrillo . . . . .Pancho
Pamela Blake . . . . Margie Holbrook
Pierre Watkin . . . . .Mr. Holbrook
Nelson Leigh . . . . .James Blake
Fred Kohler, Jr. .Steve
Forrest Taylor . . . . John Warren

CAST

CISCO KID TELEVISION PICTURES

STOLEN BONDS - CHAPTER 28
PROTECTIVE ASSOCIATION - CHAPTER 30

CISCO	DUNCAN RENALDO................STate 4-2885	
PANCHO	LEO CARRILLO..................EXbrook 5-9345	
CHRISTINE	JEAN DEAN.....................VErmont 9-9488	
	(Agent: Charles Gwynn-CR 5-0164)	
SLOAN	REED HOWES....................CRestvw 5-1907	
	(messages)HOllywd 9-2164	
	(Agent-Chas. Gwynn-CR 5-0164)	
NORTON	PIERCE LYDEN.................. HEmpstd 3005	
	(Agent-Harry Wurtzel-CR 5-6175)	
MARK	BILL HOLMES...................CRestvw 5-7390	
	(messages)HOllywd 9-2121	
	(Agent: Stemple Olenic-CR 1-7141)	
DAVE	JIM DIEHL.....................CRestvw 5-3145	
	(Agent-Chas. Gwynn-CR 5-0164)	
LEFTY #30) STAGE DRIVER #28)	BUD OSBORNE..................STate 4-0236 (Agent-Art Meyer - CR 5-7865)	
CONLON #30) SHERIFF #28)	STANLEY ANDREWS..............RUgby 6-2897 (Agent-Sam Armstrong - CR 1-1191)	

EXTRAS

HEAVY A

HEAVY B

HEAVY C

PHOTO DOUBLES

CISCO DBL.	TROY MELTON...................ARizona 3-6812
PANCHO DBL.	BILL CATCHING................RUgby 6-3521 RUgby 6-4903

Landres' cast sheets for **The Cisco Kid** episodes "Stolen Bonds" and "Protective Association" which were likewise shot at the same time with overlapping casts. (Courtesy of Paul Landres.)

George De Normand . . . . Manning
Carol Henry . . . . .Larry
Jack Ingram . . . . .Rocky
Story: Cisco and Pancho pursue the con man who killed a suspicious railroad detective and is using an innocent real estate dealer to foster a phony land promotion scheme.
Notes: Companion episodes: *Big Switch, Renegade Son*. This is the third episode with the "Oh, Pancho!" "Oh, Cisco!" ending which becomes standard from this point on.

THE WILL

Copyrighted . . . . October 31, 1950
Director . . . . Derwin Abrahams
Teleplay . . . . .Unknown
Cast
Duncan Renaldo . . . . The Cisco Kid
Leo Carrillo . . . . .Pancho
Gail Davis .Ruth Drake
Riley Hill . . . . Bob Drake
Art Dupuis . . . . .Hanley
Fred Kohler, Jr. . . . . Nixon
Robert Livingston . . . . Cantwell
Eddie Parker . . . . Barker
Forrest Taylor . . . . .Sheriff
George De Normand . . . . .Henchman
Story: Cisco and Pancho stop two gunmen from killing a young freight wagon driver who's just been released from prison after serving time for a strongbox robbery. Then they set out to prove that the young man was framed.
Notes: Companion episodes: *Convict Story, False Marriage*.

CATTLE QUARANTINE

Copyrighted . . . . November 7, 1950
Director . . . . Derwin Abrahams
Teleplay . . . . J. Benton Cheney
Cast
Duncan Renaldo . . . . The Cisco Kid
Leo Carrillo . . . . .Pancho
Peggy Stewart .Peggy
Earle Hodgins . . . . Idaho
Robert Livingston . . . . .Walter Stuart
Fred Kohler, Jr. . . . . Wiley
Forrest Taylor . . . . .Dr. Norman Slade
Art Dupuis . . . . .Utah
Luther Crockett . . . . Sheriff Jim
Riley Hill . . . . .Deputy
Story: Cisco and Pancho fight a crooked cattle buyer who's trying to gain control of a ranch by using the county livestock inspector as his tool to create a phony epidemic.
Notes: Companion episodes: *Counterfeit Money, Oil Land.*

RENEGADE SON

Copyrighted . . . . November 21, 1950
Director . . . . Derwin Abrahams
Teleplay . . . . .Betty Burbridge
Cast
Duncan Renaldo . . . . The Cisco Kid
Leo Carrillo . . . . .Pancho
Pamela Blake . . . . Joyce Henry
Pierre Watkin . . . . Sheriff
Fred Kohler, Jr. . . . . Deputy Sam
Nelson Leigh . . . . Jeff Henry
Carol Henry . . . . .Spike
Jack Ingram . . . . Henchman
Story: Cisco and Pancho try to save a young woman who's been convicted of the poison murder of her wealthy uncle.
Notes: Companion episodes: *Big Switch, Railroad Land Rush*. Betty Burbridge based her script for this episode on her screenplay for **In Old New Mexico** (Monogram, 1945), the second Cisco feature in which Renaldo starred.

FALSE MARRIAGE

Copyrighted . . . . November 28, 1950
Director . . . . Derwin Abrahams
Teleplay . . . . Betty Burbridge (?)
Cast
Duncan Renaldo . . . . The Cisco Kid
Leo Carrillo . . . . .Pancho
Gail Davis . . . . Nancy King
Mary Gordon . . . . .Mary O'Toole
Sarah Padden . . . . .Mother Smiley
Robert Livingston . . . . Duke Ralston
Russell Hicks . . . . Jasper King
Fred Kohler, Jr. . . . . Deputy
Luther Crockett . . . . Sheriff
Forrest Taylor . . . . Rev. William Smiley
Earle Hodgins . . . . Gramp
Story: Cisco and Pancho try to help a wealthy rancher prevent his niece's marriage to a notorious gambler, but when the rancher is killed they're accused of his murder.
Notes: Companion episodes: *Convict Story, The Will*. Betty Burbridge based her script for this episode on her screenplay for **The Cisco Kid Returns** (Monogram, 1945), the first Cisco feature in which Renaldo starred.

WEDDING BLACKMAIL

Copyrighted . . . . .December 5, 1950
Director . . . . Paul Landres
Teleplay . . . . .Sherman L. Lowe (?)

Cowboy MOTHER

A magazine clipping picturing Duncan Renaldo with his three children, Stephanie, Richard and Jeremy from the early 50's. (Courtesy of Charles K. Stumpf.)

Cast

Duncan Renaldo . . . . The Cisco Kid
Leo Carrillo . . . . .Pancho
Phyllis Coates . . . . Marge Lacey
Bill Kennedy . . . . .Sam Foster
Mike Ragan . . . . .Jason
David Bruce .Bill Ryan
Tom Tyler . . . . Sheriff
Story: Cisco and Pancho help out a young bank cashier whose forthcoming marriage to the bank president's daughter is endangered when two gunmen who know he's an ex-convict try to blackmail him.
Notes: Companion episodes: *Haven For Heavies, Phoney Sheriff, Uncle Disinherits Niece.*

LYNCHING STORY

Copyrighted . . . . .December 12, 1950
Director . . . . Paul Landres
Teleplay . . . . Ande Lamb
Cast
Duncan Renaldo . . . . The Cisco Kid
Leo Carrillo . . . . .Pancho
Carol Forman . . . . Pat Parker
Richard Emory . . . . Terry
Marshall Reed . . . . .Tracy
Frank Matts . . . . .Joe
Victor Cox . . . . Lou
Lane Chandler . . . . .Sheriff
I. Stanford Jolley . . . . Willard Parker
Story: When a mine owner is murdered by three employees who have been stealing gold from him, Cisco and Pancho stop a mob from lynching the dead man's prospective son-in-law for the crime.
Notes: Companion episodes: *Confession For Money, Pancho Hostage.* An uncredited Lyle Talbot plays the judge in this episode.

NEWSPAPER CRUSADERS

Copyrighted . . . . .December 19, 1950
Director . . . . .Albert Herman
Teleplay .Betty Burbridge
Cast
Duncan Renaldo . . . . The Cisco Kid
Leo Carrillo . . . . .Pancho
Ellen Hall .Elaine Jarrett
Dennis Moore . . . . .Henry Judd
Bill Henry . . . . Ben Jarrett
Steve Clark . . . . .Klondike
Ted Adams . . . . Phony Marshal
Ferris Taylor . . . . Mayor Carson
Story: Cisco and Pancho help a newspaper editor in his crusade against a crooked gambler and his cronies.
Notes: Companion episodes: *Freight Line Feud*

(first season), *Performance Bond* (listed in second season).

DOG STORY

Copyrighted . . . . .December 26, 1950
Director .Albert Herman
Teleplay . . . . .J. Benton Cheney
Cast
Duncan Renaldo . . . . The Cisco Kid
Leo Carrillo . . . . .Pancho
Tanis Chandler . . . . Melinda Weaver
Tristram Coffin . . . . Dude Cottrell
Zon Murray .Omaha
Frank McCarroll . . . . Henchman
Hank Patterson . . . . John Weaver
Kenne Duncan . . . . Townsman
Story: Cisco, Pancho and a dead prospector's dog hunt the crooked gambler who murdered the prospector for refusing to tell the location of his secret gold mine.
Notes: Companion episodes: *The Old Bum, Water Rights.*

CONFESSION FOR MONEY

Copyrighted . . . . .January 2, 1951
Director . . . . Paul Landres
Teleplay .Betty Burbridge
Cast
Duncan Renaldo . . . . The Cisco Kid
Leo Carrillo . . . . .Pancho
Carol Forman . . . . .Pat Lacey
Richard Emory . . . . Terry Ryan
Marshall Reed . . . . Tom Tracy
Frank Matts . . . . .Joe
Victor Cox . . . . Lou
Lane Chandler . . . . .Sheriff
I. Stanford Jolley . . . . A.W. Parker
Story: A lovely young lady asks Cisco and Pancho to help her fiance, who has confessed to a bank robbery and murder in return for the money needed for surgery on his mother.
Notes: Companion episodes: *Lynching Story, Pancho Hostage.*

THE OLD BUM

Copyrighted . . . . .January 9, 1951
Director . . . . .Albert Herman
Teleplay . . . . Louise Rousseau
Cast
Duncan Renaldo . . . . The Cisco Kid
Leo Carrillo . . . . .Pancho
Tanis Chandler . . . . .Paula Bonnard
Tristram Coffin . . . . .Kelly
Zon Murray . . . . .Shelby

A pre-Pancho publicity photo of Leo Carrillo. He was born in Los Angeles, California on August 6, 1881. His grandmother and her sisters made the first American flag in California. His great grandfather was the first provisional governor of California in 1837. He was a success on Broadway, made his film debut in 1929 and in addition to *The Cisco Kid* had his own TV show *Leo Carrillo's Diary*. (Courtesy of Charles K. Stumpf.)

Frank McCarroll . . . . Henchman
Hank Patterson . . . . Silas Bonnard
Kenne Duncan . . . . .Sheriff
Story: Cisco and Pancho help out a penniless derelict who unwittingly becomes a front man for rustlers when he pretends to be a wealthy rancher so as to impress his visiting daughter.
Notes: Companion episodes: *Dog Story, Water Rights*.

HAVEN FOR HEAVIES

Copyrighted . . . . .January 13, 1951
Director . . . . Paul Landres
Teleplay . . . . Warren Wilson
Cast
Duncan Renaldo . . . . The Cisco Kid
Leo Carrillo . . . . .Pancho
Phyllis Coates . . . . .Miss Doran
Bill Kennedy . . . . .Red Kelly
Mike Ragan . . . . Al Shelby
David Bruce . . . .(listed but not in cast)
Tom Tyler . . . . .Sheriff Jim Turner
Story: Cisco follows the murderer of a U.S. marshal to the haven of Twin Buttes, where outlaws enjoy immunity from the law.
Notes: Companion episodes: *Wedding Blackmail, Phoney Sheriff, Uncle Disinherits Niece*.

PANCHO HOSTAGE

Copyrighted . . . . .January 16, 1951
Director . . . . Paul Landres
Teleplay . . . . .Betty Burbridge
Cast
Duncan Renaldo . . . . The Cisco Kid
Leo Carrillo . . . . .Pancho
Carol Forman . . . . Pat Tracy
Richard Emory . . . . Terry
Marshall Reed . . . . .Frank Tracy
Frank Matts . . . . .Joe
Victor Cox . . . . Lou
Lane Chandler . . . . Sheriff Sam Dawson
I. Stanford Jolley . . . . .Parker
Story: Having jailed a bank robber, Cisco and Pancho are taken prisoners by his sister, who threatens to kill Pancho unless her brother is released.
Notes: Companion episodes: *Lynching Story, Confession For Money*.

FREIGHT LINE FEUD

Copyrighted . . . . .January 27, 1951
Director . . . . .Albert Herman
Teleplay . . . . Elizabeth Beecher
Cast
Duncan Renaldo . . . . The Cisco Kid
Leo Carrillo . . . . .Pancho
Ellen Hall . . . . .Elaine Frazer
Dennis Moore . . . . Judd
Bill Henry . . . . .Bill Jarrett
Steve Clark . . . . .Klondike
Ted Adams . . . . Cal
Ferris Taylor . . . . (listed but not in cast)
Story: Cisco and Pancho try to expose the outlaws who are attacking Bittercreek's freight line and putting the blame on a competing stage line owner.
Notes: Companion episodes: *Newspaper Crusaders* (first season), *Performance Bond* (listed in second season).

PHONEY SHERIFF

Copyrighted . . . . .February 6, 1951
Director . . . . Paul Landres
Teleplay . . . . .J. Benton Cheney
Cast
Duncan Renaldo . . . . The Cisco Kid
Leo Carrillo . . . . .Pancho
Phyllis Coates . . . . .Miss Lacey
Bill Kennedy . . . . Sam Kelly
Mike Ragan . . . . Al Shelby
David Bruce . . . . Blackie
Tom Tyler . . . . Sheriff
Story: Cisco and Pancho go after a cattle buyer who used a fake sheriff and deputies to trick them into turning over a friend's cattle herd.
Notes: Companion episodes: *Wedding Blackmail, Haven For Heavies,,Uncle Disinherits Niece*.

UNCLE DISINHERITS NIECE

Copyrighted . . . . .February 13, 1951
Director . . . . Paul Landres
Teleplay . . . . .Betty Burbridge
Cast
Duncan Renaldo . . . . The Cisco Kid
Leo Carrillo . . . . .Pancho
Phyllis Coates . . . . Marge Lacey
Bill Kennedy . . . . .Sam Foster
Mike Ragan . . . . Jason
David Bruce . . . . .Bill Ryan
Tom Tyler . . . . Sheriff
Bud Osborne . . . . Jim Lacey
Story: When a crooked lawyer murders a rancher who had threatened to disinherit his niece unless she stopped seeing her boyfriend, Cisco and Pancho try to clear the young man.
Notes: Companion episodes: *Wedding Blackmail, Haven For Heavies, Phoney Sheriff*.

Guess what famous phrase Dancer Buddy Ebsen is illustrating—with the help of Kidder Leo Carrillo.

WARNER BAXTER, LEO CARILLO, GRACE VALENTINE in "LOMBARDI, LTD."

Remember Mischa as the heavy-lidded Indian in

A scrapbook page furnished by Charles K. Stumpf that features clippings of Leo Carrillo.

PHONEY HEIRESS

Copyrighted . . . . .February 13, 1951
Director . . . . Paul Landres
Teleplay . . . . .J. Benton Cheney
Cast
Duncan Renaldo . . . . The Cisco Kid
Leo Carrillo . . . . .Pancho
Lyn Thomas . . . . Mary Stark
Vivian Mason . . . . .Stella Jackson
Jack Reynolds . . . . George Holden
Robert Bice . . . . .Turk
Mauritz Hugo . . . . Nebraska
Charles Watts . . . . .Sheriff Peabody
Joseph Granby . . . . .Judge
Story: Cisco and Pancho try to save a young woman's inherited property from a crooked lawyer who has hired an impostor to pose as the rightful owner.
Notes: Companion episodes: *Ghost Story, Water Well Oil* (both listed in second season). Quite clearly this episode, like its two companions, was filmed during the 1951-52 season. Why it was moved into the first season, and the first-season episode *Performance Bond* was released as part of the second season, is anyone's guess.

WATER RIGHTS

Copyrighted . . . . .February 20, 1951
Director . . . . .Albert Herman
Teleplay . . . . .Raymond L. Schrock
Cast
Duncan Renaldo . . . . The Cisco Kid
Leo Carrillo . . . . .Pancho
Tanis Chandler . . . . Marge Lacey
Zon Murray . . . . Sam Foster
Tristram Coffin . . . . .Tom Barton
Frank McCarroll . . . . .Jason
Hank Patterson . . . . Jim Lacey
Kenne Duncan . . . . .Sheriff
Story: Cisco and Pancho try to expose a crooked banker and lawyer who are scheming to sabotage the ranchers' water project and then foist their own project on the valley.
Notes: Companion episodes: *Dog Story, The Old Bum*.

SECOND SEASON, 1951-52

PERFORMANCE BOND

Copyrighted . . . . September 3, 1951
Director . . . . .Albert Herman
Teleplay . . . . Louise Rousseau (?)
Cast
Duncan Renaldo . . . . The Cisco Kid

Leo Carrillo . . . . .Pancho
Ellen Hall . . . . Elaine Wilson
Bill Henry . . . . Jarrett
Dennis Moore . . . . .Judd
Ted Adams . . . . Caleb Wilson
Steve Clark . . . . .Klondike
Ferris Taylor . . . . .Lem Carson
Story : Cisco and Pancho help a freight line owner who's in danger of forfeiting a $20,000 performance bond because of "accidents" preventing him from delivering ore to a smelter.
Notes: Companion episodes (both from first season): *Newspaper Crusaders, Freight Line Feud*. Quite clearly this episode, like its two companions, was filmed during the 1950-51 season. Why it was moved into the second season, and the second-season episode *Phoney Heiress* was released as part of the first season, is anyone's guess.

STOLEN BONDS

Copyrighted . . . . September 10, 1951
Director . . . . Paul Landres
Teleplay . . . . .J. Benton Cheney
Cast
Duncan Renaldo . . . . The Cisco Kid
Leo Carrillo . . . . .Pancho
Jean Dean .Christine
Reed Howes . . . . Dan
Pierce Lyden .Vic
Bill Holmes . . . . Henchman
Jim Diehl . . . . Henchman
Stanley Andrews . . . . .Sheriff
Bud Osborne . . . . Stage Driver
Story: While pursuing a man who stole $25,000 in bonds from their friend, Cisco and Pancho come to suspect that a young woman working as cook in a hotel is in league with the thief.
Notes: Companion episode: *Protective Association*.

POSTAL INSPECTOR

Copyrighted . . . . September 17, 1951
Director . . . . Paul Landres
Teleplay . . . . .J. Benton Cheney
Cast
Duncan Renaldo . . . . The Cisco Kid
Leo Carrillo . . . . .Pancho
Maris Wrixon . . . . Elaine Parker
Edward Keane . . . . Jay Willoughby
Ilse Mader . . . . (listed but not in cast)
Myron Healey . . . . .Drake
Dick Rich . . . . .Stacy
Rory Mallinson . . . . Sheriff
Steve Pendleton . . . . Inspector Sam Harris

And here's Leo Carrillo with that perennially favorite cowboy, Johnny Mack Brown, telling tall tales to the cheering throngs who came to see them at the colorful market place.

POSED BY LEO CARRILLO, DOUGLAS FAIRBANKS, JR., AND CLAIRE DODD IN "PARACHUTE JUMPER," A FIRST NATIONAL PICTURE.

Leo Carrillo, the "Cisco Kid's" partner in Law and Order, embraces his good friend Bob Cummings as they entertain shoppers at the famous Farmer's Market in Hollywood.

Duncan Renaldo as "CISCO"

4 Duncan Renaldo:

Another scrapbook page with clippings of both Leo Carrillo and Duncan Renaldo. (Courtesy of Charles K. Stumpf.)

Story: When Cisco and Pancho mail a letter in the town of Baxter Center, they're arrested as part of a gang of mail robbers.

Notes: Companion episode: *Kid Sister Trouble*. Ilse Mader gets an acting credit without actually appearing in this episode because Ziv once again decided to save a few dollars by using the cast list for the companion episode in the credit crawl for this one.

JEWELRY STORE FENCE

Copyrighted . . . . September 24, 1951
Director . . . . Paul Landres
Teleplay . . . . J. Benton Cheney
Cast
Duncan Renaldo . . . . The Cisco Kid
Leo Carrillo . . . . .Pancho
Kay Morley .Martha
Michael Whalen .Pete
Michael Mark . . . . Uncle Toby
Robert Wood .Terry
George Offerman .Ed
Steve Clark . . . . .Stage Driver
Therese Lyon . . . . .Woman on Coach
Story: While hunting for a purchaser of stolen jewelry, Cisco and Pancho encounter a crazy old man who tries to kill them with a crossbow built into an ornate clock.

Notes: Companion episode: *Water Toll*.

FOREIGN AGENT

Copyrighted . . . . October 1, 1951
Director . . . . Paul Landres
Teleplay . . . . .J. Benton Cheney
Cast
Duncan Renaldo . . . . The Cisco Kid
Leo Carrillo . . . . .Pancho
Ann Zika . . . . Diane
Carl Milletaire . . . . Wharton
Paul Hogan . . . . Henchman
Terry Frost . . . . .Dan
William M. McCormick . . . . .Panamint
John Merton . . . . .The Chief
Garnett A. Marks . . . . .Henchman
Story: Cisco uses a coded musical score to outwit foreign spies who are trying to take over a vast deposit of tungsten.

Notes: Companion episode: *The Bates Story*.

MEDICINE MAN SHOW

Copyrighted . . . . October 8, 1951
Director . . . . .Eddie Davis
Teleplay . . . . Warren Wilson

Cast
Duncan Renaldo . . . . The Cisco Kid
Leo Carrillo . . . . .Pancho
Wanda McKay . . . . .Sunny Benton
Stephen Chase . . . . Dixon
Dennis Moore .Bugsy
Ray Hyke .Henchman
Cactus Mack . . . . Henchman
George Davis . . . . .Henchman
Claudia Drake . . . . .Cheewee
Rodd Redwing . . . . .Flying Cloud
Charles Soldani . . . . .Red Moon
Story: While tracing a trunk containing guns being smuggled to the Comanches, Cisco learns that the trunk belongs to a young woman.

Notes: Companion episode: *Ride On (Black Lightning)*.

GHOST STORY

Copyrighted . . . . October 15, 1951
Director . . . . Paul Landres
Teleplay . . . . Elizabeth Beecher
Cast
Duncan Renaldo . . . . The Cisco Kid
Leo Carrillo . . . . .Pancho
Lyn Thomas . . . . .Mary Davis
Jack Reynolds . . . . George Holden
Robert Bice . . . . .Turk
Mauritz Hugo . . . . Nebraska
Charles Watts . . . . .Ben Larsen
Joseph Granby . . . . Will Harper
Story: Cisco and Pancho go after a pair of silver smugglers who killed their nervous partner, a rancher, when he tried to break with them.

Notes: Companion episodes: *Phoney Heiress* (listed in first season), *Water Well Oil*.

PROTECTIVE ASSOCIATION

Copyrighted . . . . October 22, 1951
Director . . . . Paul Landres
Teleplay . . . . Marjorie E. Fortin
Cast
Duncan Renaldo . . . . The Cisco Kid
Leo Carrillo . . . . .Pancho
Jean Dean . . . . .Peggy Conlan
Reed Howes . . . . .Dan Sloan
Pierce Lyden Vic
Bill Holmes . . . . Henchman
Jim Diehl . . . . Henchman
Bud Osborne . . . . .Henchman
Stanley Andrews . . . . Mr. Conlan
Story: Cisco and Pancho help a rancher and his daughter fight a gang of protection racketeers.

Notes : Companion episode: *Stolen Bonds*.

Duncan Renaldo .. *Rancho Mi Amigo*

974 Debra Drive
Santa Barbara, CA 93110

Telephone
(805) 687-0966

October 10, 1979

Dear Miss Downey:

Thank you very much for your kindly note, the newspaper clipping and for the "Under The Western Skies magazine. It is a very good article that Mr. Schiller wrote.

I am sending you an autographed glossy photo.

Again, thank you.

Kindest personal regards and good wishes.

Cordially yours —

Duncan Renaldo

A letter received from Duncan Renaldo when The World of Yesterday sent him a magazine with an article about him in it.

KID SISTER TROUBLE

Copyrighted	October 29, 1951
Director	Paul Landres
Teleplay	Louise Rousseau

Cast

Duncan Renaldo	The Cisco Kid
Leo Carrillo	Pancho
Maris Wrixon	Christine
Edward Keane	Conlan
Ilse Mader	Jane
Myron Healey	Sloan
Dick Rich	Martin
Rory Mallinson	Dave
Steve Pendleton	Lefty

Story: After encountering a woman gambling-house dealer doing target practice, Cisco and Pancho become involved with counterfeiters.

Notes: Companion episode: ***Postal Inspector***.

WATER TOLL

Copyrighted	November 5, 1951
Director	Paul Landres
Teleplay	J. Benton Cheney

Cast

Duncan Renaldo	The Cisco Kid
Leo Carrillo	Pancho
Kay Morley	Sondra Lindsay
Michael Whalen	Pete Sturgis
Michael Mark	Dusty
Robert Wood	Terry
George Offerman	Ed
Steve Clark	Sheriff
Brad Johnson	Johnny

Story: Cisco and Pancho help a woman rancher fight a greedy cattleman who's making unsuspecting drovers pay him for watering their stock.

Notes: Companion episode: ***Jewelry Store Fence***.

The photo that Duncan Renaldo sent with the letter on the facing page. Notice that he autographed for Diablo also.

THE BATES STORY

Copyrighted . . . . November 12, 1951
Director . . . . Paul Landres
Teleplay . . . . Sherman L. Lowe
Cast
Duncan Renaldo . . . . .The Cisco Kid
Leo Carrillo . . . . .Pancho
Ann Zika . . . . Lorraine Bentley
Carl Milletaire . . . .(listed but not in cast)
Paul Hogan . . . . Slick Wofford
Terry Frost . . . . Harry Gaines
William M. McCormick . . . . Hayden
John Merton . . . . Sheriff
Anna Demetrio . . . . Mexican Woman
Story: Cisco and Pancho are forced to switch clothes with two escaped convicts helped by a female accomplice and are later arrested as the fugitives themselves.
Notes: Companion episode: *Foreign Agent*..

WATER WELL OIL

Copyrighted . . . . November 13, 1951
Director . . . . Paul Landres
Teleplay . . . . Ande Lamb (?)
Cast
Duncan Renaldo . . . . The Cisco Kid
Leo Carrillo . . . . .Pancho
Lyn Thomas . . . . .Mary Turner
Jack Reynolds . . . . George Holden
Robert Bice . . . . Turk Martin
Mauritz Hugo . . . . Henchman
Charles Watts . . . . Sheriff
Joseph Granby . . . . Jim Turner
Story: Cisco and Pancho are shot at by a young hothead who thinks they tried to kill him because he's found oil on his ranch.
Notes: Companion episodes: *Phoney Heiress* (listed in first season), *Ghost Story*.

What senorita could resist the charms of the dashing Duncan Renaldo? Renaldo said about his costume, " I devised the costume myself, and tried to make it signify in some way each of the Latin countries. For example, the belts were Argentine and Ecuardorian. The hat was Mexican. By the time I got through with it, the whole thing was an amalgam of representation from each country. (Courtesy of Bobby Copeland.)

RIDE ON (BLACK LIGHTNING)

Copyrighted . . . . November 19, 1951
Director . . . . .Eddie Davis
Teleplay . . . . Warren Wilson
Cast
Duncan Renaldo . . . . The Cisco Kid
Leo Carrillo . . . . .Pancho
Wanda McKay . . . . Sally Emerson
Stephen Chase . . . . .Frank Larsen
Dennis Moore . . . . .Duke
Ray Hyke . . . . Steve
Cactus Mack .Utah
George Davis . . . . Doc
Chester Clute .Monty
Story: Cisco and Pancho stop a young woman from killing the wild stallion she believes has been stealing her mares, then try to find the human thieves who framed the horse.
Notes: Companion episode: *Medicine Man Show*.

VIGILANTE STORY

Copyrighted . . . . .December 4, 1951
Director . . . . Paul Landres
Teleplay . . . . .J. Benton Cheney
Cast
Duncan Renaldo . . . . The Cisco Kid
Leo Carrillo . . . . .Pancho
Lois Hall . . . . Lois Holden
Bill George . . . . .Pike
Craig Hunter . . . . .Henchman
Hugh Prosser . . . . Jed Haskell
James Kirkwood . . . . .Henchman
Earle Hodgins .Tom
Edmund Cobb . . . . John Holden
Story: Posing as a gambler and an organ grinder, Cisco and Pancho try to break up the band of masked vigilantes terrorizing the town of Buffalo Flats.
Notes: Companion episodes: *Sleeping Gas, Quicksilver Murder*.

HIDDEN VALLEY

Copyrighted . . . . .December 11, 1951
Director . . . . .Eddie Davis
Teleplay . . . . .J. Benton Cheney
Cast
Duncan Renaldo . . . . The Cisco Kid
Leo Carrillo . . . . .Pancho
Virginia Herrick . . . . .Nedra Challis
Tristram Coffin . . . . George Challis
Wee Willie Davis . . . . .Barty
I. Stanford Jolley . . . . .Jim Walker
Keith Richards . . . . .Rand

George Eldredge . . . . .Sheriff
Story: Cisco and Pancho get lost in the wilderness and discover a hidden valley run by a tyrannical ex-sea captain.
Notes: Companion episode: *Quarter Horse*.

CARRIER PIGEON

Copyrighted . . . . .December 18, 1951
Director . . . . Paul Landres
Teleplay . . . . .J. Benton Cheney
Cast
Duncan Renaldo . . . . The Cisco Kid
Leo Carrillo . . . . Pancho
Sherry Moreland . . . . .Joan Bentley
Leonard Penn . . . . .Gary Mason
Milburn Morante . . . . Tracy Parker
John Cason . . . . Henchman
Ted Mapes .Henchman
Garry Garrett . . . . .Henchman
Story: Cisco and Pancho become involved with a woman claiming to be an insurance investigator on the trail of a stolen diamond necklace.
Notes: Companion episode: *Jewelry Holdup*.

HYPNOTIST MURDER

Copyrighted . . . . .December 25, 1951
Director . . . . .Eddie Davis
Teleplay . . . . .J. Benton Cheney
Cast
Duncan Renaldo . . . . The Cisco Kid
Leo Carrillo . . . . .Pancho
Marsha Jones . . . . .Blanche Modell/Sue Prentiss
Riley Hill . . . . Bill Prentiss
Joe Forte . . . . Mr. Prentiss
Doris Merrick . . . . .Madame Lil
Denver Pyle . . . . Jerry Roark
Zon Murray . . . . .Henchman
Tom Holland . . . . .Henchman
Story: Cisco and Pancho try to stop a former carnival hypnotist who gets tired of waiting for her wealthy father-in-law to die and mesmerizes her husband into a murder attempt.
Notes: Companion episode: *Ghost Town*.

ROMANY CARAVAN

Copyrighted . . . . .January 8, 1952
Director . . . . Paul Landres
Teleplay . . . . .J. Benton Cheney
Cast
Duncan Renaldo . . . . The Cisco Kid
Leo Carrillo . . . . .Pancho
Dolores Castle . . . . Marisa
Sondra Rodgers . . . . Ilka
Craig Woods . . . . Jay Costain

Leo Carrillo earned a degree in journalism from Loyola University, and worked on a San Francisco newspaper as a cartoonist before becoming a dialect comedian. Although he played many parts in his long career, he is best remembered for his role of Pancho in the Cisco Kid films and TV series. Carrillo is shown here in a publicity photo for **The Girl From San Lorenzo** (United Artists, 1950). (Courtesy of Bobby Copeland.)

Peter Coe . . . . Danilo
Milburn Morante . . . . .Stefan
Jack George . . . . .Benji
Story: Cisco visits a gypsy camp and gets involved in a knife fight over a woman while Pancho is terrified by a dancing bear.
Notes: Companion episode: *Buried Treasure*.

ROBBER CROW

Copyrighted . . . . .January 15, 1952
Director . . . . Paul Landres
Teleplay . . . . Herbert Purdum
Cast
Duncan Renaldo . . . . The Cisco Kid
Leo Carrillo . . . . .Pancho
Mary Dean Moss . . . . .Nina Loring
Michael Vallon . . . . .Scotty
Raphael Bennett . . . . Jack Kells
Karl Davis . . . . .Gregg
Mickey Simpson . . . . Henchman
Kermit Maynard . . . . .Albuquerque Jones
Teddy Infuhr . . . . Tommy Loring
Story: Cisco and Pancho intervene in a feud between the gunmen who are guarding a placer mine and the workers from town who are suspected by the guards of stealing gold.
Notes: Companion episode: *Spanish Dagger*.

SLEEPING GAS

Copyrighted . . . . .January 22, 1952
Director . . . . Paul Landres
Teleplay . . . . .J. Benton Cheney
Cast
Duncan Renaldo . . . . The Cisco Kid
Leo Carrillo . . . . .Pancho
Lois Hall . . . . Jerry
Bill George . . . . .Joe
Hugh Prosser .Larry
James Kirkwood . . . . Fiddlin' Sam
George Eldredge . . . . Banker Wharton
Franklyn Farnum . . . . .Banker Tracy
Story: A bank holdup while Pancho is cashing a check involves Cisco with an outlaw family whose modus operandi includes a high-pitched fiddle and an ornamental globe full of sleeping gas.
Notes: Companion episodes: *Vigilante Story*, *Quicksilver Murder*.

QUARTER HORSE

Copyrighted . . . . .January 29, 1952
Director . . . . .Eddie Davis
Teleplay . . . . .J. Benton Cheney
Cast
Duncan Renaldo . . . . The Cisco Kid
Leo Carrillo .Pancho
Virginia Herrick . . . . Helen Butler
Tristram Coffin . . . . Joe Butler
I. Stanford Jolley . . . . Sam Carson
Keith Richards . . . . Terry
George Eldredge . . . . Jackson
Stanley Blystone . . . . Frank Wallace
Eddie Nash . . . . Nash
Story: Cisco steps into a revenge-motivated plot to fix a race pitting four quarter horses against a thoroughbred.
Notes: Companion episode: *Hidden Valley*.

JEWELRY HOLDUP

Copyrighted . . . . .February 5, 1952
Director . . . . Paul Landres
Teleplay . . . . .J. Benton Cheney
Cast
Duncan Renaldo . . . . The Cisco Kid
Leo Carrillo .Pancho
Sherry Moreland . . . . .Judy Winters
Leonard Penn . . . . Steve
Helene Millard . . . . Aunt Ellen Palmer
John Cason . . . . Jim
Milburn Morante . . . . Jasper Peabody
Ted Mapes .Marty
Story: Cisco and Pancho step in when jewel thieves who mailed some loot to themselves try to retrieve their package by force from an officious postal clerk.
Notes: Companion episode: *Carrier Pigeon*.

GHOST TOWN

Copyrighted . . . . .February 12, 1952
Director . . . . .Eddie Davis
Teleplay . . . . .J. Benton Cheney
Cast
Duncan Renaldo . . . . The Cisco Kid
Leo Carrillo .Pancho
Marsha Jones . . . . Sondra Spencer
Riley Hill . . . . George Hardy
Joe Forte . .Willoughby Baxter/Napoleon Gordon
Doris Merrick . . . . .Anita Hardy
Denver Pyle . . . . .Outlaw
Zon Murray . . . . Outlaw
Story: In an empty town, Cisco and Pancho meet a young woman searching for proof of her identity, a crazy hotel proprietor, an eloping young couple and some weird menaces.
Notes: Companion episode: *Hypnotist Murder*.

A full page Ad in <u>Variety</u> touting how many stations to whom *The Cisco Kid* has been sold.

QUICKSILVER MURDER

Copyrighted . . . . .February 12, 1952
Director . . . . Paul Landres
Teleplay . . . . .J. Benton Cheney
Cast
Duncan Renaldo . . . . The Cisco Kid
Leo Carrillo . . . . .Pancho
Lois Hall . . . . .Jennifer Hart
Bill George . . . . Larry Scott
Hugh Prosser . . . . .Joe Wallace
James Kirkwood . . . . .Marshal Fletcher
Joe Forte . . . . .Wharton Stone
Hunter Gardner . . . . Sam Moore
Story: Cisco goes after a corrupt public
prosecutor who steals quicksilver shipments and
uses chemical weapons to commit murder.
Notes: Companion episodes: *Vigilante Story*,
Sleeping Gas.

BURIED TREASURE

Copyrighted . . . . .February 19, 1952
Director . . . . Paul Landres
Teleplay . . . . .J. Benton Cheney
Cast
Duncan Renaldo . . . . The Cisco Kid
Leo Carrillo . . . . .Pancho
Dolores Castle . . . . .Toni
Sondra Rodgers . . . . Margot
Craig Woods . . . . Kit
Peter Coe . . . . Bernardo
Milburn Morante . . . . Girardot
Jack George . . . . Curator
Story: Cisco encounters an ancient witch-like hag
and her sons, who resort to torture and murder
while hunting the lost treasure of pirate Jean
Lafitte.
Notes: Companion episode: *Romany Caravan*.

SPANISH DAGGER

Copyrighted . . . . .February 19, 1952
Director . . . . Paul Landres
Teleplay . . . . .J. Benton Cheney
Cast
Duncan Renaldo . . . . The Cisco Kid
Leo Carrillo . . . . .Pancho
Mary Dean Moss . . . . .Shelley Drake
Michael Vallon . . . . Uncle Pete
Raphael Bennett . . . . Professor
Karl Davis . . . . Smiley
Mickey Simpson . . . . Jiggers
Kermit Maynard . . . . .Bert
Story: While Cisco is rescuing a prospector
from an explosion, he unearths a
jeweled dagger bearing a curse which

begins to work when it's stolen.
Notes: Companion episode: *Robber Crow*.

THIRD SEASON, 1952-53

MONKEY BUSINESS

Copyrighted . . . . August 3, 1952
Director . . . . Eddie Davis
Teleplay . . . . Robert A. White
Cast
Duncan Renaldo . . . . The Cisco Kid
Leo Carrillo . . . . .Pancho
Poodles Hanneford . . . . .Harry Smith
Grace Hanneford . . . . Pat Smith
Marshall Reed . . . . Slick
Zon Murray . . . . .Henchman
Jack Ingram . . . . Henchman
Story: Cisco and Pancho are arrested for
robbery after some stolen money is planted on
them by three thieves using an equestrian clown
show as their cover.
Notes: Companion episode: *Laughing Badman*.

THE PUPPETEER

Copyrighted . . . . .August 10, 1952
Director . . . . .George M. Cahan
Teleplay . . . . Irwin Lieberman
Cast
Duncan Renaldo . . . . The Cisco Kid
Leo Carrillo . . . . .Pancho
Leonard Penn . . . . .Clyde Barrows
Raymond Hatton . . . . Uncle Gitano
Mike Ragan . . . . Turk Evans
Joel Marston . . . . Marcus Meeker
Ted Mapes . . . . Sheriff Tom Enright
Louise Manley . . . . Townswoman
Story: Cisco and Pancho wonder why the
notorious Ghost Gang has never robbed the
wealthiest town in Peaceful Valley. When they
find out, they use Pancho's uncle's puppet show to
get word to the sheriff.
Notes: Companion episode: *Canyon City Kid*.

THE TALKING DOG

Copyrighted . . . . .August 17, 1952
Director .Eddie Davis
Teleplay . . . . Warren Wilson
Cast
Duncan Renaldo . . . . The Cisco Kid
Leo Carrillo . . . . .Pancho
Gail Davis . . . . .Miss Scott
Paul Livermore .Griff
Bruce Payne .Maddock
Allen Pinson . . . . Rusty

A very popular publicity photo of Duncan Renaldo from *The Cisco Kid* TV series.

Ferris Taylor . . . . Vincent C. Emerson
Cactus Mack . . . . Sheriff
Story: The first telephone in the West falls into the hands of bandits who use it to alert members of their gang when gold is being shipped. Without realizing it, Cisco and Pancho are the only ones who can break the gang's scheme.
Notes: Companion episode: *Big Steal.*

PANCHO AND THE PACHYDERM

Copyrighted . . . . October 5, 1952
Director . . . . .George M. Cahan
Teleplay . . . . . . .Elizabeth Beecher & Jack Lewis
Cast
Duncan Renaldo . . . . The Cisco Kid
Leo Carrillo . . . . .Pancho
Carole Mathews . . . . Sally Griffith
Tom London . . . . Ben Griffith
House Peters, Jr. . . . . Joe Shadden
Sheb Wooley . . . . .Roy Stokes
James Parnell . . . . Sheriff
Story: When Cisco and Pancho thwart the holdup of a one-wagon medicine show, they find themselves involved in the mystery of a stolen jade idol.
Notes: Companion episode: *Dutchman's Flat.*

KID BROTHER

Copyrighted . . . . October 12, 1952
Director . . . . .Eddie Davis
Teleplay . . . . Richard Conway
Cast
Duncan Renaldo . . . . The Cisco Kid
Leo Carrillo . . . . .Pancho
Edward Clark . . . . Doc Taylor
Linda Johnson . . . . Mrs. Hawkins
Keith Richards . . . . Brad Torrance
Robert Wilke Vic
Kermit Maynard . . . . .Henchman
Teddy Infuhr . . . . Bobby Torrance
Story: In an apparently abandoned shack, Cisco and Pancho come upon a wounded teen-age boy who tells them that outlaws murdered his brother.
Notes: Companion episodes: *Mad About Money, The Commodore Goes West.*

FACE OF DEATH

Copyrighted . . . . October 19, 1952
Director . . . . .George M. Cahan
Teleplay . . . . .J. Benton Cheney
Cast
Duncan Renaldo . . . . The Cisco Kid
Leo Carrillo . . . . .Pancho
Gloria Saunders . . . . Miss Spencer

Billy Griffith . Prof. John Ferris/Sam Chanfield
Robert Cabal .Tecla
Tom Monroe . . . . Digger
William Bakewell . . . . .Rance
Wesley Hudman . . . . Barry
Don Mahin .Henchman
Paul Marion .Henchman
Watson Downs . . . . .Quetzal
Story: Cisco and Pancho avenge an archaeologist who was murdered by his guides when on the verge of discovering the tomb of an Aztec high priest.
Notes: Companion episode: *Lost City*.

BIG STEAL

Copyrighted . . . . October 19, 1952
Director . . . . .Eddie Davis
Teleplay . . . . .J. Benton Cheney
Cast
Duncan Renaldo . . . . The Cisco Kid
Leo Carrillo . . . . .Pancho
Gail Davis . . . . .Lucille Gordon
Paul Livermore .Barry
Bruce Payne . . . . .Don Miguel Escobar
John Cason . . . . .Stewart
Story: Cisco and Pancho run into a phony U.S. land commissioner and a crooked homesteading project when they try to help their friend Don Miguel Escobar settle a dispute with a neighbor over water rights.
Notes: Companion episode: *The Talking Dog*.

LAUGHING BADMAN

Copyrighted . . . . October 26, 1952
Director . . . . .George M. Cahan
Teleplay . . . . Elizabeth Beecher
Cast
Duncan Renaldo . . . . The Cisco Kid
Leo Carrillo .Pancho
Marshall Reed . . . . Blade Meddick
Zon Murray . . . . .Sheriff Tom Brayle
Jack Ingram . . . . Homer Appleby
Billy Curtis . . . . Laughing Midget
Story: Cisco and Pancho discover a murdered deputy sheriff whose saddlebags are stuffed with $50 bills. A strange laugh, tiny footprints and a ventriloquist with a live dummy set them on the trail of the two counterfeiters who are responsible.
Notes: Companion episode: *Monkey Business*.

CANYON CITY KID

Copyrighted . . . . November 2, 1952
Director . . . . .George M. Cahan
Teleplay . . . . Warren Wilson

This blurred action shot shows Bill Catching doubling Pancho doing a horse transfer to Troy Melton doubling Cisco. (Courtesy of Bill Catching.)

Cast

Duncan Renaldo . . . . The Cisco Kid
Leo Carrillo . . . . .Pancho
Leonard Penn . . . . Curt Mathers
Raymond Hatton . . . . .Gramps
Mike Ragan . . . . Cappy
Joel Marston . . . . Kenny
Ted Mapes .Henchman
Louise Manley . . . . Lily

Story: Cisco becomes suspicious of a group staying in Canyon City. They intercept his letter of inquiry about them and then try to manipulate a local boy into challenging Cisco to a gunfight.

Notes: Companion episode: *The Puppeteer*.

DUTCHMAN'S FLAT

Copyrighted . . . . November 9, 1952
Director . . . . .George M. Cahan
Teleplay . . . . .J. Benton Cheney

Cast

Duncan Renaldo . . . . The Cisco Kid
Leo Carrillo . . . . .Pancho
Carole Mathews . . . . Debby Hansen
Tom London . . . . Dusty
House Peters, Jr. . . . . Curt Hansen
Sheb Wooley . . . . .Bill Bronson
James Parnell . . . . Ollie Hansen
Guy Wilkerson . . . . Cactus Bronson

Story: After being grubstaked by Cisco and Pancho, prospector Cactus Bronson strikes it rich. But he is murdered for his mine and his son thinks Cisco and Pancho are the killers.

Notes: Companion episode: *Pancho And The Pachyderm*.

MAD ABOUT MONEY

Copyrighted . . . . November 16, 1952
Director . . . . .Eddie Davis
Teleplay . . . . .Don Brinkley

Duncan Renaldo is trying to make the dog give him the keys to the jail cell as Leo Carrillo looks on in this scene from **Valiant Hombre** (United Artists, 1949).

Cast

Duncan Renaldo	The Cisco Kid
Leo Carrillo	Pancho
Edward Clark	Toby
Linda Johnson	Nora Blake
Keith Richards	Sandy
Robert Wilke	Barney
Kermit Maynard	Sheriff J.J. McGrew

Story: When an eccentric old man starts giving away bags of gold coins, he's suspected of murder. Cisco and Pancho try to prove his innocence. **Notes:** Companion episodes: *Kid Brother*, *The Commodore Goes West*.

LOST CITY

Copyrighted	November 23, 1952
Director	George M. Cahan
Teleplay	J. Benton Cheney (?)

Cast

Duncan Renaldo	The Cisco Kid
Leo Carrillo	Pancho
Gloria Saunders	Princess Zenda
Billy Griffith	Prof. Winston
Robert Cabal	Mathaozin
Tom Monroe	George Hardy
William Bakewell	Prof. Ralph Chaney

Story: Cisco and Pancho try to stop three men from making off with part of the treasure from a lost Inca city.
Notes: Companion episode: *Face Of Death*.

THUNDERHEAD

Copyrighted	November 30, 1952
Director	Sobey Martin
Teleplay	J. Benton Cheney

Cast

Duncan Renaldo	The Cisco Kid
Leo Carrillo	Pancho
Almira Sessions	Aunt Christine
Richard Barron	Winters

Duncan Renaldo in a publicity still for the movie series. (Courtesy of Jerry Ohlinger's Movie Material Store.)

Rodolfo Hoyos, Jr. . . . . .listed but not in cast
Edward Colmans . . . . .Jose Ramon
Everett Glass . . . . .Prado
Augie W. Gomez . . . . Manolo
Story: Cisco and Pancho open the eyes of absentee landowner Kathy Kerrigan to the corrupt practices of her ranch manager, who then holds her captive.
Notes: Companion episode: *Bell Of Santa Margarita*. The cast list on the credits of this episode is identical to the one on the credits of its companion episode even though the actual casts are different. The result is that the actress who played Kathy Kerrigan gets no credit at all, while Rodolfo Hoyos, Jr. is credited even though he's not in the film!

BELL OF SANTA MARGARITA

Copyrighted . . . . .December 14, 1952
Director . . . . .Sobey Martin
Teleplay . . . . .Edmond Kelso
Cast
Duncan Renaldo . . . . The Cisco Kid
Leo Carrillo . . . . .Pancho
Almira Sessions . . . . .Michaela
Richard Barron . . . . El Puma
Rodolfo Hoyos, Jr. . . . . .Vejar
Edward Colmans . . . . Padre Miguel
Everett Glass . . . . Don Fernando
Augie W. Gomez .Santo
Story: When the good-luck bell of Santa Margarita is stolen by El Puma and his gang, Cisco and Pancho try to recover it in time for the wedding of a friend's daughter.
Notes: Companion episode: *Thunderhead*.

LODESTONE

Copyrighted . . . . .December 21, 1952
Director . . . . .Sobey Martin
Teleplay . . . . .J. Benton Cheney
Cast
Duncan Renaldo . . . . The Cisco Kid
Leo Carrillo . . . . .Pancho
Peggy Stewart . . . . Linda Blaine
Gordon Clark . . . . Henry Duprez
Bud Osborne . . . . .Kansas
Hal K. Dawson . . . . Charles Blaine
Henry Rowland . . . . Rocky
Marshall Bradford . . . . Doc
Story: Cisco and Pancho go after a Kansas City dude who tries to kidnap the wife and daughter of a wealthy rancher and hold them for ransom.
Notes: Companion episode: *Gun Totin' Papa*.

DEAD BY PROXY

Copyrighted . . . . .December 28, 1952
Director . . . . .Eddie Davis
Teleplay . . . . Robert Clayton
Cast
Duncan Renaldo . . . . The Cisco Kid
Leo Carrillo . . . . .Pancho
Anne Kimbell . . . . .Alice Fleming
Lee Roberts . . . . .Olson
Peter Leeds . . . . Franklin Holt
Hank Patterson . . . . Jess Fleming
John Hamilton . . . . .Sheriff
Story: When a gunman hired to kill the owner of a general store is himself killed instead, Cisco persuades the intended victim to play dead as part of a scheme to flush out whoever hired the killer.
Notes: Companion episodes: *The Fire Engine*, *Fear*.

THE DEVIL'S DEPUTY

Copyrighted . . . . .January 4, 1953
Director . . . . .Eddie Davis
Teleplay . . . . Richard Conway
Cast
Duncan Renaldo . . . . The Cisco Kid
Leo Carrillo . . . . .Pancho
Myron Healey . . . . E.B. Johnson
Earle Hodgins .Sims
Salvador Baguez . . . . .Lopez
Eddie Parker . . . . .Henchman
Story: A crooked businessman hires a gunman named Lopez to impersonate Colonel Lucky Gonzales, who is to be the town's new marshal. Then Cisco and Pancho ride into town, and Pancho is mistaken by the townspeople for Gonzales and by the crooks for Lopez.
Notes: Companion episode: None.

CHURCH IN THE TOWN

Copyrighted . . . . .January 11, 1953
Director . . . . .Eddie Davis
Teleplay . . . . .Edmond E. Kelso
Cast
Duncan Renaldo . . . . The Cisco Kid
Leo Carrillo . . . . .Pancho
Tom Bernard . . . . Danny Whitacre
Bennie Bartlett . . . . .Matt Gray
Forrest Taylor . . . . Rev. Calvin Whitacre
Marshall Reed . . . . .Slade
Davison Clark . . . . Luke Gray
Lillian Albertson . . . . Townswoman
Story: Cisco and Pancho help a fighting parson build a new church, overcome the town banker's opposition and convert a sinful community.

Duncan Renaldo steps out of the woods ready for action in this publicity still for **Satan's Cradle** (United Artists, 1949.) (Courtesy of Jerry Ohlinger's Movie Material Store.)

Notes: Companion episode: None.

GUN TOTIN' PAPA

Copyrighted . . . . January 18, 1953
Director .Sobey Martin
Teleplay . . . . Irwin Lieberman (?)
Cast
Duncan Renaldo . . . . The Cisco Kid
Leo Carrillo . . . . .Pancho
Peggy Stewart . . . . .listed but not in cast
Gordon Clark . . . . .Ace
Bud Osborne . . . . Sheriff
Hal K. Dawson . . . . Eric Potter
Henry Rowland . . . . Tex
Marshall Bradford . . . . Restaurant Owner
Story: A meek little bookkeeper leaves home with his prize possession, a shotgun that once belonged to the notorious outlaw Shotgun Miller. When the gun is recognized, Cisco and Pancho try to help the man prove he's not Miller.
Notes: Companion episode: *Lodestone*. Peggy Stewart is listed in the credits because the identical cast list for the companion episode was recycled for this one.

THE FIRE ENGINE

Copyrighted . . . . January 25, 1953
Director . . . . .Eddie Davis
Teleplay . . . . Irwin Lieberman
Cast
Duncan Renaldo . . . . The Cisco Kid
Leo Carrillo . . . . .Pancho
Ezelle Poule . . . . .Rose
Bill Henry .Todd Ritter
Lee Roberts . . . . .Matt Collins
Peter Leeds . . . . Sheriff
Hank Patterson . . . . .Luke Higgins
John Hamilton . . . . John Mitchell
Story: Cisco and Pancho become involved when an old miner who's always wanted to be a fire chief buys a fire engine for his town and unwittingly interferes with the schemes of the local banker.
Notes: Companion episodes: *Dead By Proxy*, *Fear*.

THE CENSUS TAKER

Copyrighted . . . . .February 1, 1953
Director . . . . .Sobey Martin
Teleplay . . . . .Hilda & Endre Bohem
Cast
Duncan Renaldo . . . . The Cisco Kid
Leo Carrillo . . . . .Pancho
Roscoe Ates . . . . Henry Wilson

A Candid shot of Troy Melton doubling Cisco on location. (Courtesy of Mrs. Jean Melton.)

Kyle James . . . . .Floyd
Steve Wayne . . . . Jock
Alex Sharp . . . . .Brad
William Fawcett . . . . .Zeke Tobias
Edmund Cobb . . . . Hobbs
Story: Cisco and Pancho go after outlaws who pose as census takers to gather information on their potential victims.
Notes: Companion episode: None.

SMUGGLED SILVER

Copyrighted . . . . .February 8, 1953
Director . . . . .Sobey Martin
Teleplay . . . . .Unknown
Cast
Duncan Renaldo . . . . The Cisco Kid
Leo Carrillo . . . . .Pancho
John Damler . . . . .Shang Bisbee
Bill Hale . . . . .Sim Dykes
Gail Bonney . . . . .Minnie Higgins
Harvey Dunn . . . . .Cookie
Bobby Blake . . . . .Alfredo
Story: Cisco and Pancho set out after a band of silver smugglers who seem to know all of their pursuers' moves in advance.
Notes: Companion episode: None.

THE RUNAWAY KID

Copyrighted . . . . .February 15, 1953
Director . . . . .Sobey Martin
Teleplay . . . . Richard Conway

Another candid shot of Troy Melton doubling Cisco on location. (Courtesy of Mrs. Jean Melton.)

Cast

Duncan Renaldo . . . . The Cisco Kid
Leo Carrillo .Pancho
John Pickard . . . . .Layton
Harry Harvey, Jr. . . . . .Sheriff
Robert Bice . . . . .Notch
B.G. Norman . . . . .Jimmy
James Harrison Vic
Story: Cisco and Pancho encounter an eight-year-old boy running away from home and a band of outlaws looking for the hidden loot from an old crime.
Notes: Companion episode: None.

FEAR

Copyrighted . . . . .February 22, 1953
Director . . . . .Eddie Davis
Teleplay . . . . .J. Benton Cheney
Cast
Duncan Renaldo . . . . The Cisco Kid
Leo Carrillo .Pancho
Anne Kimbell . . . . Jennifer Kellin
Ezelle Poule . . . . .Matilda Kellin
Bill Henry . . . . .George Bruce
Lee Roberts . . . . .Lacey
Peter Leeds . . . . .Prescott
John Hamilton . . . . .Thomas T. Trimble
Story: Cisco and Pancho become involved in an "old dark house" mystery in which a dead man's ghost terrorizes the heirs who are required by his will to live on his ranch.
Notes: Companion episodes: *Dead By Proxy,The Fire Engine*.

THE PHOTO STUDIO

Copyrighted . . . . .March 1, 1953
Director .Sobey Martin
Teleplay . . . . .J. Benton Cheney
Cast
Duncan Renaldo . . . . The Cisco Kid
Leo Carrillo .Pancho
Rand Brooks . . . . .Clint Riley
James Seay . . . . .Harvey Price
Madeleine Burkette . . . . Donna Burdette
Walter McGrail . . . . Fred Appleby
Charles Williams . . . . .Stanley Burdette
Sandy Sanders .Juniper
Frank Jenks . . . . Marshal Sutton
Story: A rancher is shot to death while posing for a photograph. Cisco and Pancho try to clear the chief suspect, an ex-convict in love with the dead man's daughter.
Notes: Companion episode: None.

THE COMMODORE GOES WEST

Copyrighted . . . . .March 8, 1953
Director .Eddie Davis
Teleplay . . . . Robert Clayton
Cast
Duncan Renaldo . . . . The Cisco Kid
Leo Carrillo .Pancho
Edward Clark . . . . .Commodore Owens
Linda Johnson . . . . Judy Owens
Keith Richards . . . . Frank
Robert Wilke . . . . .Judd Stone
Kermit Maynard . . . . Farley
Story: On their way south to attend the wedding of Pancho's cousin, Cisco and Pancho stop to help a young woman who's worried about her father, a former Navy officer, and his embattled freight line.
Notes: Companion episodes: *Mad About Money, Kid Brother*.

FOURTH SEASON, 1953-54

BODYGUARD

Copyrighted . . . . October 1, 1953
Director .Eddie Davis
Teleplay . . . . .Barney A. Sarecky
Cast
Duncan Renaldo . . . . The Cisco Kid
Leo Carrillo .Pancho
Keith Richards . . . . Outlaw Leader
Steve Clark . . . . Henry Williams
John Merton . . . . .Wally
Riley Hill . . . . Larry
Virginia Mullen . . . . .Mrs. Williams

Story: The wife of a cantankerous old rancher asks Cisco and Pancho to watch out for her husband while he's carrying a tote-bag full of money. **Notes:** Companion episode: *Chinese Gold.*

PANCHO AND THE WOLF DOG

Copyrighted . . . . October 8, 1953
Director .Lambert Hillyer
Teleplay . . . . Warren Wilson
Cast
Duncan Renaldo . . . . The Cisco Kid
Leo Carrillo .Pancho
Gloria Talbott . . . . Suzette Duval
John Doucette . . . . Sandy Harris
Francis McDonald . . . . Frenchy Duval
Robert Livingston . . . . Miller
Bill Catching . . . . Sheriff
Story: Cisco and Pancho encounter a wild dog as they try to help an eccentric Frenchman who has built the first refrigeration plant in the West.
Notes: Companion episode: *The Faded General.*

BULLETS AND THE BOOBY TRAP

Copyrighted . . . . October 15, 1953
Director . . . . Herbert Leeds
Teleplay . . . . .Edmond E. Kelso
Cast
Duncan Renaldo . . . . The Cisco Kid
Leo Carrillo .Pancho
Rory Mallinson . . . . .Henchman
Billy Halop . . . . Cass Rankin
Bobby Blake .Davy
Lillian Albertson . . . . .Grandma
Troy Melton . . . . Winochie
Story: Cisco and Pancho chase an outlaw gang into a ghost town inhabited only by a teen-age inventor and his shotgun-toting grandmother.
Notes: Companion episode: *The Fugitive.*

THE GRAMOPHONE

Copyrighted . . . . October 22, 1953
Director . . . . Lew Landers
Teleplay . . . . Roy Hamilton
Cast
Duncan Renaldo . . . . The Cisco Kid
Leo Carrillo .Pancho
William Tannen . . . . Bix Douglas
William Boyett . . . . Henchman
Iron Eyes Cody . . . . Chief Big Cloud
Lyle Talbot . . . . R.H. Wilkerson
Rosa Turich . . . . Rosita
Story: Cisco and Pancho combat a rancher who uses a primitive record player to scare the Sioux

Another candid shot on location in 1952 picturing Troy Melton and Bill Catching and others. (Courtesy of Mrs. Jean Melton.)

into fighting the coming of the railroad.
Notes: Companion episode: *Indian Uprising.*

FREEDOM OF THE PRESS

Copyrighted . . . . October 29, 1953
Director . . . . Paul Landres
Teleplay . . . . .Lawrence Goldman
Cast
Duncan Renaldo . . . . The Cisco Kid
Leo Carrillo .Pancho
Frank Wilcox . . . . Mayor Rayburn
Paul Marion . . . . John Vine
I. Stanford Jolley . . . . .Henry Wilcox
Richard Avonde . . . . .Murdock
Bill Catching . . . . Jacks
Story: Cisco and Pancho help out an old newspaper editor who's caught in the middle of a hotly contested election battle between a corrupt mayor and a young reformer.
Notes: Companion episode: *The Raccoon Story.*

*BATTLE OF RED ROCK PASS

Copyrighted . . . . November 5, 1953
Director . . . . Lew Landers
Teleplay .Ben Markson
Cast
Duncan Renaldo . . . . The Cisco Kid
Leo Carrillo .Pancho
Rory Mallinson . . . . Sheriff Ed
William Fawcett . . . . .John Matlock
Red Morgan . . . . .Hank Dawson
Nan Leslie .Sue Matlock

Troy Melton doubling Cisco in a leap onto a moving buckboard. (Courtesy of Mrs. Jean Melton.)

Troy Melton . . . . .Henchman
Story: Cisco and Pancho try to help a retired Union Army artillery sergeant who spends his old age guarding a toll road with an old cannon but develops amnesia after being hit on the head by the outlaw Cisco is chasing.
Notes: Companion episode: *Outlaw's Gallery*. This is the episode where a rock flying the wrong way during an explosion sequence hit Duncan Renaldo and put him in the hospital for weeks. In the next several episodes filmed, which are marked with a star, Renaldo is seen only in extreme close-ups that were shot while he was recovering and most of the scripts call for him to have his face masked or bandaged so that his stunt double Troy Melton could take his place.

*BANDAGED BADMAN

Copyrighted . . . . November 12, 1953
Director . . . . .Eddie Davis
Teleplay . . . . .Donn Mullally
Cast
Duncan Renaldo . . . . The Cisco Kid
Leo Carrillo . . . . .Pancho
Christine Larson . . . . Terry Lane
Bill Henry . . . . Gold Thief
Reed Howes . . . . .Jeff Malcolm
Forrest Taylor .Sheriff
Marshall Bradford . . . . Dr. Shaw
Keith Richards . . . . Winkler
Lee Roberts . . . . Assayer
Story: When a gunman hired to kill Cisco is

blown up in an explosion, Cisco has a doctor cover his face with bandages and identify the corpse as Cisco himself.
Notes: Companion episode: *The Black Terror*.

CHINESE GOLD

Copyrighted . . . . November 19, 1953
Director . . . . .Eddie Davis
Teleplay . . . . George Callahan
Cast
Duncan Renaldo . . . . The Cisco Kid
Leo Carrillo . . . . .Pancho
Keith Richards . . . . Henchman
Steve Clark . . . . .Sheriff Joe Bowers
Judy Dan . . . . .Ming Toy
John Merton . . . . Turner
Story: Cisco and Pancho try to help a community of Chinese miners who are being systematically robbed by a masked bandit.
Notes: Companion episode: *Bodyguard*.

THE FADED GENERAL

Copyrighted . . . . November 26, 1953
Director . . . . .Lambert Hillyer
Teleplay . . . . .Donn Mullally
Cast
Duncan Renaldo . . . . The Cisco Kid
Leo Carrillo . . . . .Pancho
Gloria Talbott . . . . Amelia Lawrence
John Doucette . . . . .Sgt. Jess Corbin
Francis McDonald . . . . .Gen. Lawrence
Robert Livingston . . . . Col. Yancy Blake
Bill Catching . . . . Sheriff
Story: While trailing a gang of bank robbers wearing linen dusters, Cisco and Pancho are captured by a senile general and locked up in his private jail.
Notes: Companion episode: *Pancho And The Wolf Dog*. Director Lambert Hillyer borrowed the stunt at the climax of this episode from a Buck Jones Western feature, **One Man Law** (Columbia, 1932), which Hillyer had both written and directed.

THE FUGITIVE

Copyrighted . . . . .December 3, 1953
Director . . . . Herbert Leeds
Teleplay .Donn Mullally
Cast
Duncan Renaldo . . . . The Cisco Kid
Leo Carrillo . . . . .Pancho
Rory Mallinson . . . . .Madison
Billy Halop . . . . .Dr. Jerome Alpers
Harry Strang . . . . J.A. Kennedy

Troy Melton . . . . Val
Story: While hunting for a plague-stricken Mexican youth, Cisco and Pancho run into a wealthy rancher's plot to contaminate land with infected animals so he can buy it cheaply.
Notes: Companion episode: ***Bullets And The Booby Trap.***

INDIAN UPRISING

Copyrighted . . . . .December 10, 1953
Director . . . . Lew Landers
Teleplay . . . . .Larry Lund
Cast
Duncan Renaldo . . . . The Cisco Kid
Leo Carrillo . . . . .Pancho
William Tannen . . . . .Clyde Evans
William Boyett . . . . Henchman
Iron Eyes Cody . . . . .Chief Sky Eagle
Lyle Talbot . . . . .Thomas
Story: Cisco and Pancho go after the white men who are impersonating Chief Sky Eagle and his braves and terrorizing the farmers so they'll sell out to a local realtor for a few cents on the dollar.
Notes: Companion episode: ***The Gramophone.***

THE RACCOON STORY

Copyrighted . . . . .December 17, 1953
Director . . . . Paul Landres
Teleplay . . . . Warren Wilson
Cast
Duncan Renaldo . . . . The Cisco Kid
Leo Carrillo . . . . .Pancho
Frank Wilcox . . . . .Henry Collins
Paul Marion . . . . .Henchman
I. Stanford Jolley . . . . Gus Brown
Almira Sessions . . . . Sarah Hotchkiss
Claudia Barrett . . . . .Sally Phillips
Bill Catching . . . . Henchman
Story: Cisco and Pancho are asked to deliver miner Gus Brown's death certificate to the town of Sweetwater, and soon learn that Brown's will left all his property to his dog.
Notes: Companion episode: ***Freedom Of The Press.*** Despite the title, there is no raccoon in this episode. Most likely a dog was substituted when no trained raccoon could be found.

OUTLAW'S GALLERY

Copyrighted . . . . .December 24, 1953
Director . . . . Lew Landers
Teleplay . . . . .Ben Markson
Cast
Duncan Renaldo . . . . The Cisco Kid
Leo Carrillo . . . . .Pancho

A candid shot of Leo Carrillo and his beautiful palomino. (Courtesy of Mrs. Jean Melton.)

Rory Mallinson . . . . Will Roberts
William Fawcett . . . . Zack Marsh
Red Morgan . . . . .Gil
Nan Leslie . . . . Cynthia Marsh
John Damler . . . . Sheriff
Story: Cisco and Pancho use an express rider's hobby of painting and sketching to bait a trap for a robber gang plaguing the town of Dry River Falls.
Notes: Companion episode: ***Battle Of Red Rock Pass.***

*THE BLACK TERROR

Copyrighted . . . . .December 31, 1953
Director . . . . .Eddie Davis
Teleplay . . . . .Frank Burt
Cast
Duncan Renaldo . . . . The Cisco Kid
Leo Carrillo . . . . .Pancho
Christine Larson . . . . .Molly Cantry
Bill Henry . . . . Jed Barton
Reed Howes . . . . Hank Barton
Forrest Taylor . . . . Red Bell
Lee Roberts . . . . .Link Barton
Story: Cisco invents a masked-bandit personality for himself and uses it to join the notorious Barton Brothers gang so he can break it up from within.
Notes: Companion episode: ***Bandaged Badman.***

SKY SIGN

Copyrighted . . . . .January 7, 1954
Director . . . . .Eddie Davis
Teleplay . . . . George Callahan
Cast
Duncan Renaldo . . . . The Cisco Kid

211

A candid shot of Duncan Renaldo and Leo Carrillo. (Courtesy of Mrs. Jean Melton.)

Leo Carrillo . . . . .Pancho
Jan Bryant . . . . Miss Hardin
Mort Mills . . . . Carver
Mike Ragan . . . . .Twisty
Steve Clark . . . . Sheriff Cole
Story: Cisco and Pancho run out of ammunition and stop at a country store where an escaped convict and his gang are hiding.
Notes: Companion episode: *Marriage By Mail*.

CISCO MEETS THE GORILLA

Copyrighted . . . . .January 14, 1954
Director . . . . .Lambert Hillyer
Teleplay . . . . .Edmond E. Kelso
Cast
Duncan Renaldo . . . . The Cisco Kid
Leo Carrillo . . . . .Pancho
Robert Clarke . . . . .Johnny Boyle
Russ Conway . . . . Outlaw Leader
Max Wagner . . . . .Marvin
Troy Melton . . . . .Sheriff Mike
Bill Catching . . . . Bevins
Story: Cisco and Pancho go after the bandits who have pulled off a series of robberies while everyone in town was out searching for an escaped carnival gorilla.
Notes: Companion episode: *The Ventriloquist*.

NOT GUILTY

Copyrighted . . . . .January 21, 1954
Director . . . . Paul Landres
Teleplay . . . . .Barney A. Sarecky
Cast
Duncan Renaldo . . . . The Cisco Kid

Leo Carrillo . . . . .Pancho
Jose Gonzales Gonzales . . .
. . . Jose Gonzales de la Vega
Peter Coe . . . . .Joe
Tristram Coffin . . . . Outlaw Leader
Lyle Talbot . . . . Judge Watkins
Troy Melton . . . . Sheriff Brady
Story: Cisco and Pancho take a hand when Pancho's nephew witnesses a murder and one of the killer's pals impersonates the circuit judge in a scheme to free his friend.
Notes: Companion episode: *Horseless Carriage*.

*RODEO

Copyrighted . . . . .January 28, 1954
Director . . . . .Eddie Davis
Teleplay . . . . .Ed Gardner Jr. & Roy Engel
Cast
Duncan Renaldo . . . . The Cisco Kid
Leo Carrillo . . . . .Pancho
Keith Richards . . . . .Jim Usher
Marshall Reed . . . . .Henchman
Shirley Lucas . . . . Pat Lacy
John Cason . . . . .Phil Burleson
Bill Catching . . . . Ralph London
Sharon Lucas . . . . .Peg Lacy
Story: Cisco and Pancho try to protect two daredevil-riding sisters from a confidence man who's promoting a phony rodeo.
Notes: Companion episode: *The Steel Plow*.

MARRIAGE BY MAIL

Copyrighted . . . . .February 4, 1954
Director . . . . .Eddie Davis
Teleplay . . . . Buckley Angell
Cast
Duncan Renaldo . . . . The Cisco Kid
Leo Carrillo . . . . .Pancho
Jan Bryant . . . . Susan Marsh
Mort Mills . . . . Professor
Mike Ragan . . . . .Decker
Steve Clark . . . . Sheriff
Story: Cisco wins a bride when Pancho enters his picture in a matrimonial lottery, but the lottery turns out to be an outlaw gang's ruse to empty the town.
Notes: Companion episode: *Sky Sign*.

*THE IRON MASK

Copyrighted . . . . .February 11, 1954
Director . . . . Lew Landers
Teleplay .Donn Mullally
Cast
Duncan Renaldo . . . . The Cisco Kid

Leo Carrillo . . . . .Pancho
Dan White . . . . .Brace Hagger
John Crawford . . . . Sheriff Al White
Michael Whalen . . . . . Cain Hagger/Matt Hagger
Story: Cisco and Pancho try to rescue a sheriff who's been captured by outlaws and imprisoned in an iron mask.
Notes: Companion episode: *Cisco Plays The Ghost*.

*DOUBLE DEAL

Copyrighted . . . . .February 18, 1954
Director . . . . .Eddie Davis
Teleplay . . . . Fred Leighton
Cast
Duncan Renaldo . . . . The Cisco Kid
Leo Carrillo . . . . .Pancho
Bill Henry . . . . .Dave Langley
Edmund Cobb . . . . Brady
William Phipps . . . . .McNulty
Frank Hagney .Connors
Charles Watts . . . . Clark Jones
Bill Catching . . . . Sheriff
Story: Cisco finds himself a fugitive after an old enemy of his hires an actor to dress up as Cisco and commit a series of robberies.
Notes: Companion episode: *Powder Trail*.

HORSELESS CARRIAGE

Copyrighted . . . . .February 25, 1954
Director . . . . Paul Landres
Teleplay . . . . . . David Nowinson & Barry Cohon
Cast
Duncan Renaldo . . . . The Cisco Kid
Leo Carrillo . . . . .Pancho
Jose Gonzales Gonzales . . . . Jose
Peter Coe . . . . .Henchman
Tristram Coffin . . . . Nick Ward
Jeanne Dean . . . . .Doris
William Fawcett . . . . .Scroggins
Bill Catching . . . . Sheriff
Story: Cisco and Pancho try to help Pancho's nephew, whose newly purchased horseless carriage is used as a getaway vehicle by bank robbers.
Notes: Companion episode: *Not Guilty*.

*THE STEEL PLOW

Copyrighted . . . . .March 4, 1954
Director . . . . .Eddie Davis
Teleplay . . . . George Callahan
Cast
Duncan Renaldo . . . . The Cisco Kid
Leo Carrillo . . . . .Pancho

A Candid Shot of Duncan Renaldo surrounded by crew. (Courtesy of Mrs. Jean Melton.)

Keith Richards . . . . .William Griff
Marshall Reed . . . . John Sterns
Shirley Lucas . . . . Grace Warren
John Cason . . . . .Cavvy
Bill Catching . . . . .Farmer Jarvis
Kermit Maynard . . . . .Mr. Warren
Story: Cisco helps an inventive blacksmith make a steel plow to help the local farmers cultivate the stony soil.
Notes: Companion episode: *Rodeo*.

THE VENTRILOQUIST

Copyrighted . . . . .March 11, 1954
Director .Lambert Hillyer
Teleplay . . . . Roy Hamilton & Barry Cohon
Cast
Duncan Renaldo . . . . The Cisco Kid
Leo Carrillo . . . . .Pancho
Robert Clarke . . . . .Bud Thatcher
Russ Conway . . . . E.W. Akers
Max Wagner . . . . Webster
Rankin Mansfield . . . . .Hiram Thatcher
Story: Cisco uses Pancho's voice-throwing skill to expose a crooked assayer who kidnaps prospectors after they've filed their claims.
Notes: Companion episode: *Cisco Meets The Gorilla*.

*POWDER TRAIL

Copyrighted . . . . .March 18, 1954
Director . . . . .Eddie Davis
Teleplay . . . . George Callahan

Another candid shot of Duncan Renaldo on location. (Courtesy of Mrs. Jean Melton.)

Cast
Duncan Renaldo . . . . The Cisco Kid
Leo Carrillo .Pancho
Bill Henry . . . . .Blount
Edmund Cobb . . . . Mr. Adams
William Phipps . . . . Henchman
Frank Hagney . . . . Lon
Shirley Tegge . . . . .Celia Adams
Patsy Moran . . . . .Townswoman
Story: Cisco and Pancho try to find out why outlaws are stealing wagonloads of the petrified-wood curios on which the economy of the virtual ghost town of Padera depends.
Notes: Companion episode: *Double Deal.*

*CISCO PLAYS THE GHOST

Copyrighted . . . . .March 25, 1954
Director . . . . Lew Landers
Teleplay . . . . Warren Wilson
Cast
Duncan Renaldo . . . . The Cisco Kid
Leo Carrillo . . . . .Pancho
Dan White . . . . Alan Moxley
John Crawford . . . . .Sheriff Todd
Michael Whalen . . . . .Hank Winters
Bennie Bartlett . . . . .Jimmy Winters
Byron Foulger . . . . .Claude Bobkins, Jr.
Troy Melton . . . . .Henchman
Story: Cisco uses a player piano and spook effects to convince a superstitious killer that he's being haunted by his victims.
Notes: Companion episode: *The Iron Mask.*

A SIX-GUN FOR NO-PAIN

Copyrighted . . . . September 25, 1954
Director . . . . .Lambert Hillyer
Teleplay . . . . .Barney A. Sarecky
Cast
Duncan Renaldo . . . . The Cisco Kid
Leo Carrillo . . . . .Pancho
Dennis Moore . . . . Henchman
Earle Hodgins . . . . .No-Pain Norton
Henry Rowland . . .Steve Potter/Blackie Dawson
Joey Ray . . . . .Briggs
Mickey Simpson . . . . Patient
Zon Murray . . . . .Sheriff
Story: Cisco enlists the aid of a traveling dentist to track down a notorious killer who's set up a new identity as a cattle dealer.
Notes: Companion episode: *Sundown's Gun.*

THE HAUNTED STAGE STOP

Copyrighted . . . . October 2, 1954
Director . . . . .Lambert Hillyer
Teleplay . . . . Robert Clayton
Cast
Duncan Renaldo . . . . The Cisco Kid
Leo Carrillo . . . . .Pancho
Nan Leslie . . . . .Judy MacPherson
John Cason . . . . Henchman
Bill Kennedy . . . . Hank Jaggett
Myron Healey . . . . .Don White
Bob Woodward . . . . .Henchman
Story: What purports to be the ghost of way station master Angus MacPherson summons Cisco and Pancho to trace the gold shipment that vanished when Angus did.
Notes: Companion episode: *Pot Of Gold.*

GOLD STRIKE

Copyrighted . . . . October 9, 1954
Director . . . . .Eddie Davis
Teleplay . . . . Ande Lamb
Cast
Duncan Renaldo . . . . The Cisco Kid
Leo Carrillo . . . . .Pancho
Jacquelyn Park . . . . Dolly Ferguson
Sandy Sanders . . . . Gary Austin
James Anderson . . . . .Tap
Marshall Reed . . . . .Fred
Ed Hinton . . . . Outlaw
Story: Cisco and Pancho are escorting a safecracker to jail when their stagecoach is captured by bandits who take all the passengers to a ghost town.

214

Notes: Companion episode: *Caution Of Curley Thompson.*

TROUBLE IN TONOPAH

Copyrighted . . . . October 16, 1954
Director . . . . .Lambert Hillyer
Teleplay . . . . Oliver Drake
Cast
Duncan Renaldo . . . . The Cisco Kid
Leo Carrillo . . . . .Pancho
Edwin Parker . . . . Jeff Donovan
Kenneth MacDonald . . . . Henry Blake
Gregg Barton . . . . Mike Dugan
Kermit Maynard . . . . Phil Dugan
Edward Clark . . . . Doc
Dan White . . . . Sheriff
Story: Cisco and Pancho try to outwit a robber who has somehow learned the combination to the express office's burglar-proof safe and pulled off a series of baffling thefts.
Notes: Companion episode: *Fool's Gold.* Oliver Drake borrowed the plot of this episode from his script for the B Western feature **Trouble In Sundown** (RKO, 1938), starring George O'Brien.

HARRY THE HEIR

Copyrighted . . . . October 23, 1954
Director . . . . .Lambert Hillyer
Teleplay . . . . Robert Clayton
Cast
Duncan Renaldo . . . . The Cisco Kid
Leo Carrillo . . . . .Pancho
I. Stanford Jolley . . . . .Roderick Lamoreux
Fay Morley . . . . .Antoinette Lamoreux
James Parnell . . . . Sheriff
Leonard Penn . . . . .Jed Proctor
Keith Richards . . . . London Harry Hanley
Story: While trying to save an egotistical actor who's confessed to bank robbery and murder, Cisco and Pancho find that the grave of the supposed murder victim is empty.
Notes: Companion episode: None.

THE LOWEST BIDDER

Copyrighted . . . . October 30, 1954
Director . . . . .Lambert Hillyer
Teleplay . . . . Ande Lamb
Cast
Duncan Renaldo . . . . The Cisco Kid
Leo Carrillo . . . . .Pancho
Bill George . . . . Greg Sayer
Kenneth Terrell . . . . Paul Blackwell
Lane Bradford . . . . .Hayne
Eddy Waller . . . . Eli Oliver

Duncan Renaldo poses with tourists on location. (Courtesy of Mrs. Jean Melton.)

Jack Ingram .Stableman
Story: Cisco and Pancho confront a scheming well-digger who's out to steal the funds a thirsty town has raised to secure a water supply.
Notes: Companion episode: *The Hospital.*

MINING MADNESS

Copyrighted . . . . November 6, 1954
Director . . . . .Lambert Hillyer
Teleplay . . . . Gerald Geraghty
Cast
Duncan Renaldo . . . . The Cisco Kid
Leo Carrillo . . . . .Pancho
Raymond Hatton . . . . Jeff Hanby
Marshall Reed . . . . .Todd Wheeler
Ted Mapes .Augie
Lee Roberts . . . . .Sheriff
Story: When an old prospector friend of theirs is cheated by a crooked gambler, Cisco and Pancho kidnap the gambler and make him work a worthless but salted gold claim.
Notes: Companion episode: *Three Suspects.*

SUNDOWN'S GUN

Copyrighted . . . . November 13, 1954
Director . . . . .Lambert Hillyer
Teleplay . . . . .Wilbur S. Peacock
Cast
Duncan Renaldo . . . . The Cisco Kid
Leo Carrillo . . . . .Pancho
Dennis Moore . . . . Sheriff Fred
Henry Rowland . . . . Matt Barlow
Earle Hodgins . . . . .Purdy
B.G. Norman .Billy
Story: Cisco and Pancho try to straighten out a

Troy Melton doubling Cisco is about to jump off a roof. (Courtesy of Mrs. Jean Melton.)

12-year-old boy who's disappointed in his father, a workmanlike sheriff, and worships his dead grandfather, a famous gunfighter.
Notes: Companion episode: *A Six-Gun For No-Pain*.

POT OF GOLD

Copyrighted . . . . November 20, 1954
Director . . . . .Lambert Hillyer
Teleplay . . . . .Wilbur S. Peacock
Cast
Duncan Renaldo . . . . The Cisco Kid
Leo Carrillo . . . . .Pancho
Nan Leslie . . . . .Mary Andrew
John Cason . . . . Frank
Bill Kennedy . . . . .Deputy Cogley
Myron Healey . . . . .Jim Gault
Hank Patterson . . . . .Wind River Bill
William Vedder . . . . .Pete Andrew
Bob Woodward . . . . .Jake
Story: When a half-crazy old man is killed by a deputy sheriff trying to make him reveal the location of a buried Civil War treasure, Cisco and Pancho and a traveling snake-oil peddler help the dead man's daughter find the fortune.
Notes: Companion episode: *The Haunted Stage Stop*.

CAUTION OF CURLEY THOMPSON

Copyrighted . . . . November 27, 1954
Director . . . . .Eddie Davis
Teleplay . . . . Barry Cohon
Cast
Duncan Renaldo . . . . The Cisco Kid
Leo Carrillo . . . . .Pancho

Jacquelyn Park .Ruth
Sandy Sanders . . . . Whitey Thompson
James Anderson . . . . Jack Hanley
Marshall Reed . . . . Wilson Ford
Ed Hinton . . . . .Muley
Story: Cisco and Pancho help an ex-convict track down the leader of his old gang, who has started a new life as the owner of a general store.
Notes: Companion episode: *Gold Strike*. Director Eddie Davis must have changed the Thompson character's first name from Curley to Whitey after giving the part to Sandy Sanders, whose hair was light-colored and straight.

FOOL'S GOLD

Copyrighted . . . . .December 4, 1954
Director . . . . .Lambert Hillyer
Teleplay . . . . Gerald Geraghty
Cast
Duncan Renaldo . . . . The Cisco Kid
Leo Carrillo . . . . .Pancho
Edwin Parker . . . . Outlaw Leader
Kenneth MacDonald . . . . J.L. Webster
Gregg Barton . . . . Grady
Kermit Maynard . . . . Booth
Karolee Kelly . . . . Cindy
Story: Cisco and Pancho trap some outlaws by making them believe that their hideout is the center of a major gold rush.
Notes: Companion episode: *Trouble In Tonopah*.

THE HOSPITAL

Copyrighted . . . . .December 11, 1954
Director . . . . .Lambert Hillyer
Teleplay . . . . .Wilbur S. Peacock
Cast
Duncan Renaldo . . . . The Cisco Kid
Leo Carrillo . . . . .Pancho
Bill George . . . . Dr. Bob Randall
Kenneth Terrell . . . . Jason Turnbull
Lane Bradford . . . . Blackie
Eddy Waller . . . . Dr. Bender
Jack Ingram . . . . .Sheriff
Story: Cisco and Pancho help a young doctor who's been framed for attempted murder by a fund-embezzling trustee of the town hospital.
Notes: Companion episode: *The Lowest Bidder*.

THREE SUSPECTS

Copyrighted . . . . .December 18, 1954
Director . . . . .Lambert Hillyer
Teleplay . . . . Kenneth A. Enochs
Cast
Duncan Renaldo . . . . The Cisco Kid

Leo Carrillo . . . . .Pancho
Lee Roberts . . . . .Jim
Marshall Reed . . . . Whit Jameson
Raymond Hatton . . . . .Morgan
Ted Mapes . . . . .Burke
Story: With his only clue a bandit's hat found near the scene of a robbery, Cisco tries to figure out which of three suspects is the bandit.
Notes: Companion episode: *Mining Madness*.

PANCHO'S NIECE

Copyrighted . . . . .December 25, 1954
Director . . . . .Lambert Hillyer
Teleplay . . . . Barry Cohon
Cast
Duncan Renaldo . . . . The Cisco Kid
Leo Carrillo . . . . .Pancho
J. P. O'Donnell . . . . Dolores James
John Pickard . . . . Riddle
Julian Rivero . . . . Juan/Fernando Ramirez
William Tannen . . . . Roland McCard
Roy Engel . . . . .Sheriff
Story: Cisco has Pancho pose as the uncle of a half-Mexican young woman whose banker father apparently killed himself after losing most of the bank's money.
Notes: Companion episode: None. This episode is a remake of the B Western feature **The Fighting Code** (Columbia, 1933), which was written and directed by Lambert Hillyer and starred Buck Jones.

EXTRADITION PAPERS

Copyrighted . . . . .January 1, 1955
Director . . . . .Lambert Hillyer
Teleplay . . . . Kenneth A. Enochs
Cast
Duncan Renaldo . . . . The Cisco Kid
Leo Carrillo . . . . .Pancho
John Beradino . . . . Jess Martin
Dayton Osmond . . . . .Tommy Martin
Mitchell Kowal . . . . Henchman
Henry Rowland . . . . .Henchman
Sam Flint . . . . Sheriff
Story: While taking a captured bandit leader to trial, Cisco and Pancho are ambushed by his gang while passing through a ghost town.
Notes: Companion episode: *Son Of A Gunman*.

NEW EVIDENCE

Copyrighted . . . . .January 8, 1955
Director . . . . .Lambert Hillyer
Teleplay . . . . Ande Lamb

Troy Melton doubling Cisco jumps from the rocks onto a shack. (Courtesy of Mrs. Jean Melton.)

Cast
Duncan Renaldo . . . . The Cisco Kid
Leo Carrillo . . . . .Pancho
Sandy Sanders . . . . .Dorsey Knudsen
Edwin Parker . . . . Gibbs
Fay Morley . . . . .Carmel Tracy
Earle Hodgins . . . . .Judge Elias Kendall
Edmund Cobb . . . . Henry Tracy
Story: When a rancher is murdered and his daughter's boyfriend is put on trial for the crime, Cisco uses a Farmer's Almanac and a full moon and the Army signal system to trap the real killer.
Notes: Companion episode: None. The plot device in this episode is lifted bodily from the classic **Young Mr. Lincoln** (20th Century-Fox, 1939), directed by John Ford and starring Henry Fonda.

DOORWAY TO NOWHERE

Copyrighted . . . . .January 15, 1955
Director . . . . .Lambert Hillyer
Teleplay . . . . Robert Clayton
Cast
Duncan Renaldo . . . . The Cisco Kid
Leo Carrillo . . . . .Pancho
Lillian Albertson . . . . Mrs. Collins
Nan Leslie . . . . Blanche
Kenneth MacDonald . . . . Ralph Hammond
Lane Chandler .Sheriff
Story: Cisco escorts a wealthy old Boston lady to her daughter-in-law's ranch but is charged with kidnapping and robbery when both women disappear.
Notes: Companion episode: None.

Troy Melton doubling Cisco fights with a bad guy in the back of wagon. (Courtesy of Mrs. Jean Melton.)

STOLEN RIVER

Copyrighted . . . . .January 22, 1955
Director . . . . .Lambert Hillyer
Teleplay . . . . Barry Cohon
Cast
Duncan Renaldo . . . . The Cisco Kid
Leo Carrillo . . . . .Pancho
Nancy Hale . . . . Mady Barbour
I. Stanford Jolley . . . . .Slim Lennox
Zon Murray . . . . King
Thayer Roberts . . . . .Sheriff
Rory Mallinson . . . . Surveyor
Story: Arriving at the ranch of their old friend Wayne Barbour, Cisco and Pancho find that Wayne has been murdered and that his widow is ready to sell the ranch and move back east.
Notes: Companion episode: *Montezuma's Treasure*.

SON OF A GUNMAN

Copyrighted . . . . .January 29, 1955
Director . . . . .Lambert Hillyer
Teleplay .Rik Vollaerts
Cast
Duncan Renaldo . . . . The Cisco Kid
Leo Carrillo . . . . .Pancho
John Beradino . . . . Buck Lundigan
Mitchell Kowal . . . . Johnny Nestor
Sam Flint . . . . Sheriff
Henry Rowland . . .Will Foresby/Will Knowland
Story: When the son of a famous gunfighter is run out of town, Cisco and Pancho try to help the young man outlive his father's reputation.
Notes: Companion episode: *Extradition Papers*.

JUGGLER'S SILVER

Copyrighted . . . . .February 3, 1955
Director . . . . .Lambert Hillyer
Teleplay . . . . Barry Cohon
Cast
Duncan Renaldo . . . . The Cisco Kid
Leo Carrillo . . . . .Pancho
Fortune Gordien . . . . .Danny Harris
Rodd Redwing . . . . .Nimble Nick Carr
Leonard Penn . . . . Judd
Kenneth MacDonald . . . . . . Marshal Ed Watson
Story: Cisco and Pancho are shot at by a former circus juggler who bought what he claims is a worthless mine.
Notes: Companion episode: None.

THE KIDNAPPED CAMERAMAN

Copyrighted . . . . .February 10, 1955
Director . . . . .Lambert Hillyer
Teleplay . . . . Barry Cohon
Cast
Duncan Renaldo . . . . The Cisco Kid
Leo Carrillo . . . . .Pancho
Tom Irish .Ted Miller
Terry Frost . . . . Chuck Farley
Keith Richards . . . . Red Farley
Kermit Maynard . . . . .Sheriff
Chuck Cason . . . . .Tracy
Story: When a photographer inadvertently takes a picture of a murder at the Lone Mountain mine, Cisco uses the lantern slide to trap the killer.
Notes: Companion episode: *The Two-Wheeler*.

CISCO AND THE GIANT

Copyrighted . . . . .February 17, 1955
Director . . . . .Lambert Hillyer
Teleplay . . . . Bill George
Cast
Duncan Renaldo . . . . The Cisco Kid
Leo Carrillo . . . . .Pancho
Dennis Moore . . . . Sheriff Sam Johnson
Glenn Strange . . . . .Curly Peters
Rex Thorsen . . . . .Judd Casey
Kenneth Terrell . . . . .Lobo
Patricia Tiernan . . . . Ann Johnson
Story: A huge and dim-witted man who thinks he killed his lawman brother-in-law takes refuge with an outlaw gang. Then Cisco and Pancho join the gang in an attempt to solve a series of well-planned stagecoach robberies.
Notes: Companion episode: None.

The two sides of a post card sent to Cisco TV fans by their sponsor, The Tip Top Bakers. (Courtesy of Bobby Copeland.)

MONTEZUMA'S TREASURE

Copyrighted . . . . February 24, 1955
Director . . . . .Lambert Hillyer
Teleplay . . . . .Wilbur S. Peacock

Cast

Duncan Renaldo . . . . The Cisco Kid
Leo Carrillo . . . . .Pancho
Thayer Roberts . . . . .Prof. Bradley
I. Stanford Jolley . . . . .Prof. Danforth
Zon Murray . . . . .Bull
Ferris Taylor . . . . .Sheriff

Story: A professor, hunting for the Aztec emperor's fabulous treasure, discovers its location but is attacked by outlaws and wounded. A code message on a deck of cards leads Cisco and Pancho to the treasure.

Notes: Companion episode: _Stolen River_.

VENDETTA

Copyrighted . . . . .March 3, 1955
Director . . . . .Lambert Hillyer
Teleplay . . . . Ande Lamb

Cast

Duncan Renaldo . . . . The Cisco Kid
Leo Carrillo . . . . .Pancho
Alan Wells . . . . Gil Parker
Claudia Barrett . . . . .Terry Monahan
Kenneth MacDonald . . . . .Frank Guthrie
Leonard Penn . . . . .Warren Sturgis

Story: Cisco and Pancho try to settle an old family feud between neighboring ranchers which has been secretly fanned by a mercenary uncle.

Notes: Companion episode: None. Based on an original story by J. Benton Cheney.

THE TWO-WHEELER

Copyrighted . . . . .March 10, 1955
Director . . . . .Lambert Hillyer
Teleplay . . . . Barry Cohon

Cast

Duncan Renaldo . . . . The Cisco Kid

219

A publicity photo of Duncan Renaldo used for *The Cisco Kid* TV series. (Courtesy of Old West Shop.)

Leo Carrillo . . . . .Pancho
Tom Irish . . . . Albert Taylor
Sally Fraser . . . . .Martha
Keith Richards . . . . Frank Douglas
Terry Frost . . . . Webb
Story: Cisco and Pancho help out a quick-tempered bicycle-riding young Easterner who has struck it rich with a gold claim but is being cheated by claim jumpers.
Notes: Companion episode: *The Kidnapped Cameraman.*

THE TUMBLERS

Copyrighted . . . . .March 17, 1955
Director . . . . Leslie Goodwins
Teleplay . . . .Harry S. Franklin & Otto Englander
Cast
Duncan Renaldo . . . . The Cisco Kid
Leo Carrillo . . . . .Pancho
Loren Janes . . . . .Tim Siebert
Ward James . . . . Hearn
Harry Cody . . . . Hank Siebert
Maureen Cassidy . . . . Kitty Noonan
William Fawcett . . . . Sheriff Len Cooper
Story: Cisco and Pancho teach an acrobat some riding and shooting skills so he can fight the bully who runs the town of Smoky Gap.
Notes: Companion episode: None.

SIXTH SEASON, 1955-56

A QUIET SUNDAY MORNING

Copyrighted . . . . October 6, 1955
Director . . . . Leslie Goodwins
Teleplay . . . . .Barney A. Sarecky & Barry Cohon
Cast
Duncan Renaldo . . . . The Cisco Kid
Leo Carrillo . . . . .Pancho
Frank Richards . . . . .Grant
Richard Castle . . . . Kenny Marsh
Elsie Baker . . . . June Sims
Margie Moran . . . . Mrs. Sims
Chuck Cason .Rancher
Story: Cisco and Pancho go after three robbers—one of them a teen-age boy on his first job—who killed the sheriff while making their getaway.
Notes: Companion episode: *Young Blood.*

ARROYO MILLIONAIRE'S CASTLE

Copyrighted . . . . October 13, 1955
Director . . . . .Lambert Hillyer
Teleplay . . . . Barry Cohon
Cast
Duncan Renaldo . . . . The Cisco Kid

Leo Carrillo . . . . .Pancho
Wayne Mallory . . . . .Carl White
Britt Wood . . . . .Grampus White
Mort Mills . . . . Sheriff Tom Roscoe
Gene Covelli . . . . .Steve
Story: While hunting the gunman who murdered a young prospector, Cisco and Pancho find an eccentric millionaire living in a castle in the desert.
Notes: Companion episode: *(Cisco And The Tappers.)*

WITNESS

Copyrighted . . . . October 20, 1955
Director . . . . Leslie Goodwins
Teleplay . . . . Kenneth A. Enochs
Cast
Duncan Renaldo . . . . The Cisco Kid
Leo Carrillo . . . . .Pancho
Tristram Coffin . . . . Chet Morton
Terry Frost . . . . Dorf
Russell Whitney . . . . Mr. Cartright
Melinda Plowman . . . . Carol Cartright
Story: Cisco and Pancho try to persuade a teen-age girl who witnessed a robbery to admit that she recognized the bandit leader as her uncle.
Notes: Companion episode: *New York's Finest.*

CHOCTAW JUSTICE

Copyrighted . . . . October 27, 1955
Director . . . . .Lambert Hillyer
Teleplay . . . . Robert Clayton
Cast
Duncan Renaldo . . . . The Cisco Kid
Leo Carrillo . . . . .Pancho
Bill Pullen . . . . .Charlie Ponca
Margaret Cahill . . . . Molly
Paul Fierro . . . . Fred Tofo
James Anderson . . . . Curly
Chief Yowlachie . . . . .Indian Judge
Story: Cisco receives an urgent letter asking him to follow Choctaw custom and serve as the executioner of his friend Charlie Ponca, who's been convicted of murder by an Indian court. Instead he and Pancho set out to prove Charlie's innocence.
Notes: Companion episode: *Ambush.*

NEW YORK'S FINEST

Copyrighted . . . . November 3, 1955
Director . . . . Leslie Goodwins
Teleplay .John Krafft
Cast
Duncan Renaldo . . . . The Cisco Kid

Another publicity photo of Duncan Renaldo, Diablo and friend used for **The Cisco Kid** TV series.

Leo Carrillo . . . . .Pancho
Tristram Coffin . . . . .Saunders
Terry Frost . . . . .Morgan
Charles Maxwell . . . . Jeff Adams
Anna Navarro . . . . .Ruth Mallory
Story: Cisco and Pancho help a young New York policeman who has come west to search for the murderer of his former commander.
Notes: Companion episode: *Witness*.

(CISCO AND THE TAPPERS)

Copyrighted . . . . November 3, 1955
Director . . . . .Lambert Hillyer
Teleplay . . . . .Wilbur S. Peacock
Cast
Duncan Renaldo . . . . The Cisco Kid
Leo Carrillo . . . . .Pancho
Wayne Mallory . . . . .Harry
Britt Wood . . . . .Sheriff
Mort Mills . . . . .Bart Stevens
Bill Catching .Whitey
Story: Cisco and Pancho help an old sheriff and his young deputy capture a group of outlaws who tap telegraph wires to learn of gold shipments.
Notes: Companion episode: *Arroyo Millionaire's Castle*. This is the only episode in the entire series for which the Copyright Catalog does not provide a title. Therefore I've made up one of my own.

YOUNG BLOOD

Copyrighted . . . . November 10, 1955
Director . . . . Leslie Goodwins
Teleplay . . . . Kenneth A. Enochs
Cast
Duncan Renaldo . . . . The Cisco Kid
Leo Carrillo . . . . .Pancho
Richard Castle .Dan
Elsie Baker . . . . .Mrs. Parry
Gerald Olken . . . . Buck
Tim Johnson . . . . .Ray
Story: Cisco and Pancho help a widow whose young hired hand is associating with a pair of teen-age bandits.
Notes: Companion episode: *A Quiet Sunday Morning*.

SCHOOL MARM

Copyrighted . . . . November 17, 1955
Director . . . . .Lambert Hillyer
Teleplay . . . . .Barney A. Sarecky & Barry Cohon
Cast
Duncan Renaldo . . . . The Cisco Kid
Leo Carrillo . . . . .Pancho
Elaine Riley . . . . .Irene Moore

Sydney Mason . . . . .Abner Craig
Marshall Reed . . . . .Dick
Joel Ashley .Mr. Bond
Kenneth Miller . . . . Jay Jones
Story: Cisco and Pancho try to rescue the town of Madera's new schoolteacher, who's been kidnapped and held for ransom.
Notes: Companion episode: *Gold, Death And Dynamite*.

BOUNTY MEN

Copyrighted . . . . November 24, 1955
Director . . . . Leslie Goodwins
Teleplay . . . . Ande Lamb
Cast
Duncan Renaldo . . . . The Cisco Kid
Leo Carrillo . . . . .Pancho
Frosty Royce . . . . .Pat Pierce
Earle Hodgins . . . . .Dr. Owen Desmond
Zon Murray . . . . . Ron Copeland/Norman Castle
Mickey Simpson . . . . .Wade/Sgt. Quinn
Story: Cisco and Pancho trail a wanted killer to an Army recruiting station where they encounter a corrupt military doctor who enlists outlaws in the service under dead men's names.
Notes: Companion episode: *Jumping Beans*.

QUICK ON THE TRIGGER

Copyrighted . . . . .December 1, 1955
Director . . . . .Lambert Hillyer
Teleplay . . . . .Barney A. Sarecky & Barry Cohon
Cast
Duncan Renaldo . . . . The Cisco Kid
Leo Carrillo . . . . .Pancho
Peter Mamakos . . . . Sheriff Carter
Robin Short . . . . Joe Wilcox
John Compton .Barnes
Sue England . . . . Laura Wilcox
Story: Cisco and Pancho try to help an expectant father who stole back the horse he sold to a crooked animal dealer in order to pay for medical care for his pregnant wife.
Notes: Companion episode: *Six Gun Cupids*.

GOLD, DEATH AND DYNAMITE

Copyrighted . . . . .December 8, 1955
Director . . . . .Lambert Hillyer
Teleplay . . . . .Barney A. Sarecky & Barry Cohon
Cast
Duncan Renaldo . . . . The Cisco Kid
Leo Carrillo . . . . .Pancho
Elaine Riley . . . . .Millie Stone
Steven Clark . . . . Mel Baldwin
Marshall Reed . . . . .Dobie

Joel Ashley . . . . .Clem
Sydney Mason .Sheriff
Story: Cisco and Pancho become involved when the desperate owner of a stagecoach line substitutes dynamite for a gold shipment in hope of blowing up the outlaws who have been robbing his coaches.
Notes: Companion episode: *School Marm*.

JUMPING BEANS

Copyrighted . . . . .December 15, 1955
Director . . . . Leslie Goodwins
Teleplay . . . . Jack Rock
Cast
Duncan Renaldo . . . . The Cisco Kid
Leo Carrillo . . . . .Pancho
Earle Hodgins .Lang
Robert Strong . . . . .Menkin
Zon Murray . . . . Bailey
Mickey Simpson . . . . .Judd
Frosty Royce .Brewster
Story: Cisco and Pancho arrive in Rimtown too late to prevent a robbery by three escaped convicts but try to catch the trio by using a handful of Mexican jumping beans as a lie detector.
Notes: Companion episode: *Bounty Men*.

AMBUSH

Copyrighted . . . . .December 22, 1955
Director . . . . .Lambert Hillyer
Teleplay . . . . .Stuart Jerome & Barry Cohon
Cast
Duncan Renaldo . . . . The Cisco Kid
Leo Carrillo . . . . .Pancho
Paul Fierro . . . . .Ricardo Gomez
Bill Pullen . . . . Cheyenne Jones
James Anderson . . . . .Iceberg Ike
Joe Dominguez . . . . .Uncle Alberto
Anna Navarro . . . . Elena
Story: Cisco encounters three rival outlaws who have joined forces to do away with him by using Pancho as bait for a clever ambush.
Notes: Companion episode: *Choctaw Justice*.

SIX GUN CUPIDS

Copyrighted . . . . .December 29, 1955
Director . . . . .Lambert Hillyer
Teleplay . . . . Buckley Angell
Cast
Duncan Renaldo . . . . The Cisco Kid
Leo Carrillo . . . . .Pancho
Robin Short . . . . Ted Landry
Paula Houston . . . . Isabel Landry
John Compton . . . . .Emery

Jackie Loughery . . . . Ellen Marland
Peter Mamakos . . . . .Leach
Story: Cisco and Pancho learn that a wealthy old woman has forbidden her son to associate with the housemaid he loves, and try to help the young couple find happiness.
Notes: Companion episode: *Quick On The Trigger*.

STRANGERS

Copyrighted . . . . .January 5, 1956
Director . . . . .Lambert Hillyer
Teleplay . . . . .Donn Mullally
Cast
Duncan Renaldo . . . . .The Cisco Kid
Leo Carrillo . . . . Pancho
John Cliff . . . . .Matt Pearson
Pierce Lyden . . . . Carl Barton
John Halloran . . . . Brace Haskell
Don Gardner . . . . .Jerry Haskell
Story: Cisco and Pancho are ambushed and their horses stolen but when they try to buy fresh horses everyone drives them away.
Notes: Companion episode: *Mr. X*.

THE JOKER

Copyrighted . . . . .January 12, 1956
Director . . . . Leslie Goodwins
Teleplay . . . . .Barney A. Sarecky & Barry Cohon
Cast
Duncan Renaldo . . . . The Cisco Kid
Leo Carrillo . . . . .Pancho
Terry Frost . . . . Porter
John Beradino . . . . .Crane
Lee Morgan .Muscles
Joyce Jameson . . . . Jill Stewart
Story: Cisco and Pancho go after a prankster who has made a fortune selling ranches he doesn't own.
Notes: Companion episode: *Roundup*.

MAN WITH THE REPUTATION

Copyrighted . . . . .January 19, 1956
Director . . . . .Lambert Hillyer
Teleplay . . . . Ande Lamb
Cast
Duncan Renaldo . . . . The Cisco Kid
Leo Carrillo . . . . .Pancho
Steven Clark . . . . Branch Kennedy
Marilyn Saris . . . . Juanita Harris
Paul Hahn . . . . Trent Wilson
Joel Smith . . . . Constable Slate
Lane Bradford . . . . John Mason
Story: A newspaper editor accuses Cisco and

Pancho of taking bribes from a criminal in order to get them into town so he can ask their help in cleaning up local political corruption.
Notes: Companion episode: *Kilts And Sombreros*.

THE EPIDEMIC

Copyrighted . . . . January 26, 1956
Director . . . . Leslie Goodwins
Teleplay . . . . Kenneth A. Enochs
Cast
Duncan Renaldo . . . . The Cisco Kid
Leo Carrillo . . . . .Pancho
George Meader .Doc
Leo Needham .Mackey
Jack Littlefield . . . . Trim
Ward C. James . . . . Ward
John B. Duncan . . . . .Mail Rider
Story: Cisco and Pancho pursue the outlaws who are holding a bottle of vital smallpox vaccine for ransom.
Notes: Companion episode: *West Of The Law.*

MR. X

Copyrighted . . . . .February 2, 1956
Director . . . . .Lambert Hillyer
Teleplay . . . . .Barney A. Sarecky & Barry Cohon
Cast
Duncan Renaldo . . . . The Cisco Kid
Leo Carrillo . . . . .Pancho
Diana Welles . . . . Alice Blake
Gene Roth . . . . .Tom Blake
Pierce Lyden . . . . .Dana
Don Gardner . . . . .Johnny Clark
Story: Cisco rescues a mine owner who's been buried alive in a collapsed tunnel, then discovers that the apparent accident was a murder attempt and is himself trapped by the killer.
Notes: Companion episode: *Strangers.*

ROUNDUP

Copyrighted . . . . .February 9, 1956
Director . . . . Leslie Goodwins
Teleplay . . . . Barney A. Sarecky & Barry Cohon
Cast
Duncan Renaldo . . . . The Cisco Kid
Leo Carrillo . . . . .Pancho
Joyce Jameson . . . . Arizona Williams
John Beradino . . . . .Rick Johnson
Terry Frost . . . . .Ned
Lee Morgan . . . . Grubstake
Story: Cisco and Pancho help a young woman who has come West to take control of the ranch she inherited, only to encounter trouble in the

shape of a jealous foreman and some rustlers.
Notes: Companion episode: *The Joker.*

HE COULDN'T QUIT

Copyrighted . . . . .February 16, 1956
Director . . . . Leslie Goodwins
Teleplay . . . . Ande Lamb
Cast
Duncan Renaldo . . . . The Cisco Kid
Leo Carrillo . . . . .Pancho
Lillian Molieri . . . . Gypsy
Charles Maxwell . . . . Sheriff Paul Jackson
James Seay . . . . Roy Dillon
William Fawcett . . . . .Hunt
Story: Cisco and Pancho become involved when an outlaw who's in love with a gypsy palmist returns to town to visit his now respectable former partner in crime and collect his share of the loot from their last robbery.
Notes: Companion episode: *The Magician Of Jamesville.*

KILTS AND SOMBREROS

Copyrighted . . . . .February 23, 1956
Director . . . . .Lambert Hillyer
Teleplay . . . . Kenneth A. Enochs
Cast
Duncan Renaldo . . . . The Cisco Kid
Leo Carrillo . . . . .Pancho
Ian Murray . . . . .MacDougall
Barry Froner . . . . Billy
Sydney Mason . . . . .Sheriff
Lane Bradford . . . . Outlaw Leader
Joel Smith . . . . Henchman
Story: Cisco and Pancho help a Scotsman who was fired from his job as a Wells Fargo courier after being ambushed by bandits.
Notes: Companion episode: *Man With The Reputation.*

WEST OF THE LAW

Copyrighted . . . . .March 1, 1956
Director . . . . Leslie Goodwins
Teleplay . . . . Buckley Angell
Cast
Duncan Renaldo . . . . The Cisco Kid
Leo Carrillo . . . . .Pancho
John B. Duncan . . . . Mickey Doan
Leo Needham . . . . .Camden
Ward C. James . . . . .Durango
Fay Morley . . . . .Marla Fontaine
Story: Cisco and Pancho help a friendless young man who's been accused of stealing an opera singer's jewelry.

Teala Loring is romanced by Gilbert Roland in **Riding the California Trail** (Monogram, 1947). (Courtesy of Bobby Copeland.)

Notes: Companion episode: *The Epidemic.*

DANGEROUS SHOEMAKER

Copyrighted . . . . .March 8, 1956
Director . . . . .Lambert Hillyer
Teleplay . . . . .Ed Gardner Jr.
Cast
Duncan Renaldo . . . . The Cisco Kid
Leo Carrillo . . . . .Pancho
Sandy Sanders . . . . Duke Martin
Keith Richards . . . . Simon Telford
Bruce Payne . . . . .Tom Jordan
Glenn Strange . . . . .Blake
Story: Cisco and Pancho stop off at a shoemaker's shop to get Pancho's boots fixed and become entangled in a plot by the shoemaker to blackmail a man who thinks he's a murderer.
Notes: Companion episode: None.

THE MAGICIAN OF JAMESVILLE

Copyrighted . . . . .March 15, 1956
Director . . . . Leslie Goodwins
Teleplay . . . . .Larry Lund
Cast
Duncan Renaldo . . . . The Cisco Kid
Leo Carrillo . . . . .Pancho
Earle Hodgins . . . . Orlando
Charles Maxwell . . . . .Mayor Brandon
William Fawcett . . . . .Joe/Grampaw
James Seay . . . . Hardy
Bert Rumsey . . . . Sheriff
Story: Cisco uses a boomerang from a traveling magician's kit to expose a crooked mayor and a mysterious blowgun killer.
Notes: Companion episode: *He Couldn't Quit.*

TANGLED TRAILS

Copyrighted . . . . .March 22, 1956
Director . . . . Leslie Goodwins
Teleplay . . . . .J. Benton Cheney
Cast
Duncan Renaldo . . . . The Cisco Kid
Leo Carrillo . . . . .Pancho
William Vaughan . . . . .Outlaw Leader
Ann Duncan . . . . Trudy Banning
Don Mathers . . . . Williams
Max Wagner . . . . .Nevada
Lee Morgan . . . . Henry Banning
Story: Cisco and Pancho try to clear an old friend who has disappeared along with a shipment of money.
Notes: Companion episode: None.

Index

227

WARNER BAXTER 1942

Leo Carrillo, 81, Dies Of Cancer

SANTA MONICA, Calif. (P)—Leo Carrillo, a movie star for three decades who made his biggest hit as the lovable Pancho of television's Cisco Kid series, died Sunday of cancer. He was 81.

The end came at the Mexican-style ranch house where Carrillo had lived with his daughter, Antoinette. His wife, Edith, died in 1953 after 40 years of marriage.

Born in Los Angeles, Carrillo was a newspaper cartoonist before turning actor in his early 20s. He played in vaudeville, toured with stock companies and appeared on Broadway before he turned to Hollywood and movie roles.

In early years he specialized in Spanish and Italian roles, but finally became typed as a hard-riding Spaniard of the border days. His trademarks were a flat-brimmed sombrero and carefully waxed mustache.

Carrillo appeared in hundreds of silent movies, short subjects and talkies. He made more than 150 of the Cisco Kid TV films co-starring as Pancho, the Western Robin Hood's Fat, funny sidekick —from 1949 to 1955.

WARNER BAXTER, 59, FILM STAR, IS DEAD

Winner of 'Oscar' in 1929— Best Known for Cisco Kid and 'Crime Doctor' Portrayals

BEVERLY HILLS, Calif., May 7 (P)—Warner Baxter, veteran motion-picture actor, died at his home tonight after a long illness. His age was 59. He had suffered from arthritis for years and a lobotomy was performed three weeks ago to alleviate his pain. Bronchial pneumonia set in recently.

In recent years, he was chronically ill, suffering pain which made eating difficult and induced malnutrition. In April, he underwent cranial surgery at St. John's Hospital in Santa Monica, then returned to his Beverly Hills home. He and his second wife, the former Winifred Bryson, stage actress, celebrated their thirty-third wedding anniversary in January.

Began as Juvenile Lead

Mr. Baxter, whose career began with the talking films, was most widely remembered for his creation of the Cisco Kid movie role. In 1929 the Academy Award for the best actor of the year went to him for his portrayal of this role in "In Old Arizona."

Well known as a juvenile lead in his early screen days, Mr. Baxter attained even greater popularity as a character actor. In 1949 he appeared in the role of Victor Burnell in "Prison Warden," a Columbia Pictures production.

Although he received some acclaim for his part in "Lady in the Dark" in 1944, it was as the Cisco Kid that he established himself in the hearts of America's more romantic film-goers. The Cisco Kid was a Robin Hood with a six-gun. In later years the role of Dr. Robert Ordway in the "Crime Doctor" series kept him before the nation's motion-picture fans.

Mr. Baxter was born in Columbus, Ohio, on March 29, 1893. A star in amateur theatricals, he was graduated from high school in Columbus and then became a salesman of farm implements. His big chance came when the partner of Dorothy Shoemaker became ill while the company was playing in Louisville and it was necessary to draft young Baxter to take his place. He remained on the stage in small parts for about four months until his disapproving mother found out what he was doing and made him return home.

Played Stock in Dallas

To please his mother he became an insurance man and before he left the business was head of the Philadelphia office of the Travellers Insurance Company. With the money he saved on the job he struck out for the West. In Tulsa, Okla., he invested his money in a garage and lost all of it.

His next move was to Dallas, Tex., where he joined the North Brothers stock company at $30 a week, a fair salary in those days. With a little stake saved from the Dallas stock company venture he went on to California, where he tried to get into motion pictures. He played on the stage for seven more years before he crashed Hollywood.

His nearest approach to a stage success was in Oliver Morosco's "Lombardi, Ltd.," in which he played the feature role in New York. After that Mr. Baxter again tried Hollywood, this time with success. He appeared with Ethel Clayton in a Paramount picture, "Her Own Money," and after one return to the stage in Morosco's "A Tailor-Made Man," he began his long series of successful Hollywood roles.

Pictures in which he appeared included "The Cisco Kid," "Six Hour to Live," "Paddy, the Next Best Thing," "Forty-second Street," "Stand Up and Cheer," "King of Burlesque," "Slave Ship" and "Kidnapped."

In the late Nineteen Forties Mr. Baxter was devoting only a small part of his time to the screen. He operated a real estate office in Malibu, where he had served as Mayor.

The obituaries of Warner Baxter and Leo Carrillo as they appeared in newspapers. (Courtesy of Bobby Copeland.)

Barnes, Binnie – 47
Barrat, Robert – 51, 52, 56
Barry, Don – 119
Barry, Tom – 24
Barrymore, Ethel – 25, 81
Barrymore, Lionel – 81
Barthelmess, Richard – 33, 36
Bartlett, Lanier – 36
Bartlett, Virginia Stivers – 36
Barton, Buzz – 23, 33
Barton, Charles – 40, 41
Bass, Sam – 9
"Battle of Red Rock Pass" (*Cisco Kid* episode) – 148
Batman (TV series) – 68, 161
Baxter, Warner – 20, 24, 25-26, 27, 28, 29, 30, 31, 33, 34, 38, 39, 45, 47, 48, 50, 51, 55, 64, 81, 104, 147, 157
Beach, Guy – 108
Beach, John – 56
Beal, John – 145
Beaton, Kenneth C. – 35
Beau Bandit (RKO, 1930) – 33-34, 37, 38, 76
Beauty And The Bandit (Monogram, 1946) – 82, 88-90
Beck, Jackson – 69
Beebe, Ford – 105, 115-116, 119-120
Beecher, Janet – 62
Beery, Noah – 41, 104
Belden, Charles S. – 83, 86
Bell, Hank – 108
Bell, Rex – 40, 45, 71
"Bell of Santa Margarita" (*Cisco Kid* episode) – 146
Bellamy, Madge – 25
Bells Of San Fernando (Screen Guild, 1947) – 42, 103
Bendix, William – 50
Bennet, Spencer Gordon – 36, 86, 132
Bennett, Constance – 80
Bennett, Raphael – 64, 85, 137
Benton, Jack – 116
Berke, William – 42
Bernerd, Jeffrey – 93
Bernstein, Isadore – 40
Betrayed (Fox, 1917) – 7, 21, 24
Bettinson, Ralph – 76
Bickford, Charles – 40, 42
Big Trail, The (Fox, 1930) – 36
Billingsley, Barbara – 108
Billy The Kid (MGM, 1930) – 35, 36
Binney, Constance – 25
Birell, Tala – 106
Birth Of A Nation, The (Epoch, 1915) – 21
Black Cat, The (Universal, 1934) – 43
Black Gold (Allied Artists, 1947) – 93
"Black Terror, The" (*Cisco Kid* episode) – 150

Blake, Bobby (Robert) – 146, 148
Blane, Sally – 58
Block, Ralph – 35
Blue, Monte – 21
Bluebeard (PRC, 1944) – 43
Blystone, John – 26
Boehm, Sydney – 42
Boetticher, Budd – 26, 100-101
Bogart, Humphrey – 45
Bogdanovich, Peter – 23, 43
Bohr, Jose – 36
Bold Caballero, The (Republic, 1936) – 40
Bonanza (TV series) – 101, 134
Bond, Ward – 51, 52, 56, 57
"Boomerang" (*Cisco Kid* episode) – 125, 131
Booth, Edwin – 20, 21
Booth, Edwina – 69, 107
Booth, John Wilkes – 21
Border Terror, The (Universal, 1919) – 21
Border Vigilantes (Paramount, 1941) – 120
Born To The West (Paramount, 1937) – 41
Borzage, Frank – 131
Boston Blackie (TV series) – 125, 133, 135, 142, 144,145
Bosworth, Hobart – 21
Bow, Clara – 80
Boyd, William – 45, 116
Boyer, Charles – 131
Bradbury, James, Jr. - 28, 30
Bradbury, Robert N. - 41
Bradford, Lane – 152
Brady Bunch, The (TV series) – 145
Brand, Max – 42
Branded (Paramount, 1951) – 42
Brave Eagle (TV series) – 133
Brenon, Herbert – 25, 104
Brent, Evelyn – 95, 96, 116
Bridge Of San Luis Rey, The (MGM, 1929) – 69
Britton, Barbara – 42
Broken Arrow (20th Century-Fox, 1950) – 50
Bronco (TV series) – 133, 154
Brooks, Rand – 146
Brooks, Richard – 100
Brower, Otto – 62
Brown, Harry Joe – 35
Brown, Johnny Mack – 26, 37, 41, 45, 71, 72, 77, 79, 90, 100, 104, 108, 115, 116, 120, 133, 153
Bruce, Nigel – 37
Bryson, Winifred – 25
Buchman, Harold – 64
Buffalo Bill Jr. – 23
Buffington, Adele – 38, 108
"Bullets and the Booby Trap" (*Cisco Kid* episode) – 148
Bullets For Bandits (Columbia, 1942) – 107
Bullfighter And The Lady (Republic, 1951) – 100

230

Girl From San Lorenzo, The (Inter-American/ United Artists, 1950) – 120-123, 125, 131, 157
Girl Of The Rio (RKO, 1932) – 41, 104
Girls In Chains (PRC, 1943) – 26
Gish, Lillian – 94
Glasser, Albert – 9, 71, 106-107, 125, 130, 136
Gleason, Jackie – 50, 153
"Gold, Death and Dynamite" (*Cisco Kid* episode) – 152
Golden Boy (Paramount, 1939) – 54
Golden Trail, The (Monogram, 1940) – 131
Goldin, Pat – 97
Gonzales Gonzales, Jose – 151
Goodwin, Harold – 58
Goodwins, Leslie – 49, 153, 154
Gordon, C. Henry – 37, 51
Gordon, Richard – 75
Gould, William – 89
Grable, Betty – 25, 60
Grand Canyon (Lippert, 1949) – 133
Grandville, Marcelle – 92
Grant, Cary – 100
Grant, Kirby – 108
Great Dictator, The (Chaplin/United Artists, 1940) – 58
Great Gatsby, The (Famous Players-Lasky, 1926) – 25
Green Hornet, The (TV series) – 58
Greene, Angela – 97
Greppi, Michelle – 161
Grey, Zane – 23, 40, 41, 45, 62
Griffith, D.W. – 21, 33, 94
Gross, Jack – 127
Guizar, Tito – 38, 41
Gun Packer (Monogram, 1938) – 107
Guns And Fury (alternate title for **The Daring Caballero**) – 157
Gunsmoke (TV series) – 146, 152
Gunsmoke Trail (Monogram, 1938) – 41
Haig, Douglas – 30
Hadley, Reed – 40
Half Angel (20th Century-Fox, 1936) – 48
Hall, Jon – 115
Hall, Lee "Red" – 9, 10
Halton, Charles – 113
Hammett, Dashiell – 26
Hammond, Victor – 76
Hands Across The Border (Republic, 1943) – 70
Harrison, June – 117
Hart, John – 108, 143
Hart, William S. – 23, 33, 76, 153
Hartigan, Pat – 28
Harvey, Don C. – 122
Harvey, Harry – 21
Harvey, Paul – 67
Hathaway, Henry – 68
Hatton, Frederic and Fanny – 25

Hatton, Raymond – 36, 41, 70, 79, 131, 144, 152
Hawaiian Eye (TV series) – 133
Hawkey, Rock – 40
Haycox, Ernest – 42
Hayden, Russell – 144
Hayworth, Rita – 39
Healey, Myron – 137, 143, 152
Hearn, Edward – 37
Hearts Of The West (O. Henry collection) – 10
Hecht, Ted – 91
Heflin, Van – 95
Heller In Pink Tights (Paramount, 1960) – 26
Hemingway, Ernest – 101
Henry, Bill – 133, 143
Henry, O. (William Sidney Porter) – 7, 9-10, 17, 20, 24, 28, 29, 35, 41, 67, 69, 81, 145
Henry, Orrin – 10
Herman, Albert – 131-133, 134
Heyburn, Weldon – 37
Hi, Gaucho! (RKO, 1935) – 38
"Hidden Valley" (*Cisco Kid* episode) – 142
High Chaparral, The (TV series) – 101
Hill, Doris – 35
Hill, Riley – 142
Hill, Robert F. – 40
Hill Street Blues (TV series) – 157
Hillyer, Lambert – 23, 25, 26, 33-34, 37, 42, 76-77, 116, 117, 147, 148, 151, 152, 153
History Is Made At Night (Wanger/United Artists, 1937) – 131
Hitchcock, Alfred – 101
Hitler, Adolf – 58
Hodgins, Earle – 131, 137, 143, 152
Hoeffer, Norman – 58
Hoffman, Otto – 61
Hohl, Arthur – 67
Holden, Gloria – 77
Holden, William – 20, 54
Hollywood Corral (Miller book) – 31, 62, 69, 81, 83, 86, 95, 112
Hollywood Western, The (Everson book) – 28, 35-36, 37, 38, 39, 40, 41, 55, 69, 81, 83, 94-95
Holt, Jack – 23
Holt, Tim – 41, 42, 104, 148
Hopalong Cassidy (TV series) – 131
Hopalong Cassidy Returns (Paramount, 1936) – 116, 119
"Horseless Carriage" (*Cisco Kid* episode) – 151
Horton, Robert – 42
Hot Pepper (Fox, 1933) – 26
Howes, Reed – 137, 150
Hoxie, Al – 23
Hoxie, Jack – 23, 62
Hudman, Wes – 122
Hughes, Howard – 20
Hughes, J. Anthony – 56
Hughes, Mary Beth – 60, 61, 67, 133

234

LaRue, Frank – 84
LaRue, Jack – 95, 96
LaRue, Lash – 79, 159
"Lasca" (Desprez poem) – 37
Lasca Of The Rio Grande (Universal, 1932) –
   26, 37, 38, 104
Lash, The (First National, 1930) – 36
Last Of The Mohicans, The (Mascot, 1932)–116
Last Outlaw, The (RKO, 1936) – 94-95
"Laughing Badman"(*Cisco Kid* episode)–143, 145
Laughton, Charles – 80
Laurenz, John – 75
Law And Lead (Colony, 1937) – 40
Law Of The Plainsman (TV series) – 133
Law Of The Range, The (MGM, 1928) – 82
Lease, Rex – 131
LeBorg, Reginald – 42
Leeds, Herbert I. – 47-50, 51, 55, 64, 67, 105,
   147, 148, 153
Leiber, Fritz – 72
Leonard, David – 112
Leslie, Nan – 148, 152
Lesser, Budd – 42
Lester, Bill – 121
Levine, Nat – 33, 115
Levy, Herbert – 48
Levy, Melvin – 39
Lewis, George J. – 37, 38, 76, 77, 82, 86, 90
Lewis, Joseph H. – 90
Lewis, Mitchell – 33
Life And Legend Of Wyatt Earp, The (TV
   series) – 133, 152
Life Of General Villa, The (Mutual, 1914) – 21
Life Of Riley, The (TV series) – 49, 153
Lightning Carson Rides Again (Victory, 1938) –
   40
Lillian Russell (20th Century-Fox, 1940) – 105
Lindbergh, Charles – 67
Lindsay, Vachel – 10
Litel, John – 108
Little, Mickey – 112
Livingston, Robert – 40, 41, 46, 70, 71, 131, 148
Llano Kid, The (Paramount, 1939) – 38, 41
Lloyd, Frank – 36
Lloyd, Harold – 131
Logan, Helen – 60
Lombard, Carole – 35
Lombardi, Ltd. (stage play) – 25, 104
London, Tom – 58, 64, 66, 144
Lone Defender, The (Mascot, 1930) – 33
Lone Ranger, The (TV series) – 133, 136, 137,
   143, 157
Lone Ranger Rides Again, The (Republic,
   1939) – 41, 70
Lone Star Vigilantes, The(Columbia, 1941)–107
"Lonely Runner, The" (*Bonanza* episode) – 101
Loner, The (TV series) – 58

Long, Hal – 58
Long, Walter – 33
Loren, Sophia – 26
Loring, Teala – 91
Lorre, Peter – 48
"Lost City" (*Cisco Kid* episode) – 144
Lost In Space (TV series) – 146
Lovejoy, Frank – 68
Lowe, Edmund – 26-27, 30, 35, 45, 46, 60
Lowery, Robert – 67
Loy, Myrna – 34, 36
Lubitsch, Ernst – 68
Lucky Cisco Kid (20th Century-Fox, 1940) – 60-
   62, 67, 110
Luden, Jack – 45
Lugosi, Bela – 77, 82
Lupino, Ida – 40
Lyden, Pierce – 137
MacDonald, Edmund –62
MacDonald, Kenneth – 110, 152
MacGregor, Jock – 69
Mack, Willard – 41
MacLane, Barton – 42
MacMurray, Fred – 42
Magaloni, Honorato – 159
Mahoney, Jock – 115
Malaya (MGM, 1950) – 100
Mallinson, Rory – 100, 152
Maloney, Leo – 115
Mamoulian, Rouben – 40
Man From God's Country (Allied Artists, 1958)
   – 93
Man From Hell's River, The (Cummings &
   Smith, 1922) – 25
Man From Texas, The (Monogram, 1939) – 131
Mann, Anthony – 100, 101
Mapes, Ted – 144
Marcus, James – 27, 35
Margo – 39
Marin, Cheech – 158-161
Maris, Mona – 33, 34, 35, 37
Mark, Mel – 133
Mark Of Zorro, The (Fairbanks/United
   Artists, 1920) – 33, 36
Mark Of Zorro, The (20th-Fox, 1940) – 40
Marked Trails (Monogram, 1945) – 71
Marshall, Herbert – 104
Marti, Jose – 46
Martin, Chris-Pin – 30, 38, 46, 50, 51, 70, 94,
   103, 104-105
Martin, Sobey – 145, 146
Martin, Richard – 42
Martinez, Al – 81
Martini, Nino – 40
Marx, Groucho – 25
Mason, Leroy – 58, 59, 60
Mason, Lesley – 35

Olmos, Edward James – 158
O'Malley Of The Mounted (Hart, 1920) – 76
One Man Law (Columbia, 1932) – 76, 148, 152
Orth, Marion – 33
Osborne, Bud – 58, 71, 137, 146
Our Betters (RKO, 1933) – 80
Outcasts Of Poker Flat, The (RKO, 1937) – 95
Outlaw (Haycox collection) – 42
Outlaw, The (Hughes/United Artists, 1941) – 20
Painted Stallion, The (Republic, 1937) – 70
"Paiute War, The" (*Bonanza* episode) – 134
Paiva, Nestor – 96
Palange, Inez – 65
Pals Of The Silver Sage (Monogram, 1940) –131
"Pancho and the Pachyderm" (*Cisco Kid* episode) – 143
"Pancho and the Wolf Dog" (*Cisco Kid* episode) – 148
"Pancho Hostage" (*Cisco Kid* episode) – 135
"Pancho's Niece" (*Cisco Kid* episode) – 151
Pandolfo, Tony – 158
Parker, Willard – 42
Pascal, Ernest – 38
Patterson, Hank – 133, 143, 152
Payne, Bruce – 158-161
Payne, Edna – 17
Peach, Kenneth – 125, 130
Pecos Dandy, The (Security, 1934) – 38, 43
Pegg, Vester – 21
Penn, Leonard – 121, 144, 152
Percival, Walter – 37
Perlman, Ron – 158
Peters, House, Jr. – 144
Peters, Ralph – 108
Petersalia, Patrick – 38
Phantom Empire, The (Mascot, 1935) – 62
Phantom Of Santa Fe, The (Burroughs-Tarzan, 1936) – 40
Phelps, Lee – 121
Phillips, Lou Diamond – 158
"Phoney Heiress" (*Cisco Kid* episode) – 136
Piaz, Ysabel Ponciana Chris-Pin Martin – 30
Pickard, John – 146
Pickford, Lottie – 24
Pidgeon, Walter – 101
Pioneertown – 139
Pitts, ZaSu – 26
Plastic Age, The (Schulberg, 1925) – 80
Pony Post (Universal, 1940) – 132
Ponzanneli, Valentina – 159
Porter, Algernon – 9
Porter, Clarke – 9
Powdersmoke Range (RKO, 1935) – 107
Powell, Dick – 101
Power, Tyrone – 40, 50
Prairie Gunsmoke (Columbia, 1942) – 77
Prisoner Of Shark Island, The (20th Century-Fox, 1936) – 25
"Protective Association" (*Cisco Kid* episode) – 137, 138, 139, 141, 150
Pryor, Roger – 71
Puig, Eva – 65, 72
"Puppeteer, The" (*Cisco Kid* episode) – 143
Pyle, Denver – 142
Quartaro, Nena – 40
Quinn, Anthony – 26, 93
Racers, The (20th Century-Fox, 1955) – 68
Rafferty, Frances – 42
Ragan, Mike – 135, 144
Raiders Of The Border (Monogram, 1944) – 71
Raiders Of The Lost Ark (Lucasfilm/Paramount, 1981) – 159
Ramar Of The Jungle (TV series) –115, 133
Ramona (Inspiration/United Artists, 1928) – 25
Randall, Jack – 41, 45, 79, 107
Range Rider, The (TV series) – 115, 150
Rangers Of Fortune (Paramount, 1940) – 42, 80
Rangers Take Over, The (PRC, 1943) – 133
"Ransom of Red Chief, The" (O. Henry story) – 9
Rathbone, Basil – 37, 148
Rauh, Stanley – 55
Rawhide (TV series) – 144, 146
Realm Of Unknowing (Rudman book) – 48
Rebellion (Crescent, 1936) – 39
Red Desert (Lippert, 1949) – 119
Reed, Donald – 40
Reed, Marshall – 135, 143, 152
Reed, Philip – 42
Reed, Rod – 157
Reed, Tom – 37
Reid, Dan (character on *Lone Ranger*) – 151
Renaldo, Duncan – 9, 38, 39, 40, 41, 42, 48, 69-71, 72, 75, 77, 79, 80, 81, 103, 105-106, 110, 125, 127, 131, 133-135, 138, 141, 142, 143, 144, 145, 146, 147, 148, 149, 150, 153, 155, 157
Renaldo, Tito – 78
"Renegade Son" (*Cisco Kid* episode) – 131
Renfrew Of The Royal Mounted (Grand National, 1937) – 131
Renfrew On The Great White Trail (Grand National, 1937) – 131
Rennie, James – 36
Return Of The Cisco Kid, The (20th Century-Fox, 1939) – 41, 46, 47, 50-55
Revere, Paul – 159
Revier, Dorothy – 37
Reynolds, Burt – 161
Rich, Dick – 60
Richards, Keith – 142, 152
Richmond, Kane – 51, 52
"Ride On Vaquero" (song from **Romance Of The Rio Grande**, 1941) – 65
Ride On Vaquero (20th-Fox, 1941) – 67-68

Valdez, Luis – 158-161
Valdez, Marisol – 159
Valens, Ritchie – 158
Valentino, Rudolph – 33, 36, 47, 72
Valez, Kippee – 113
Valiant Hombre (Inter-American/United Artists, 1949) – 108-110
Vanishing Frontier, The (Paramount, 1932) – 72
Varconi, Victor – 36
Variable Harvest, A (Tuska collection) – 36
Velez, Lupe – 153
Venable, Evelyn – 60, 61
Vengeance Of The West (Columbia, 1942) – 42
Venturini, Edward D. – 41
Vera Cruz (Flora/United Artists, 1954) – 68
Vidor, King – 35
Vigilante, The (Columbia, 1947) – 108
"Vigilante Story" (*Cisco Kid* episode) – 137, 143
Villa, Pancho – 20, 21, 80
Viva Cisco Kid (20th-Fox, 1940) – 58-60
von Eltz, Theodor – 35
von Sternberg, Josef – 47
Voyage To The Bottom Of The Sea (TV series) – 146
Wagon Tracks (Hart, 1919) – 76
Wakely, Jimmy – 69, 77, 100, 120
Walker, Alexander – 23, 24
Waller, Eddy – 51, 58, 152
Walsh, George – 21
Walsh, Raoul – 17, 20, 21, 23-24, 25, 26, 27, 29, 45, 47, 94, 115
Walt Disney Presents (TV series) – 101
WAR (rock group) – 145, 146
"War of the Silver Kings" (*Maverick* episode)–26
Warde, Anthony – 72, 98
Warner, Jack – 48
Warren, Earl – 105
"Water Rights" (*Cisco Kid* episode) – 133
"Water Toll" (*Cisco Kid* episode) – 137, 138, 151
Waterfront (TV series) – 133
Waters, John – 25
Watson, Minor – 58
Watt, Nate – 116
Wayne, John – 41, 45, 116
We Were Strangers (Horizon/Columbia, 1949) – 100
Weaver, Marjorie – 55, 57
Wee Willie Winkie (20th-Fox, 1937) – 47
Week-end Marriage (First National, 1932) – 48
Welles, Orson – 58
Wellman, William A. – 23, 25, 39
Wells, William K. – 36
Werker, Alfred – 37
West, Victor – 42
Western Justice (Supreme, 1934) – 41
Westward Ho (Republic, 1935) – 41
Whalen, Michael – 48, 138, 151

What Price Glory (Fox, 1926) – 26
White, Gloria Ann – 56
White, Lee "Lasses" – 73, 108
White, Stewart Edward – 34
Wide Open Town (Paramount, 1941) – 116
Wife, Husband, And Friend (20th Century-Fox, 1939) – 47
Wilde, Oscar – 145
Wildfire (1908 stage play) – 24
Wiley, Jan – 72
Wilke, Bob – 143
Wilkerson, Guy – 133, 144
Williams, Bob – 42
Williams, Big Boy – 131
Williams, Guy – 38, 101
Williams, John – 147
Willis, Norman – 73
Wilson, Whip – 77, 115
Wind In The Willows, The (Kenneth Grahame book) – 70
Window, The (early one-reel movie) – 24
Withers, Jane – 48, 49, 50
Witney, William – 40, 41, 70, 81, 85, 101
Women Of All Nations (Fox, 1931) – 26
Wood, Sam – 42
Woodbury, Joan – 67
Woods, Donald – 42
Woods, Harry – 82, 86
Wooley, Sheb – 144
Woolrich, Cornell – 60
Worden, Hank – 58
Wray, Fay – 35, 36
Wyman, Jane – 68
Yaconelli, Frank – 41, 82, 86, 90, 94
Yates, Herbert J. – 70
Yellow Dust (RKO, 1936) – 107
Yellow Streak, A (Metro, 1915) – 81
Yesterday's Newsreel (TV series) – 125
Yost, Robert – 40
Young, Clarence Upson – 41, 90
Young, Loretta – 47
Young Man Of Manhattan (Paramount, 1930) – 58
Young Mr. Lincoln (20th-Fox, 1939) –152
Young Rajah, The (Famous Players-Lasky, 1922) – 72
Your Show Time (TV series) – 145
Ziv, Frederick – 125, 127, 129, 135, 140, 141, 142, 157
Zoot Suit (1978 stage play) – 158
Zoot Suit (Universal, 1981) – 158
Zorro (TV series) – 38, 58, 101
Zorro Rides Again (Republic, 1937) – 40, 70
Zorro's Fighting Legion (Republic, 1939) – 40, 81, 85, 159